Advance Praise for
The Black Scholar Travelogue in Academia

"How fortunate we are that in *The Black Scholar Travelogue in Academia* Professor George Jerry Sefa Dei provides a timely, comprehensive guide for practical/critical Black theorizing and counter-hegemonic knowledge production as a weapon of change and social transformation. Unapologetically embedded in his African Indigeneity, drawing on a powerful body of decolonizing scholarship, and deftly posing and courageously answering politically complex questions about race, identity and coloniality, his journey exemplifies the solidarity we need. My students really need this book. It is a *tour de force*."
—Joyce E. King, Benjamin E. Mays Endowed Chair for Urban Teaching, Learning & Leadership, Georgia State University

"George J. Sefa Dei is known internationally for his scholarship and activism, in pursuit of social justice and meaningful antiracist education, in a world disfigured by oppression and coloniality. In this landmark publication Dei reflects on his journey through academia; the past battles and continuing struggles that face anyone who is serious about challenging the Global forces of anti-Blackness. A powerful personal reflection on a storied career."
—David Gillborn, Editor-in-Chief of the international journal *Race Ethnicity and Education*

"A powerful plea from the heart for a respectful, peaceful, truly decolonised world from Nana, our foremost beloved Indigenous African scholar and sage. There can be no better message of love and hope for our times."
—Heidi Safia Mirza, Professor Emerita, University College London, author of *Race, Gender, and Educational Desire*

"Throughout his working life, Prof. Nana George Sefa Dei has engaged in liberatory scholarly praxis that extends beyond the academy and cuts across international frontiers. He has been fierce in challenging Euro-centric hegemonic discourses in education, and at the forefront of epistemic intervention in studies of race, racism, and coloniality/decoloniality. In this pursuit

Dr. Dei has generated ideas, texts, and pedagogies as part of his offerings to ensure the creation a future worth living. His work is exemplary. And with it, he has changed the world.

In this current work, as Canada's leading anti-colonial and critical race studies scholar, Dei fleshes out the problem of colonial violence in education, scholarship, and in social systems as a whole. At the heart of this work is the author's examination of global anti-Black racism that has held the world in thrall. Dei critiques how this has robbed Black people of life, liberty, and happiness. Yet, influenced by his Akan cultural understandings and concepts of African indigeneity, Prof. Dei offers a vital antidote to this state of affair. This balm not only can heal Black trauma and pain, but also usher in a liberatory future for us all."

—Afua Cooper, Killam Research Professor, Dalhousie University

The Black Scholar Travelogue in Academia

Studies in Criticality

Shirley R. Steinberg
General Editor

Vol. 541

George Jerry Sefa Dei
[Nana Adusei Sefa Tweneboah]

The Black Scholar Travelogue in Academia

PETER LANG
Lausanne • Berlin • Bruxelles • Chennai • New York • Oxford

Library of Congress Cataloging-in-Publication Control Number: 2023017433

Bibliographic information published by the Deutsche Nationalbibliothek.
The German National Library lists this publication in the German
National Bibliography; detailed bibliographic data is available
on the Internet at http://dnb.d-nb.de

Cover design by Peter Lang Group AG

ISSN 1058-1634
ISBN 9781636674261 (hardback)
ISBN 9781433199479 (paperback)
ISBN 9781433199486 (ebook)
ISBN 9781433199493 (epub)
DOI 10.3726/b20855

© 2024 Peter Lang Group AG, Lausanne
Published by Peter Lang Publishing Inc., New York, USA
info@peterlang.com - www.peterlang.com

All rights reserved.
All parts of this publication are protected by copyright.
Any utilization outside the strict limits of the copyright law, without the permission of the
publisher, is forbidden and liable to prosecution.
This applies in particular to reproductions, translations, microfilming, and storage and
processing in electronic retrieval systems.

This publication has been peer reviewed.

This book is dedicated to courageous Black, Indigenous and racialized intellectuals working tirelessly to break down institutional barriers and dismantle, in particular, anti-Black and Indigenous racisms, and all other forms of inequities in academia and beyond.

CONTENTS

	Preface	ix
	Acknowledgement	xv
	Introduction	1
Chapter 1	The Beginning	11
Chapter 2	Black Theorizing: Towards a Broader Self and World	27
Chapter 3	Framing the Anti-Colonial for Blackcentricty	53
Chapter 4	Black Lives Matter: Finding My Black African Voice	81
Chapter 5	Indigeneity, Decoloniality and the Anti-Colonial Paradigms: Convergences, Divergences and Synergies	101
Chapter 6	A View of Social Justice Education	121
Chapter 7	Teaching African History to Fight Anti-Black Racism	149

Chapter 8	The Intersections of Anti-Colonial Solidarities	165
Chapter 9	The Black Scholar and Academic Mentorship	187
Chapter 10	The Ugly Face of a New "Diversity Play"	209
	Index	223

PREFACE

It is an honor and with immense appreciation to be on this Land of the traditional shared territories of the Huron-Wendat, Petun First Nations, the Seneca, and most recently, the Mississauga of the Credit River of Turtle Island. I locate myself as an African Canadian scholar, affirming my cultural rootedness while acknowledging residence in Toronto. I live and work on this Land that has through the years continued to sustain countless souls, spirits, and bodies even through times of ingratitude. I situate myself as part of a decolonial storytelling, always mindful of the complexities, complicities, and responsibilities to think through, write about, and do the work required of anyone who claims to be "anti-colonial" and "anti-racist." In this work, I reflect on the sacrifices and magnanimity of the Indigenous peoples of Turtle Island that made it possible for a great number of us to be on this Land. I reflect on the promises and the challenges of getting to the promised Land. I reflect on the ancestors who continue to guide me through these troubled and unsettling times. I reflect on the pain, and suffering from the colonial past and its continuing legacies. Underneath the smile, joy, possibilities, and desires, I also feel a spiritual yearning and regeneration. The colonial wound needs healing and restoration. The Land has allowed me to tell stories that both guide and guard knowledge for action. The Land has also been a place and space of sharing knowledge and dialogue for our collective *Living Well* through subjective politics. The Land as geo-political, social, spiritual, emotional, and cultural has ensured building relationships with living and non-living beings, learning from the wisdom of ancestors and Elders while appreciating organic Earthly teachings.

In paying homage to Turtle Island, I am anchored in other geographies in spiritual, political, and intellectual ways that allow me to reclaim my African Indigeneity. I belong to the traditional Asakyiri clan of Ghana. My African and Ghanaian Indigeneity is rooted in the family clan and lineage history that traces our descent way back to/from a putative female ancestress even prior to Euro-colonialism. The Asakyiri clan is one of the eleven major clans in the Asante Kingdom of Ghana and our totem is the vulture. The vulture is noted for seeping through leftovers to reclaim what is of value. But the proverbial saying is that the vulture never forgets family and the importance of keeping some things in storage for future needs. My African Indigeneity grounds me in the connection to Land, seas, water, and the sky. It gives me a sense of purpose in the sanctity of life, strengthening my pursuit of education and search for knowledge through academic research, teaching and scholarly writing. This is intellectual power that nobody can take away, not even the colonizer. I reiterate in strong terms that being Black and African impacts everything I do as a Canadian scholar, community worker, family member and citizen of the global nation.

I want readers to be moved by this book. My hope is to model different approaches to writing, offering readers a necessary break from traditional academic writing. I also take this space and time as an opportunity to consolidate some of my early ideas that dance with already existing scholarship. As an oppositional gaze to hegemonic Western knowledge, my objective is to centre my experiences as a Black scholar in the Western academy, schooling, and education, and what it means to seriously consider the requirements and benefits of knowledge as generated through the body, Land, spaces, and politics of Black, Indigenous, and racialized peoples.

I offer a counter-theorizing of ideas in relation to anti-colonial knowledge production. In addition, I contribute to reducing epistemic violence that Black, African, Indigenous, and racialized bodies encounter in academic spaces. Consequently, the book should be read like a conversation and lay of academic theorizing. An important thesis is that we need critical dialogues regarding counter-hegemonic thought in education and the possibilities for the future. Given the state of the world in relation to the continual murders of Black people, our academic engagements need to center race, anti-Black racism, and global Blackness. Hence, the significance of a critical conceptual orientation, one which brings to the fore the possibilities of Black and Indigenous social thought. I contend that Indigenous knowledges help us counter the dominance of Western science knowledge in academia, especially if we ensure that our discursive practices are informed by anti-colonial elaborations and intersectional identities such as race, gender, sexual orientation, dis/ability and class.

We live in a world of deep cynicism. We must continually resist the temptation of simply letting our work/scholarship be a "trend," or simply adding currency. It is time to shine the light on us. For Black, Indigenous, and racialized scholars our truths are sometimes frivolously and needlessly questioned. The challenges that come and are encountered with doing anti-racist work is ever-present, for the Western academy prefers silence around race and racism. In trying to navigate these challenges, I ask myself; are we prepared to face the risks and consequences of doing anti-Black racism work? What are the risks of becoming a "distinct Black voice" in my academic community? Academic spaces are not innocent, and Black scholars' complicities and responsibilities need to be examined, from the seduction of the political economy of academia to the ongoing studying of our communities from a distance, and Black denouncements. As a Black scholar, one must master the quotidian practice of Black refusal in academia (Moten & Harney, 2013; Butler & Athena, 2013), and continue to question those who deny it.

We should insist on asserting our truths and authentic knowledges grounded in our everyday lived experiences. Family, community, culture, and history have always been important to me. There are ideals and virtues that emerge from upholding family, community, culture, and history which have guided and continue to guide my sojourn in the Western academy. These ideals and virtues have made me understand what social responsibility truly means. In this project, I pay tribute to my birth parents who instilled ideals and virtues in me as a child, for it has been my family, community and culture that have helped me survive the treacherous life of academia.

Informed by a strong cultural upbringing I can only appreciate my Africanness, as I speak from the heart and a place of gratitude. Even as I have become increasingly critical of society in my work on racism and social justice, I have reflected upon my Black African subjectivity and agency, and what it truly means to be a Black scholar in the Western academy. One thing has been clear and did not take me long to realize, barriers do not exist for everyone, nor do they fall for everyone. You get knocked down, only to get up, dust off and continue the next challenge. As a Black scholar in the Western academy, I expect criticisms and the delegitimizing of my work. I also know I face questions over excellence. I am often viewed as always whining and stand accused of being anti-intellectual when speaking about race and anti-racism in the academy. Everything about being a Black academic in the Western academy is politics. And yes, it must rightly be so. It is for us to understand what politics means and what politics we choose to play, how, why, when and with whom. We also learn that one must be angry if we want to get things done. Nothing is ever handed down to us gleefully. This is the essence of Black rage and anger. We cannot solve a problem we deny. Denials are not simply being complicit, but they serve to sustain the problem we face. We need a public acknowledgement of the disparities, and such acknowledgement to be unapologetic.

Moving through different cultural, national, geographical, and/or onto-epistemological borders in my life, my engagements with and understandings of the concepts of race, justice, equity, diversity, and difference, necessitated a recommitment to anti-colonial politics. I have witnessed the commitment to diversity and postcolonial education in Africa, the Canadian state's lip service to multiculturalism, the domestication and the resiliency of anti-racism and pointed notion of difference, the power of anti-colonial difference, and the implications of identity for knowledge production. I have also become familiar with the rhetoric of national images and imaginaries of inclusion, belonging and citizenship and institutional avoidance. To speak about race, racism, and anti-Blackness, like all other oppressions, is about becoming a true patriot who, notwithstanding their critique, loves their community and nation and wants them to be better than they currently are. Why is this so difficult to understand? As an African Canadian who has witnessed and experienced anti-Black racism and anti-Blackness, I feel the love for community and nation. But sometimes one can be left wondering whether our nation loves us. I see this particularly in the United States where African Americans are deeply patriotic about their country, but as American professional basketball coach and former player Doc Rivers recently said, "…we keep loving this country and this country does not love us back" (2020).

Rhetorically, we would say we want justice for all. But there is no one model of social justice; and the idea of treating everyone the same, only an aspiration. "Treating everyone the same" is something to hope for, but we are not there yet. To get there we must acknowledge history, the severity of issues for certain bodies and groups, and the necessity to target our responses to the most disenfranchised, disadvantaged segments of our communities.

On educational change, how do we go about disrupting the perception of education today as a core avenue for "global redistributive justice," (Mundy, 2008), particularly the ways conventional discourses of "democracy," "good governance," and "human rights," are linked with education, specifically, in the Global South and mired in the primacy of globalized markets and capitalism (global capital). There is the Western preoccupation with democracy, good governance, and education with the underlying liberal notions of freedoms and rights. But how much have we learned of Indigenous leadership to help our understanding of governance and democracy, rights, and responsibility?

These concepts and issues of justice, equity, freedom, inclusion, diversity, and democracy are not just theory. They have lived experiences. The issues ring home to me given my Black body and African humanhood in the global context of anti-Blackness, and in the coloniality of the Western academy. This is even more reason to challenge the colonial appellation of Indigenous teachings and learnings and to reaffirm cartographies of Indigeneity. There are new or continuing questions, challenges, and insights we continually need to work through. There are new questions to be asked:

- How do we begin to speak about our colonial investments and inheritance in the scourge of anti-Blackness and anti-Indigeneity?
- What do we see as our respective ethical-political responsibilities in contemporary times?
- How do we talk about our exclusions, negations and absences and the impact these have on our own learning?
- How do we begin to trouble our deeply held assumptions that serve to maintain the social order?
- How do we openly address race, equity, and oppressions, and not merely engage the language that dances around race, social difference, and oppression?
- What speculative imaginaries are called for as we collectively envision a new, different world an idea that "something else is possible"!?
- How do we speak with each other in ways that make "critical friends" possible?
- What does it mean to pursue "pedagogies of subversion?"
- How do we co-produce knowledge with our varied communities in ways that make social and educational change possible?

This manuscript will approach these questions from my personal, political, and intellectual standpoints. We need our institutions to be committed to the ideals and values of Indigenous collective leadership and the role of public intellectuals, Black, racialized, and Indigenous scholars working for change. With these thoughts, ideas, and questions in mind, I invite you to read this book with an openness and understanding that I am who I am today because of our lived histories. I hope you appreciate these ideas, sit with them, and allow yourself to deeply and sincerely reimagine alongside me.

References:

Butler, J., & Athanasiou, A. (2013). Dispossession the performative in the political : conversations with Athena Athanasiou. Polity.

Harney, S., & Moten, F. (2013). *The undercommons : fugitive planning & black study*. Minor Compositions.

Mundy, K. (2008). Global education in Canadian elementary schools: An exploratory study. *Canadian Journal of Education, 1*(1), 6–15.

ACKNOWLEDGEMENT

I want to thank the many students who have taught me along my academic journey as graduate faculty over the years. Some of these people are established full-time tenured Professors in their own right at Canadian, American and overseas universities. Others are budding intellectuals who I continue to interact with daily as I teach at the University of Toronto.

Marycarmen Lara Villanueva and Dr. Danica Vidotto provided tremendous editorial assistance as they revised, edited, and took the lead through the publication of this book. Without them, and particularly Danica Viditto, this book will not have come out so soon. I am forever grateful. Great thanks to Ayaan Hasshi, and Rukiya Mohammed who read and revised chapters throughout the editing process.

Special thanks to Cristina Jaimungal, Ximena Martinez Trabucco, Andrea Vasquez-Jimenez, of the Department of Social Justice Education, at the Ontario Institute for Studies in Education, University of Toronto and to Leroy King of Freedom Time Media at York University as I received feedback on various chapters.

I also want to give a shout-out to Grace Garlow, Ilar Haydarian, Jinepher Koduah, Huda Salha, Wambui Karanja, Grace Erger, Asna Adhami, Julie Usih, Jessica Vassiliou, Alessia Cacciavillani, Dr. Suleman Demi and Phiona

Lloyd Henry who have been in my corner through current and on-going educational research.

I also acknowledge the support of family, friends and colleagues in Ghana and other African institutions whom have also been mentors: Daniel Nana-Ampaw, the late Dickson Darko, Nana Abrase, Kwasi Clement, Paa Nii, Alfred Agyarko, Nana Adwo Oku-Ampofo, Regina Ampadu, Kalayna Belladoma Dhamphyr, Lashanda Durowaah Dei, Yashita Agyarkoah Dei, Eric Kojo of University of Development Studies (UDS) Tamale; as well as Professors Kolawole Raheem and Jophus Anamuah-Mensah formerly of the Centre for School and Community Science and Technology Education (SACOST) and the Institute for Educational Research and Innovation Studies [IERIS], University of Education, Winneba, Ghana.

Finally, I am thankful for Peter Lang Publishing and, particularly, the editors for bringing this manuscript into publication.

INTRODUCTION

Looking at all the developments around us locally, nationally and globally today I think it is an understatement to say we are living in very troubling times. While writing this manuscript, I have witnessed far-right extremism becoming a global threat; a resurgence of White Supremacist forces, including a so-called "Freedom convoy" (MacDonald, 2022), and an unparalleled reversal to racial progress led by Critical Race Theory opponents (Weinberg, 2021). All of this comes about, as we grapple with the devastating impact of climate change on racialized communities worldwide, making it clear that inaction to global warming amounts to racism (Takei, 2016; Waldron, 2018). The list of alarming and unprecedented challenges historically rooted in a colonial past only grows. In fact, as I write these paragraphs, I mourn the ten Black people who were massacred in Buffalo, New York on May 14, 2022. A hate crime, and an anti-Black racist attack perpetrated just a few days before the second anniversary of George Floyd's murder g. Black death and Black loss continue to be immeasurable.

I cannot help but worry about the political venom, heated partisanship, frivolous bickering and all the hate and violence we are seeing today. What all this has in common is a reproduction of colonialism in an on-going coloniality of Being (Maldonado-Torres, 2007), subjects and relationships.

Notwithstanding the resistance and struggle to carve new futures, one should be excused in saying aloud that we seem to have lost a global will to do what is right by ourselves and each other. We have become so insular and looking out for ourselves and asking what it is for me that we lose what makes us a community. Of course, there are specific geo-locations and daily engagements of the issues of today that place different complicities, accountabilities and responsibilities on different bodies. I do not expect the community to be without contestations and conflicts. But it is a problem when all we are doing is to tear ourselves and communities down rather than build ourselves up from our differences. We can no longer continue to sweep these issues under the carpet and simply claim those who bring attention to the social ills of racism, patriarchy, oppressions, and White supremacy are actually fomenting a problem. There are no two sides to the issue of social and racial injustice. Racism and White supremacy are wrong and there are no, "good people of both sides[1]". I am sorry. To push against cries for justice, equity and fairness is wrong. To discredit voices that speak out on issues of racism, Black Lives Matter and other social oppressions is flat wrong. History will be unforgiving.

Amidst all the turmoil I also see rising voices undeterred by the push back, criticism, violence, and hate. I see it in the voices of those who now openly condemn racism, White supremacy, police brutality without being afraid. I recall not long ago saying "anti-racism" was met with derision. Today people not only say it, but also name the particularities of anti-Black racism. I see the young on the streets fearlessly protesting. It is a sea of rainbow colours and it gives hope. People are no longer willing to stay silent. The only fear they know now is not to speak out. We must extend these voices to a broader critique of the state, institutions and the economic systems that continue to hold people back. We must ask for state and political leadership accountability. The rising voices must be matched with concrete action to avoid disappointment to our youth. We need action for local and national political leadership. We need a sincere commitment to act for change. We need grassroot mobilized action to ensure our ideas and protest movements translate into concrete change. The nation state cannot shirk its responsibilities to a larger citizenry, responsibilities to the dignity, survival, and humanity of all its peoples.

---

1 In a press conference on August 15, 2017, U.S. President Donald Trump, held a press conference where in response to violent protests in Charlettosvile, Va., he said "you also have people who were very fine people on both sides", referring to neo-Nazis White Supremacists, and counter-protests.

While I do not staunchly believe we can educate people out of their oppressions and coloniality, I strongly believe that the academy (e.g.: schools, colleges, and universities) all have a role to play in this struggle. I see the role as about possibilities. What we teach, how and why, who is teaching, what and how, and the objectives of our academic work are all equally implicated in this discussion. The academic space must address its own decolonization efforts, including the relevance of academic scholarship to respond to the challenges of our time. The politics of the academy is in the rearview mirror more so than ever before. We are all implicated as learners, educators, community workers and knowledge producers. We must make ourselves complicit to understand the challenges ahead of us. How we bring attention to these issues is as critical, relevant, and important as how we go about solving problems through our politics and political work. The time for intellectual cowardice is over. We cannot hide behind nice big words and academic jargons intended to show our academic brilliance and win kudos with dominant validation and acceptance. We must be prepared to ruffle feathers and make people uncomfortable and upset. Hopefully, our anger will move people to get up from their comfort zones and sense of complacency and begin to act. The current situation calls for more than being "woke". It is about action *now*! Talking about race and oppression by itself means action is required. Otherwise, the talk is meaningless.

This book is a reflexive undertaking on how through the years I have come to understand the Black scholar identity in academia, and the role and responsibilities of scholarship to speak to communities' myriad concerns and aspirations. It is a reflexive exercise on the academic journey and the learning that I have received from others as well as what I have impacted. In this process I reflect on what it means to reclaim and work with my African Indigeneity as a site and source of knowledge even while residing on the Lands of the Indigenous peoples of Turtle Island. This is so important given the strengths from the impact of the Land and the Earthly teachings on the Black and Indigenous subject. In later chapters I explore the implications of Indigeneity and Black subjectivity in coming to know, and act in socio-political contexts. In this book I also write about what discursive frameworks I have chosen to work with over the years, and the implications of our scholarship to promote a politics of solidarity across our differences.

Building epistemic and political communities through our shared and interconnected history and struggles is critical for surviving academia. The impact of our work also must be revealed in what we set out to do not just by way of theorization, but also, political practice of sharing knowledge to enhance our collective development and relevance. I broached one particular area of academic mentorship (i.e., scholarly publishing) for it's the lessons gained from colleagues and students who have been my best teachers over the years in a journey of academic decolonization.

Bolivian anti-colonial activist and sociologist, Silvia Rivera Cusicanqui argues that decolonization must be a group task and that we cannot decolonize on our own. I wholeheartedly agree (see also Gago, 2016, p. 5). Therefore, we must see and take all discursive practices and projects including the use of "epistemology" as both a "radical critique" and a "decolonizing practice" (Gago, 2016, p. 5). This knowledge extends to an important teaching for me; that the nostalgia with my African Indigenous ancestry must be political and transformative. I have found my voice through reading, writing, and pursuing politics, and more importantly, using knowledge as resistance for personal and collective survival. In thinking through these difficult moments and particularly the current social movement struggles for justice, the whole idea of "coming to know" must be a "political practice", while also bearing in mind that every knowledge carries "living traces of colonialism" within (Gago, 2016, p. 8). The challenge is how we set our minds to the task of ridding ourselves of colonial relations, including hierarchies of knowledge and practice. It is about what vision we chose to align ourselves with and whether we are prepared to do the work required for a realization of our dreams. To quote Cusicanqui, I only "dream on the condition of firmly believing in [my] dreams" to become a reality (Gago, 2016, p. 1).

We must continually reflect on our practices if we want to be on the journey of decolonization. We have collective responsibilities, complicities and implications to address in our everyday practice. Redressing is taking risks. Part of the "redressing" is also asking uncomfortable questions. In anti-colonial, decolonial and anti-racist work, there are always provocative and destabilizing questions to contend with. These questions disturb status quo thinking and can make us edgy. One such question is whether so-called people "of colour" can be racist, and if so, what is the context? My short answer is no. But I do believe that racialized communities can, and at times, do work with racist, colonial, and colonizing tropes indicating discrimination and bias even among ourselves. It is a form of internalized colonialism rooted in the ideology of White racism. But as Black, Indigenous, racialized, and colonized peoples we generally do not have that ability to reproduce and gain meaningfully through racist and colonial power and privilege the way dominant groups can.

It is also significant that we do not liberalize racism and make it a common practice for everyone. To be deemed "racist" is a heavy burden to carry for anyone who is of conscience. It is more than guilt. Racism is also having institutionalized and systemic power working on your side. It is to have that ability to reproduce one's action of injustice and oppression and have it backed up by institutional forces. But we should not be distracted with these contentions. The key is to speak of racism and colonizing acts as social systemic practices that work with (i.e., operationalized through) racial and colonial hierarchies and supported by institutionalized power.

We have seen that, especially in North America, it is quite literally deadly to advocate for anti-racism practice. There is a vast cross-section of our community who regard claims of anti-racism and "Black lives matter" with so much contempt, disdain, and outrage. Still, we must understand the outrage and confront it. For example, anti-racism highlights the violence of society and racism. There is discomfort for many in speaking about racism. Racism has a history which is unpleasant for everyone. This is compounded by the fact of capitalist social logics of the "cult of individualism", the thought that everyone can pull themselves up by the bootstrap and that there is no system holding anyone behind. This is powerful and seductive. It gets a morale boost from a principle of meritocracy where individual hard work and achievement is all that matters for one to succeed. We see it in the defense of colonial privilege which denies history claiming no one group has been given a head start by history. We must also not forget the role of the nation state in seeking safety and security through the promotion of inter and intra-group relations. The mantra is a yearning for peace and harmony which glosses over the need to address systemic inequities, power and histories of entitlement certain groups have. This is the on-going coloniality of racism and oppression. Many people have become very uncomfortable with the politics of decolonization and social activism, especially, when we develop a sense of complacency that the system is working fine and to one's benefit.

Anti-Black racism has a central placement in the anti-racist and anti-colonial struggle. In looking at anti-colonial solidarity, Black struggles have informed political movements such as the Civil rights struggles. And anti-Black racism has not receded to the background even in times of global stress such as the on-going Covid-19 pandemic. We see that health, poverty and body politics are linked revealing racialization and feminization of poverty. Although Covid-19 has no eyes, the pandemic has successfully read and discerned society to the extent of disproportionately attacking our most vulnerable segments. Covid-19 has also been revealing of the inequities in health care and social service delivery. It has impacted the weak in terms of those with pre-existing conditions of heart risk, diabetes, blood pressure, old age etc. But Covid-19 is also revealing disparities in housing, employment, education etc. And, most importantly, we are disproportionately in the frontline service sector.

In the midst of all the despair and discontent there is a glimmer of hope. In both Canada and the US, police and policing have long been connected to a White politic of anti-Blackness and anti-Indigenous oppression. It is not a simple Black-White bifurcation. And so, we must appreciate and welcome the fact that so many White people are joining in solidarity to resist all oppressive forces of society. There is the awareness that it is the culture of policing that creates the White body politics of anti-Blackness. The growing collective push for change among several of today's youth, particularly Generation Z and millennials, is a healthy development. Youth from all stripes, races, ethnicities, class, gender, sexuality, dis/ability, religion, etc. are not willing to see injustice without a fight. They are choosing to hope over fear and have come to understand that movements such as "Black Lives Matter" are registering broadly social justice struggles in law and order, health, housing, employment, education and social welfare. Today's Generation Z and millennials are using social media in productive ways to raise collective consciousness. One can only admire and be optimistic that there are energetic, smart, and young integrative anti-racists and anti-colonial workers expressing themselves. As a pedagogue this development gives me hope. It allows me to write, teach and speak about the "politics of possibilities", while also, recognizing that disappointment and being let down is too heavy a price for us to pay. People simply want new futures, and they are willing to fight for it.

We must continually search for our roots and refuse being defined by our circumstances. The creativity of thought and practice is this constant search for an identity and politics to transform our living conditions. It is continually insisted by anti-colonial thinkers that the world did not begin with Europe, and neither is colonialism our only story. Colonialism, in effect, cannot be our only reference point. How then do we present colonialism as more than a historical narrative (see Alfred, & Corntassel, 2006, p. 601)? We must see Indigenous continued existence even in the current context as a historical, political, and spiritual narrative. This narrative is about power, resistance, relationality, and a symbolic and political yearning to do good for the common case alongside others. For example, doing racial justice work calls for welcoming open arms even amidst a clenched fist protesting injustice. We must open our hearts for the good of humanity rather than building walls around us. We must challenge the coloniality of (our) Being (Maldonado-Torres 2007) through a discursive and political unsettling (this) coloniality of Being (Wynter, 2003).

A colleague taught me a lesson. As academics we must always be grateful for knowledge shared oftentimes in very powerful, eloquent, and meaningful ways by our students and local communities. We must all be emboldened, enlivened, and empowered by the subversive teachings for educational and social change. Our collective task must encompass offering a broad-reaching foundational way of thinking for our educational practice for liberation, against anti-Blackness, White supremacy, capitalism, patriarchy, and all other isms, and more importantly, for a humanizing, complex, and authentic practice that liberates us all. Western modernity has been created through genocide of Black and Indigenous peoples and the seize of our Lands and possessions. To reclaim Land is power and working with our repressed knowledge to begin to "know our pasts, presents and futures as relational, [political] and as pedagogical" (Byrd, 2019, p. 209) is fundamentally important. The White nationalism of today is crude White Nativism that has nothing to do with fighting for existence. It is about maintaining White supremacy.

We must strive to make our institutions more human and humane. The Western academic culture including its scholars have long participated in the colonial (political and intellectual) oppression of Black, Indigenous, racialized, and colonized peoples' histories, cultures, experiences, and knowledges. As Black, Indigenous, and racialized subjects (workers), learners and scholars we cannot engage in academic projects that continually marginalize our existence or openly exclude us from the academic narrative. We need to reclaim our existence in these spaces as political arenas and political spheres for anti-colonial change. There is a problem in our participating in the practice of depoliticizing our knowledges (including placing our knowledges in the service of the political economy of the academy and the interest of Western capital) rather than focusing on an anti-colonial critique and transformation of these colonial structure and the political economic culture itself. As Black, Indigenous, and racialized academics and learners unless we are prepared to name the forces that have continually threatened our existence, knowledges, and humanity and to subvert "the colonizing forces currently within the academy" any talk of "decolonization will certainly fail" (Simpson, 2004, p. 378; see Mbembe, 2016).

We cannot understand decolonization as only a "thought or a discourse"; it is an academic political practice (Cusicanqui, 2012, p. 100). For the academy to be a truly anti-colonial and decolonial space it must be "an arena of resistance and conflict, a site of development of sweeping counter hegemonic strategies, and a space for the creation of new Indigenous languages and projects of modernity [as well as] offering a condition of possibility" (Cusicanqui, 2012, p. 95).

We must begin by seeking and knowing our truths about Indigeneity, colonialism, and decolonization. We must uphold the power of our ways of knowing and unknowing and understand the relationality of Land and Indigeneity in decolonization and, particularly, the place of race and the body in both anti-colonial and decolonial (settler) politics. Decolonization must be about Land, bodies, our labour and the relationalities of knowledge as the unifying processes around which we can construct the principles and politics of anti-colonial and decolonial struggles. Bringing such extended meanings to "Land" as physical, cultural, social, spiritual, and emotional grounds "we stand on" will help capture the relationalities and complexities of space, body, labour, knowledge. As has been noted repeatedly, Indigenous peoples globally have a particular relation to the Land, and "Land is the common ground that unites colonial projects of control and decolonial projects of reclamation" (Garba & Sorentino, 2020, p. 767). Furthermore, Land grounds colonial, as well as "settler projects and decolonial futures" (Garba & Sorentino, 2020, p. 767; see Tuck & Yang, 2012). Land is about life and bodies and the labour of the human body has continually sustained life.

The project of rediscovering the Black self and the African collective to courageously define and interpret our histories, experiences, and scholarship as learners is important as it allows us to tell the stories ourselves and not by others. I see my Blackness as a perspective to bring into critical conversations. My Blackness is about the power of our ways of knowing and unknowing in particular spaces and moments in time. Geography is not simply a "discursive attachment to statis and physicality" (Garba & Sorentino, 2020, p. 764), but also, about how we make sense of our worlds, including particular identifications with Land and space and their representations. For a people whose "Blackness is performatively appropriated" for consumption (Garba & Sorentino, 2020, p. 773) we must continually strive for the "figurative capacities of Blackness" (Hartman, 1997, p. 7) beyond the material and symbolic to transform our collective humanhood. Politically, our claims of Blackness can be an evocation of words which must be used productively to change circumstances because words are powerful. Garba and Sorentino (2020, p. 776) allude to Hortense Spillers revision of the schoolyard chant, "Sticks and stones <u>might</u> break our bones, but words will most certainly <u>kill us</u>" (Spillers, 2003, p. 209). We see Blackness and Canadianess/Americaness always in "dialectical opposition" (Harris, 2019, p. 219). Similarly, "Black" and "Blackness" have been categories defined through slavery and enslavement, the African humanhood and peoplehood revealing a process of subordination and colonial erasure of Black and African humanity (Harris, 2019, p. 219). Furthermore, "belonging" to the nation state has never been "unambiguous" for Black subjects in the diaspora because of processes on inclusion, exclusion, and formations of "race, nation and citizenship" (Harris, 2019, p. 220).

While the Black experience is more than a history of racism, we cannot minimize the impact on Black existence notwithstanding decolonial resistance. Racism has a long history, and it continues to be real, consequential, and impactful in the lives of Black bodies. It is an irrelevant debate as to whether slavery was "born out of racism" or "racism was the consequences of slavery" (see Harris, 2019, p. 217). Colonialism continues to be a modern problem. Byrd (2019) makes the interesting point regarding "the causality between racism and colonialism, to spatialize and disturb slightly the recursive assumption that empire racializes to colonize and that it colonizes because it has already racialized" (p. 208). Historically, slavery and colonialism were pursued with the Euro-supremacist logics of African (racial) inferiority and White (racial) superiority (see Kelley, 2017). In contemporary colonial relations and hierarchies still circulate using the dominant tropes of inferiority and superiority well laid out in human history. "Capitalism and racism grew together, both as processes grounded in Western civilization, not just post-Enlightenment phenomenon" (Harris, 2019, p. 218 referencing the works of Williams, 1944, Robinson, 2000) is as much appropriate today as it was in history. The relevance of this discussion lies in the challenge to the thesis of making colonialism and human exploitation as a universal, natural human practice that would have happened outside of any intervention.

References Cited:

Byrd, J. A. (2019). Weather with you: Settler colonialism, antiblackness, and the grounded relationalities of resistance. *Journal of the Critical Ethnic Studies Association, 5*(1–2), 207–213.

Cusicanqui, S. R. (2012). Ch'ixinakax utxiwa: A reflection on the practices and discourses of decolonization. *South Atlantic Quarterly, 111*(1), 95–109. doi: 10.1215/00382876-1472612.

Gago, V. (2016). Silvia Rivera Cusicanqui: Against internal colonialism. Retrieved from: https://www.viewpointmag.com/2016/10/25/silvia-rivera-cusicanqui-against-internal-colonialism

Garba, T., & Sorentino, S. M. (2020). Slavery is a metaphor: A critical commentary on Eve Tuck and K. Wayne Yang's "Decolonization is Not a Metaphor." *Antipode, 52*(3), 764–782. https://doi/abs/10.1111/anti.12615

Harris, C. I. (2019). Of Blackness and indigeneity: Comments on Jodi A. Byrd's "Weather with you: Settler colonialism, antiblackness, and the grounded relationalities of resistance." *Journal of the Critical Ethnic Studies Association, 5*(1–2), 215–227.

Hartman, S. V. (1997). *Scenes of subjection: Terror, slavery, and self-making in 19th century America*. Oxford University Press.

Kelley, R. D. G. (2017). The rest of us: Rethinking settler and native. *American Quarterly, 69*(2), 267–276. doi:10.1353/aq.2017.0020.

MacDonald, F. (2022, June 30). What the truck? The 'freedom convoy' protesters are heading back to Ottawa. The Conversation. Retrieved from What the truck? The 'freedom convoy' protesters are heading back to Ottawa (theconversation.com)

Maldonado-Torres, N. (2007). On the coloniality of being: Contributions to the development of a concept. *Cultural Studies, 21*(2–3), 240–270.

Mbembe, A. (2016). Decolonizing the University: New directions. *Arts and Humanities in Higher Education, 15*(1), 29–45.

Robinson, C. (2000). *Black Marxism: The making of the Black Radical Tradition*. University of North Carolina Press.

Simpson, L. (2004). Anti-colonial strategies for the recovery and maintenance of Indigenous knowledge. *The American Indian Quarterly, 28*(3–4), 373–384.

Spillers H J (2003) Mama's baby, papa's maybe: An American grammar book. In id. Black, White, and In Color(pp 203–229). Chicago: University of Chicago Press

Takei, M. (2016). Global warming as North-South conflict: The role of unconscious racism 1. In *Emergent Possibilities for Global Sustainability* (1st ed., pp. 50–56). Routledge. https://doi.org/10.4324/9781315737478-8

Tuck E., & Yang K. W. (2012). Decolonization is not a metaphor. *Decolonization: Indigeneity, Education & Society, 1*(1), 1–40.

Waldron, I. (2018). *There's something in the water : Environmental racism in Indigenous and Black communities*. Fernwood Publishing.

Weinberg, T. (2021). *Missouri independent – States newsroom: Opponents of 'critical race theory' urge missouri lawmakers to take action*. Singer Island: Newstex. Retrieved from http://myaccess.library.utoronto.ca/login?qurl=https%3A%2F%2Fwww.proquest.com%2Fblogs-podcasts-websites%2Fmissouri-independent-states-newsroom-opponents%2Fdocview%2F2625279445%2Fse-2%3Faccountid%3D14771

Williams, E. (1944). *Capitalism and slavery*. University of North Carolina Press.

Wynter, S. (2003). Unsettling the Coloniality of Being/Power/Truth/Freedom: Toward the human, after man, its overrepresentation – An argument. *The New Centennial Review, 3*(3), 257–337.

· 1 ·
THE BEGINNING

I grew up in a loving extended family household. Along with my siblings, we never had much, but my parents were loving and took care of us. In Ghana, secondary school was viewed as exceptional, for a family had to have financial means and extended familiar support to do so. Upon the death of my biological father, I had other fathers and mothers who helped along the way.

Death laid its icy hands on our father so suddenly; my mother, siblings and I were very young. I recall my father sent me to Ghana National College, Cape Coast as a boarding student in early September 1967. He wanted to avoid or minimize the usual initiation rites and "punishment" for new students at school so decided not to send me on that same Friday to campus. Instead, he left me in Cape Coast with his close friend Mr. Tumi and took me to school the following Monday to begin my residency.

My father was the usual protective father. I recall our Headmaster, the late Mr. Mensah-Kane, announcing at the morning assembly in late October 1967 that he would like to see me in his office. When I got there, I saw that both the late Mr. Tumi and his driver looked uneasy. The headmaster said, "Dei, you are going with Mr. Tumi as you are needed home". Heavy silence prevailed as we rode the long journey from Cape Coast to Asokore, Koforidua. Upon reaching the outskirts of the Asokore- Koforidua vicinity, I started seeing people wearing *kobene*, *Kuntunkuni* and other traditional mourning clothing. My worst fears about death were soon to be realized. My guttural heartache however was my mother.

The gravity of death loomed as I thought of how my dad had written to me earlier. My mother suffered from chronic and regularly occurring stomach ulcers; we were used to it, but somehow the seriousness of his writing seemed different. I began to mourn for my mother as tears flowed from my deep brown eyes.

So, readers, no words can describe my shock when Mr. Tumi turned from the front seat of his Land Rover and said "*Kwaku*[2], something terrible has happened. Your dad has passed away!" My Dad? He was the last person I expected to hear. The words were so startling that I could have jumped out of the jeep. We were on the way home for the one-week funeral celebration. Adorned still in my white shorts and short-sleeved uniform, I spent just a few hours at the celebration. The wailing faces, sorrowed eyes and the shared emotional frenzy were present when I went to our family house. But the haunting sight of my fragile mother calling out and questioning faith, "oh God why did you take away the man looking after the children? You should have taken me instead!" are words and scenes etched in my memory.

I always recant in tears. Perhaps it was because I could not attend the main funeral and burial, never given the time and space to heal and grieve. There is solace in knowing that my mother's stomach ulcer would never bother her again. We would later say, our dad took it with him to heaven, where God gave him the cure. Our mother would never remarry, explaining to us that in her heart, "no one can replace our Dad."

My mother was nicknamed "*Nnipa nso ye den*" or "what is a human being after all?" In my mind, my mother's being is strength. She ably took charge until her own death in July 2015. She toiled doing all kinds of trades, going around from house to house in the town, selling chewing sticks, kerosene, and other small items. She did her best to support us, as my father's side of the family ensured my continued education at Ghana National College upon his death.

Upon completion of my undergraduate studies at the University of Ghana, Legon. In 1979, I gained a Canadian scholarship from McMaster University to pursue a Master of Arts. Later in 1986, I completed a Ph.D. at the University

---

2 Kwaku, in Twi, given name for male children born on a Wednesday

of Toronto. With secure employment, I sponsored my mother and siblings to Canada in the early 1990s.

My mother lived a life of love and strength. She remained close with her family until she passed away in 2015. I hold fondly to her teachings, "Try to take care of your siblings ... stay united always and act as the leader of the family." My mother's last advice connects back to the early teachings of community and responsibility that she and my father impressed on us when we were very young. Her words, spoken in our last moments together at a nursing home remind me of the identity challenges that come with being an African Canadian settler.

Growing up as an African and later immigrating to Canada, I have always seen how cultures clash over values. I have spoken in the past about one of the things I struggled to come to terms with when I first arrived from Ghana to study in Canada. It was the sight of Canadians taking their elderly parents into nursing homes. Coming from Ghana, our Elders are always near where we are because of their teachings. So, I did not understand why a child of an aging family member would take their parents or an elderly relative into a nursing home rather than be with them in the house. In later years, I grappled and understood the pressures that made this decision possible. But I also learned that no matter where our parents are, we all respect our parents as Elders.

A funny thing happened quite recently. I was at a thrift shop buying clothes to send to family relatives in Ghana. Seniors are entitled to a 10% discount, the cashier implied toward me. I not only looked upset that she was impressed with this idea but was outright defensive in my reply. As to why, I could never tell. Was it the thought of me getting old, or that someone saw me as being that old? I was resisting that image or idea. I concluded later it was me seeing myself young and never wanting to be called a "senior citizen." It was my problem, not the salesperson. Such refusal to aging, later transformed and became an appreciation for the inevitable, because time and experience is a gift. Especially, when premature death for Black people often denies us the right to become Elders.

There are many lessons for me to share, that I learned from my parents. But one in particular stands out as I remember and speak about Elders' teachings. It was during my elementary school days in Ghana when I was near the top of my class. There was one outstanding assignment before computing our final marks. It was an item revealing the learner's handicraft. We were all supposed to bring something we created to school to show our teacher. I had been molding a clay pot for the assignment and I brought it to class. It turns out my closest scholarly rival and classmate brought a cat for his handicraft. He won and got a higher mark. I ended up coming second in my class. Going home that afternoon, my father was furious when I told him. The next day we marched straight to school to complain, why was a cat seen as a handicraft and why did it win over my work? The teacher argued that the pupil who brought the cat claimed he reared the little cat in the house to become a grown cat. My father turned to me and said, "I hope you learn something from this." The lesson was never extended, nor was it ever explicit. He just expected me to learn from the experience. Throughout the years I have thought about it and made my own reasoning, shifting stances, and interpretation, trying to make sense of this lesson with time. I now conclude that maybe the lesson was to use my knowledge and wisdom to always figure out why people do what they do and that even if I am wrong, at least I tried to understand and reason from multiple viewpoints. After all, as is customary to present a teacher with an end of year present, the cat was then gifted to the teacher.

Drawing Inspiration for My Scholarship on Race, Anti-Blackness, Indigeneity and Anti-Colonial Studies

Let me share some stories, many of which have been repeated in some earlier writings. I came to a critical decolonizing consciousness about race, anti-Black racism, and anti-colonial studies in the 1980s. It is a fact that for a number of us, as African learners born on the continent, we have either shunned away from directly engaging race or feel speaking race brings a negative focus on our scholarship. As a beginning graduate student arriving in Canada, I had unevolved reactions to racial issues where I prioritize my end goal: "Oh this is not my issue I will leave it to the Caribbean and Indigenous Black Canadian students to fight racism. For me, upon graduation I am going back to 'Africa'".

I recall in 1988, the police killing of an unarmed 44-year-old Black man, Lester Donaldson, and the protest of the Black community in Toronto. I listened to the words of community activists and stalwarts like Dudley Laws and Charles Roach of the Black Action Defence Committee (BADC) of blessed memory demanding justice. It was their words that registered, opened my eyes, and impressed upon me a need to be involved in the fight against racism. As a postgraduate student later at the University of Toronto, I would join student protests demanding the university to divest its holding from South Africa organized by the Anti-Apartheid Network. The words of community leaders such as anti-apartheid activist Lennox Farrell, as well as colleagues, Keren Brathwaite, Bernard Moitt, the late Charles Mills informed and inspired my activism and scholarship. Later, a new generation of community members, such as leaders from the Ontario-based of Parents of Black Children (OPBC) in Toronto also reminded me of why this work is so necessary.

From these experiences, I began to reflect on my early graduate research in "Development Studies." I questioned what the concept of "development" taught or did not teach me about race, specifically, discourses and conceptions of "development" and the denial of White complicity. There is a denial of White identity as privilege position/location in "development" work in the Global South. We have the portrayal of Africa as a "basket case" and the powerful refrain of "crisis" as a metanarrative in Africa. The celebrations of Whiteness stood out starkly as I traveled home to Ghana. As such, my research on local strategies and practices of development lead to a realization of the devaluation of local cultural knowledge. Theorizing Africa beyond its physical boundaries (Dei, 2010) is so important when advancing the Black and African global cause. Africa is everywhere today. Such understanding has implications for our re-reading of conventional explanations of Africa as Africa does not suffer from a lack of experts on the continent. The problem is we do not respect our own experts and expertise.

Graduate school experiences shaped by discussion and the processes of knowledge validation and privileging remain with me. It was frustrating to be asked time and again to repeat myself. Often my thoughts or attempts to partake in conversations were ignored. My comments were then repeated from the mouths of White or English-speaking colleagues who were then praised for my idea. I now often hear from Black, racialized and Indigenous students who echo these complaints, including linguistic inequities, having to go through the lack of validating other knowledges, experiences and stories in the school system.

Even my early teaching career was not easy. As a postdoctoral candidate and teacher at the University of Windsor in 1990, I experienced pain as many, mostly White students, in my *Introduction to Sociology* course left the class when they realized my accent was going to be difficult for them to follow discussions. There was no attempt or effort made to learn from me, the same way I made the effort to listen to students speaking English as their mother tongue. Speaking differently is hard for some to appreciate and accept. I have been fortunate to have colleagues stand at my side when I've been critiqued unfairly for my use of language. For example, Helen Lenskyj rallied with me when I was unfairly attacked by a colleague for what I had written in a University Bulletin (see Dei, 2006). Along the way, on this intellectual journey, I have learned a lot from other scholars, my own students, local community workers and leaders, parents, teaching me about the importance of building upon such knowledges that is received. These narratives, stories, and experiences have shaped my work in anti-racism, anti-Black racism, and African education.

As a member of the Organization of Black Parents of Black Children [OPBC] in Toronto in the 1990s, the question of Black youth's education was foremost on the minds of Black mothers. I recall one mother finding out I was a newly hired faculty at the Ontario Institute for Studies in Education (OISE), University of Toronto. Beaming, she said, "good, now one of our own can study the issue of Black youth and school dropouts because I believe there is more to be told!" This Black mother inspired our later studies on "school pushouts" (see Dei, 1995; Dei, Mazzuca, McIsaac, & Zine, 1997).

With time, my experiences of living abroad have also informed my work on race and African education. I have come to appreciate that issues crosscut geographical boundaries. There is an urgent need to develop a comparative lens to discussions of race and racisms (i.e., globalization of racisms). I see vestiges of colonial education in post-colonial African education. Elsewhere (see Dei, 1996) I have shared some reflections. For example, while growing up in Ghana, I learned more about Niagara Falls, in New York and Ontario than the local rivers in my village where my mother caught the fish we ate. I have also examined postcolonial African schooling and education with its goal and purpose of national integration and nation building.Consequently, there has been denial of difference and/or sweeping differences under the carpet. The story of African monuments and landmarks named after colonizers: European discoveries and colonial naming (e.g., Victoria Waterfalls in Zimbabwe and Zambia, Cecil Rhodes imperialists exploits in Southern Africa), brought me to the question: why do we honor our abusers? If we insist on continuing to teach the history of those who fought to preserve slavery, why not include Black resistance movements and narratives that speak to Black humanity? Many of us have been written out of history for far too long (Dei & Lara-Villanueva, 2021).

My Academia

In my early work on anti-racism and anti-Black racism, I was read as the "race man" who sees the world in only Black/White terms. A graduate student named Bhumush, joked, "Prof Dei, do not let race get to you. I don't want to hear in your obituary that "race" was the last word you typed on your computer!" A colleague and I made quips about how with our passion for studying race and anti-racism, we could have invented the term, should it not have previously existed in the dictionary. We view ourselves as operating through a "Black-White" prism, rather than a binary. The prism argues a closer proximity to Whiteness, is rewarded globally, and as a counter proximity to Blackness is punished (see Dei & Jimenez, 2017). I also write about "integrative anti-racism" meaning one cannot understand the full effects of race without its connection with other forms of difference: class, gender, sexuality, dis/ability, etc. (Dei,1995).

To be frank, as anyone who does critical race scholarship will tell you, there are huge risks in academia for the Black scholar. Your life can be at risk with threats. There are personal attacks and lives in peril– lodging complaints that you are teaching students to hate White people. You are perceived as a separatist and being asked "why are you teaching at our university?" My experiences promoting Africentric schooling in Canada is a testament for me. I was portrayed as an anti-intellectual, only concerned with Black and race issues. Other risks have to do with the spiritual and emotional wounds produced by institutional hypocrisy – non-performativity of anti-racist work (Ahmed, 2006). The anti-racist policies that exist in the books are only for show. This disappointment can be harsh for Black academics when compounded with attempts to seek legitimation, validation, and acceptance in white colonial spaces.

The culture of denialism and the silencing of courage is evident, as Black academics face subtle and blatant push-back. We navigate success by standing on the shoulders of those before us- their work, teachings, and sacrifices. These wave makers and Elders strengthen us spiritually, intellectually, and politically, working with communities both local and epistemic. From this I have personally developed a necessary awareness of the important conceptual and political distinction between being an "African/Black scholar" and engaging in Black scholarship. I find students' support and mentorship very healing, alongside being purposeful and intentional with the battles I choose to fight, and with whom I work with as a critical friend.

Writing in This Moment

There is a big story to tell. Judith Butler (1988) long ago mentioned the importance of theorizing the experiential. To me, "theorizing the experiential" is to connect our experiences to a larger conversation of the moment. Allow me to situate the book in the moment I find myself writing. We are living in an era of two global pandemics: Covid-19 and structural anti-Black racism. 2020 has been difficult for all of us. We are witnessing the disproportionate effects of Covid-19 on Black, Indigenous, and racialized communities. In the beginning of summer 2020, we have all been part of the "shelter in place" and constantly saturated with news and information of Covid-19 through the television, radio, Internet and even through personal text messages and emails. The communication about death has been emotionally and physically wrenching for most people. Black healthcare workers in Great Britain, United States and Canada emotionally advising the global Black and African community, especially in the Diaspora, to take the virus very seriously was frightening given the pandemic's heavy toll on our communities. As reiterated in Dei (2021) who can forget their words, "Covid-19 is killing our Black people." I recall a viral email where a Black nurse, in tears, not only complained about the lack of available resources like PPEs, but also, about how she feared for her own health and life. In the video, this nurse further describes the distraught and intense sadness she feels about losing her patients overnight to the virus. It is clear then, that no words can truly describe the emotional, physical, and psychological toll Covid-19 has brought onto many. In July 2020, Toronto Public Health released socio-demographic Covid-19 data which stated racialized people make up 83% of those infected with Covid-19. Specific to Black communities, Black people are only 9% of Toronto's population but are 48% of people with Covid-19[3].

The nightmare is not over. Many of us fear the possible Covid-19 resurgence with the seasonal flu during the autumn and winter seasons. Therefore, those who pit wealth against health are making a false foolhardy choice. Death is irrevocable when it happens. Property can always be rebuilt. The fact of the matter is, the few who are on the side of wealth, those dissatisfied with job losses, mortgages and businesses shutting down, while the pain cannot be diminished, have a great number of wealthy folks among them. These

---

3 https://www.toronto.ca/news/toronto-public-health-releases-new-socio-demographic-covid-19-data/

folks are merely afraid of losing their wealth and privileged living conditions. It is not cruel to make this assertion. In a society like ours, where there is some degree of a safety net, it can be guaranteed that the rich people will not go hungry overnight. However, one cannot say that the same applies to many poor, working families who have gone hungry for *many* nights. Thus, these privileged few constitute the loud voices who are upset about the "shelter-in place" because their privileged way of life has been affronted suddenly. This is the sad part of our world today. The privileged class is guaranteed to make loud noises and the masses are expected to listen to their cries. Unfortunately, in North America, the privileged are aided by political leadership where elected officials are more concerned about winning political elections than devoting energies to saving human lives (see also Dei, 2021).

Concurrently, we have witnessed unprecedented public voicing and uprising on "Black Lives Matter" (BLM). The murder of Breonna Taylor by police while asleep on March 13, 2020, the killing of D'Andre Campbell who called Peel Regional police for help in April, the senseless social death of George Floyd in Minneapolis on May 25, 2020, the death of an Afro-Indigenous woman, Regis Korchinski-Paquet two days later in Toronto, the shooting of Jacob Blake in August, all register sadness and rage. While Black bodies are surveilled and policed, a seventeen-year-old White Wisconsin teen with a rifle is allowed to roam free on the streets under the full gaze of police officers after he kills two people who are protesting for justice! Why is the same humanity extended to a White mass murderer who has lunch purchased for him by authorities before he is sent to prison not afforded to Black people?

As a Black/African scholar and man, the Black Lives Matter protests have affected me powerfully. I ask myself: What will I remember in terms of this moment, time, and space of Black Lives Matter? How will I honour and remember the countless victims of state violence? How does one remember past, present and futures, and the place of cultural narratives and spiritual memories? How can I develop critical consciousness of our diverse and complex realities as Black and African peoples? How can I ensure that developing such consciousness means to be aware of our complex existence and the complexities of our identities and the politics we seek to play?

As we argue elsewhere (see Dei, Anamuah-Mensah, Kolawole, & Mohamed (in press); Dei & Mohamed, 2022) Black Lives Matter very well matters for all Black people, including Africa itself. This is because Black Lives Matter protests are fundamentally (but not exclusively) about anti-Black racism. Protest is the weapon of the oppressed and downtrodden. People hardly protest over their privilege. They, of course, protest when they fear losing their privilege. But I will not call that protest. It is an exercise of self-entitlement. For the oppressed, our protest is informed by a history of neglect, abuse, violence, and inhumanity. We protest anti-Black racism and police brutality because of the abuse, neglect, violence, and the inhumanity shown to the Black body. In fact, anti-Black racism reveals itself in the enduring legacies of colonialism and enslavement and the afterlife of slavery. Anti-Black racism supports capitalism. The continuing perception of the imperial savior, Africa as the Whiteman's burden. Discourses of "crisis" where we cannot put our house in order. The flattening and cheating of Africa outside its complexities and heterogeneities. We also have the denial of African Indigeneity – there was no Africa before colonialism. We should also not forget the internalized racism that reveals itself under anti-African racism.

Black Lives Matter is a national conversation about racism, unlawful police brutality and movement against injustice. With Black Lives Matter mobilized online, the objective of the hashtag #Blacklivesmatter was to spark a conversation locally and internationally around systems of power that allow Black lives and communities to be disproportionately victims of over- surveillance, police brutality, daily microaggressions and racial profiling. The Black Lives Matter global movement acknowledges those marginalized: "Black queer and trans folks, disabled folks, undocumented folks, folks with records, women, and all Black lives along the gender spectrum" (BLM, 2020). Today the hashtag #Blacklivesmatter has become a collective human rights movement, rallying for cultural resistance, and resilience. Racism and anti-Blackness have been an American and European problem for centuries since the enslaved Africans were forcibly transported across oceans in the 1600s.

The Significance of the Moment

We need to develop priorities as a society to combat our social ills. We need a multi-pronged approach to fighting anti-Black racism. All gestures are significant and personally I would not deny or downplay the symbolism of painting Black Lives Matter on streets. In Toronto, Canada, in front of the city's police department BLM protesters held up traffic, shut down the street and painted in large, capital, pink letters "DEFUND THE POLICE." There is always the problem of speaking racial justice in a pro-capitalist society. But how do we play new songs, dance to a new tune, and create a new rhythm? Our politics must be to protect ourselves from more colonial harm and injuries. For bodies always fighting racism, we don't need any moment to awaken us.

In these challenging times, not only must we offer intellectual leadership around issues of anti-Black racism in our institutions, but also, we must contribute to public awareness of systemic anti-Black racism and the need for this destructive reality to be addressed at all levels of our society. As a community of scholars, we not only have a collective responsibility to contribute to new knowledge, but to share this knowledge with the world and to seek change.

Selfishness and disregard for Black lives has reached a saturation point. We cannot leave this moment even more disappointed. This is concerning considering our society's short attention span. There is also a real concern as the current global reckoning on race and anti-Black racism has not come without a backlash, push back, or hostile resistance.

At this moment we are confronted with the rising tide of racial hostility. There is a systemic application of White supremacist logic to regulate social action. Blackness is deemed menacing. It is demonized and perceived as a threat to Euro-civility. Our silence reveals the normalizing, rationalizing and deafening gaze of White racism on our collective psyche. We must counter the interpretation of White privilege as about White hate or dislike. The denial of White privilege, White supremacy and structural racism is intended to individualize social problems and blame individuals rather than structures. One can benefit from White privilege, White supremacy, and structural racism without being consciously aware. White fears and anxieties are unfounded. It is about protecting White privileges and power. History gives them no reason to be afraid. Colonialism, like slavery, is not a football match for us to say that the game has ended. Colonialism is a structure. This structure continues to be in place to keep Blacks at the bottom of the social and racial hierarchy. There is an erroneous perception that perhaps, except for the descendants of enslaved Africans, we as Black people are all settlers.

Anti-Black racism has a long history. In fact, anti-Black racism is implicated in the creation of the Canadian settler colony. We need to teach and understand the use of enslaved Black labor and making Black bodies as property class in the nation building project. A lot of our anti-Black racism politics should start from our settler commitments and responsibilities in support of Indigenous sovereignty movements.

Racism is a bigger pandemic than Covid-19. We do not, and neither have we even tried, to develop a vaccine for racism. The pursuit of a health equity response to the pandemic is significant. But we must develop a critical lens to address social inequity across the board because Covid-19 has been able to read how we treat each other in society and take due advantage of this fact. We need to maintain a critical gaze, and fight to ensure structural change on the institutions that sustains and maintains the status quo. We must examine how systems are set up to marginalize, render invisible and ensure the perpetuation and continuation of systemic inequities and injustice. Our denials of racism activate invisibilization of bodies.

Thinking and Working Collectively to Create New Decolonial Futures

Coming to critical scholarship is not easy. Like decolonization it begins with asking new questions: How do discern de-politicizing projects work? What constitutes anti-racist responses to colonial actions? What is the place for the radicalization of thought if it is for a decolonization objective? How do we connect oppressions and shares histories such that we connect anti-racism with anti-Black racism, anti-Indigeneity, anti-Semitism, and that we see the threat to Arabs as more than directed at Islam, just as anti-Islam violence is more than violence against Arabs?

We cannot find new futures in a hopeless place. The permanence of our existence is an apt descriptor that does not obscure our different and contesting histories. It is important to acknowledge the varying geographies of home, place, and Land. When we ask who and what is a Black subject, we are visually discerning this subject as complex and multiple subjectivities. The desire to investigate all our subjectivities is about a fundamental quest for place, belonging and identity. Our histories are intertwined, and they do not necessarily fit oneself in a giant narrative.

How we insert ourselves into the slippery terrain is as important as how conceptualizing race beyond the visual optics. The visual conceptions of race presented in the binaries of Black and White are no longer tenable. But it does not mean black and white are meaningless categories. Neo-liberalism and multiculturalism play a deep role in the construction of Blackness and other identities today. The threat to the White nation is presented both in ideology and practice. In exploring anti-racist and anti-colonial futurities we must deal with White fantasies and curiosities and the seductive practices of domesticating progressive politics which are nothing more than sophisticated ways of pushing back against the tide of social change. There is a way to conceptualize race outside of the visual regimes and representation. While there is merit in arguing for us to think about race beyond visual regimes, part of the anti-colonial strategies to recuperating decolonial discourses for anti-racist futures is to connect histories, cultures, identities, and politics. We do not need to be a Muslim or Arab to develop a strong affinity to anti-Islamophobia resistance. Similarly, not every discourse has redemptive qualities.

An interrogation of the ways we use the social construction of race to dismiss anti-racism or using anti-religion stance to dismiss Islamophobia, is necessary. Hiding under the cloak of anti-religion to spew anti-Muslim hate and violence. Similarly, we see the subtle and conniving ways Western rationality is used to justify the colonial order (e.g., "Black on Black" crime). In the sociology of desirability, Black bodies are desired to serve White curiosity and entertainment. We are tired in the sense of being an emotional sponge for anyone's taste and consumption. There is the absurdity of the idea that getting people to talk on both sides of the issue is the only way to flesh out the truth. These smacks of moral equivalence stances run amok. We must be bold to take stances and condemn oppression. There has always been a wider climate of racist, sexist, homophobic hate and violence and that current Trumpian politics is a mere symptom and not just a fueling of hate.

Interrogating the pathologies around emotions and the psychology of attraction will lead us to understand our anger as well as why there are the rewards for being complicit in upholding White supremacist values. In thinking and working collectively to create new decolonial futures we must question ourselves whether we are better at theorizing or framing the end of the world than the beginning of new futures? The idea of decolonizing, unchaining, and changing the mind (Womack, 2013) is powerful. Change is not inevitable. Change must be imperative because a lot has happened but not a lot has changed. Colonialism has been an interrupter of history. For all colonized peoples we will never know what might have happened. This is because we have never known a world outside of colonialism.

So, what do we want to happen? Are we working towards the end of capitalism, to be human again, to self-define one's own existence, to get rid of the falsity of Western democracy and the hypocritical claims of freedoms, liberty, rights, etc.? The answer may well be working towards all these goals. Whichever answer we search for, it is important that we shape the change we want. Futures are liberatory and require that we act in the present, making new imaginations, and action. We must also accentuate agency rather than denying them. We must understand that the representations we seek to make since representations have material, spiritual, psychological, and political consequences.

There is always the possibility of change. We must figure out how we talk about decolonial futures outside of Western corporate hegemony or ideologies, shaping the change we want by relying on the communal relations we make. Therefore, decolonization becomes a question of relationships and the understandings we bring to the community. We face fundamental political challenges and the transformative actions we pursue must truly represent a serious challenge and subversion of White supremacy. It may require that we work with/draw upon African and Indigenous spiritual ontologies and epistemes and to talk about Afro-futurity that is built on dreams, visions and what it means to dream and re-envision differently. It won't be a magical futurity but one that we collectively work to bring it into being. In situating the nexus of knowledge, practice and politics, the goal is to delink from the structures and processes of "coloniality of Being" (Maldonado-Torres, 2007; Wynter, 2003), colonial existence, knowledge, and practice. We must insist on our own self definitions since we can no longer be deemed "empty signifiers". We must disturb stereotypes about Africa, Black(ness), the racialized and the Indigenous existence. We must aim to de-Westernize thought and practice

Positionality is significant in searching for new futures. That is to work with both "politics of position" and "position of relation" (Rowe, 2008). This is a position in relation to one's work, as well as a reflexive exercise on what this means to be a learner, scholar and community worker and the roles, responsibilities, and expectations of the position (see Rowe, 2008). This allows one to engage in the difficulty of reflexivity. The identities we hold, produce, reproduce must help subvert privilege and promote change. This goes beyond the recognition of relative positions of power and privilege.

We also need a theorization of modernity. Colonialism as a precursor of modernity. The universalization of Euro-modernity has been a huge problem for anti-colonial resistance. We need a more decolonial tradition that sees coloniality and modernity as inherently linked. There is no modernity without coloniality notwithstanding the fact that Western modernity itself is fundamentally dependent on the suppression of other ways of knowing.

We must also flesh out the racial-colonial matrix/network, Mignolo's idea of "coloniality is constitutive of modernity. Colonial modernity has suppressed the epistemologies and ontologies of Black/African, Indigenous, and racialized peoples and it is important to subvert a traditional-modernity split. It means a lot for us to delink from Western Europe-colonial modernity as a starting point to facilitating epistemic shifts away from Western science/knowledge systems.

We must begin to pay attention to Black/African nationalist sensibilities, specifically, the specificity of anti-colonial nationalism and its distinctions from other nationalisms (e.g., White nationalism). White nationalism is about the reinforcement of coloniality. The power of Black nationalist epistemologies is to subvert colonial dominance of thought and practice. True freedom is essential to the survival of any democracy. There must be a place of ideas, where knowledges competes for us to come to a better understanding of our societies (i.e., the idea of what it means or what it means to be human – the capacity to live well as human). True freedom is about competency and responsibility and there must be checks and balances of any rights and freedoms given human abuses. So collectively we insist on freedoms and responsibilities.

Liberal democracies have been overrated and freedom has not always been about truth seeking. It is in such a context that we must understand the rise in political extremism, populism and nationalism. We need freedom and integrity to be nurtured, actively and defended but within certain considerations and understandings. Freedom cannot be a hollow pursuit in search of knowledge. Freedom can only survive if we uphold the humanity of all learners and local communities. There is a long history of the coloniality of science and scientific knowledge like pursuing knowledge on the bags of disadvantaged communities. Our pursuit of anticolonial freedom must be made meaningful and relevant to local communities. It must be buttressed with the pursuit of equity and social justice education viewed as not anti-intellectualism nor an unfounded interrogation of science knowledge. Everywhere, we sustain freedom through social responsibility, integrity, and competence. It is only when we abide by these ideals that we begin to open new frontiers of knowledge as we navigate new worlds. I will take up these frontiers of knowledge in the succeeding chapters, starting with Black theorizing in academia.

References Cited

Afful-Broni, A. J., Anamuah-Mensah, K. R., & Dei, G. J. S. (2020). "Introduction." In A. J. Afful-Broni, R. Anamuah-Mensah, & G. Dei (Eds.), *Africanizing the school curriculum: Promoting an inclusive, decolonial education in African contexts*. Myers Educational Press.

Black Lives Matter. (2020). "Herstory." *Black Lives Matter*. Black Lives Matter. https://blacklivesmatter.com/

tler, J. (1988). Performative acts and gender constitution: An essay in phenomenology and feminist theory. *Theatre Journal*, 40(4), 519–531.

Butler, J., & Athanasiou, A. (2013). *Dispossession: The performative in the political.* Cambridge: Polity Press.

Dei, G. J. S., (1995). "Integrative anti-racism and the dynamics of social difference." *Race, Gender and Class*, 2(3), 11–30.

Dei, G. J. S., (1996). *Anti-Racism education in theory and practice.* Halifax: Fernwood Publishing.

Dei, G. J. S., (2006, May, 29). "Speaking Out, Differently." *University of Toronto Bulletin.* Number 18, page 12.

Dei, G. J. S., (2010). Theorizing Africa beyond its boundaries. In G. Dei (Ed.), *Teaching Africa. explorations of educational purpose*, vol. 9. Dordrecht: Springer.

Dei, G. J. S., Anamuah-Mensah, J., Kolawole, R., & Mohamed, E. (in press). *Anti-Black racism, Black lives matter and Africa today: Scholars and activists in conversation about new strategies for social change.* Myers Educational Press.

Dei, G. J. S., Holmes, L., Mazzuca, J., McIsaac, E., & Campbell, R. (1995). *Push out or drop out?: The dynamics of Black Students' disengagement from school.* University of Toronto.

Dei, G. J. S., Mazzuca, J., McIsaac, E., & Zine, J. (1997). *Reconstructing 'Dropout': A critical ethnography of the dynamics of Black Students' disengagement from schools.* Toronto: University of Toronto Press.

Dei, G. J. S., & Mohamed, R. (2022). *Mapping the contours: African perspectives on anti-Blackness and anti-Black Racism.* DIO Press.

Dei, G. J. S., & Vasquez Jimenez, A. (2017). "The foundations of transformative anti-racism: A conversation with George J. Sefa Dei." *Canada Education*, 57(3), 50–52.

Harney, S., & Moten, F. (2013). *The undercommons: Fugitive planning & Black Study.* Minor Compositions.

Maldonado-Torres, N. (2007). On the coloniality of being: Contributions to the development of a concept. *Cultural Studies*, 21(2), 240–270.

Mbembe, A. (2016). Decolonizing the University: New directions. *Arts and Humanities in Higher Education*, 15(1), 29–45.

Womack, Y. (2013). *Afrofuturism: The world of Black Sci-Fi and fantasy culture.* Lawrence Hill Books Press.

Wynter, S. (2003). Unsettling the coloniality of being/power/truth/freedom: Towards the human, after man, its overrepresentation-an argument. *The New Centennial Review*, 3(3), 257–337.

· 2 ·

BLACK THEORIZING: TOWARDS A BROADER SELF AND WORLD

Introduction

An important learning objective from ongoing discussion is how our lives, even as we resist daily, can still be scripted by relations of domination as Black, Indigenous, and racialized learners. I will begin this chapter with some basic questions: How then do we make sense of our lives and educational experiences as Black learners? How much longer can we be apologists for racism and anti-Black violence? For how long do we want to see others lower the bar of human decency to protect themselves? How long are we going to be silent on the continuing assault on Black/African humanity? Silence has never been an option for some of us. We have come to a place where we all must be loud and insist on being heard through theory and practice. In other words, it is not enough to simply insist that all voices be heard. We must engage in concrete practice to make our voices heard and actualize in action. This means working with our received knowledge in collective transformation. The privileged voices among us can no longer stay silent and oblivious with the continuing injustices around us. We owe it to ourselves and our collective moral, ethical and spiritual fortitudes to speak out against racism and other social oppressions. We cannot be complacent anymore. In the age of social media, we must resolve to use technology effectively to combat White supremacy, racism, and all forms of systemic violence.

This chapter is a discussion of "coming to theory" that embraces the power of Black theorizing. I want to start by laying the groundwork for "coming to theory" and the particularity of "Black theorizing". We cannot confuse White supremacy with patriotism. Neither can we confuse White nationalism with Black and Indigenous nationalist struggles intended to reaffirm our humanity and existence as a people. White nationalism and White privilege are about oppression. They are about the denial of the fundamental freedoms of those historically oppressed by dominant society. It never ceases to amaze me how the study of the Black experience or the Black and African human condition can be a subject of inquiry where everyone can claim to be an "expert" or have knowledge on. To claim to know, we must bring an embodied commitment to Black and African people and our shared causes. After all that is what Blackness is about.

Of course, I have been curious and disappointed even with myself, because at times our own writings do not seem to fully explain or capture what is happening to Black lives. I refuse to accept the thinking that the economic times we live in today explain away everything about us. It is simply not enough. We cannot afford to be material determinists and lay everything at the foot of economics. As I followed the 2020 U.S.A election, I kept hearing people talk about "how it will all come to economics and how people feel in their pocketbooks." Really? What about human moral decency and character to do right by people? If the stock market is rising but people face the harsh realities of everyday systemic racism making them humans to be disposed of, is it a case of a job well done? The phenomenon of President Donald Trump has a lot to do with how the White supremacist colonial project speaks to racism and the particularity of anti-Blackness and the Black subject and body. "Shit hole" countries[4], people with low IQs, communities that are ridden with crime and insects, demonstrating how languages demean a people and a person. I have also heard a reasoning that President Trump and the subsequent reiterations and reactions is a direct response to President Barack Obama, a Black man in the U.S. White House. I want to think this is deeper than that. The fear of losing power and privilege is at the heart of politics of division that keep tearing our communities apart. I still believe our myriad identities can be a shared

---

4   Oval Office Speech, January 11, 2018; https://www.theatlantic.com/politics/archive/2019/01/shithole-countries/580054/

ground for critical conversations about solidarity, bringing the oppressed fighting injustice and the dominant consumed by their fears and anxieties together for common purpose. We may critique "identity politics" but it is the real politics and political agenda of our identities that matter.

In 2019, chants of "blood and soil" rang from the KKK and White supremacists march in Charlottetown, U.SA. These chants were deeply disturbing, not only for the untruths but for their violence and hatred. Yet, we should not have been all that amazed or surprised by this vitriol. My initial reaction upon hearing those chants was to respond, "Really? Whose blood and soil? Is this historical amnesia?" The history of colonial genocide, land dispossession, displacement and other forms of violence makes any claims of "blood and soil", especially on stolen Lands, very ridiculous, if not laughable. But what was at play was a particular brand of body politics all decent people should despise.

We should look at body politics in a way that can be uplifting and subversive. For example, how do we speak about the genealogies of Black thought? How do we account for the colonial encounter and experience, and the before the encounter of Black thought? How is Black and Blackness understood in the prism of an African Indigeneity? Racism, like colonialism, continues to be a problem of Western civilization. It does not mean only the West has a monopoly on racism. The West is the genesis of the problem. Racism makes the "thingification" of the Black body (Césaire, 1972) real and consequential. If racism is to be challenged, the claiming of humanity for the Black subject is essential politics. Hence, a need to understand body politics differently and to acknowledge the importance of taking Blackness and Whiteness both as conceptual framings and as epidermal schema, which is not the opposites, but a continuum. That is, a sort of Black-White prism for reading the world. As argued elsewhere (Dei & Vasquez, 2017) this prism is not a duality but a lens that affirms a close proximity to Whiteness is rewarded, while a proximity to Blackness is punished.

In the new bodily schemata, we must read the curious interface of the skin, body, psyche, hegemonies, and politics. The visceral reaction to Black skin, body and representations matters equally and significantly (Dei, 2017). There is a racist reaction to the Black skin and body and the images and resistance evoked, as in showing up in unwanted or transgressed spaces. We must produce counter readings of the Black body as an embodiment of knowledge- as a set of ideas, values, expressions, and histories- and as resistance and consciousness rather than conventional racist, essentialist, unchanging and fixed readings as deviant, criminal, degenerate and contaminated (see Dei, 2017,

2018). In effect, we need a new body politic to counter the perceived Black transgressions. We need to counter how the Black, Indigenous, and racialized body is disciplined when shown up in "unwanted spaces".

The Black and Indigenous body is associated with place-based knowledges. For the Black subject, our Blackness is significant in the ways of seeing and thinking (e.g., body in relation to our thought processes), experiencing the Black body is central in our lived experiences. If the Black body does not question spaces and places, we get into then our politics will always be suspect. Long ago, Fanon (1963) poked at the idea of a Black body being one that questions in spaces. For example, when we get into academic and social spaces, we can question the way Western corporate modernity interrogates and validates our Black intellectuality. We must promote the idea that the study of Blackness must be for us and the community, and not simply in furtherance of an "intellectual agenda" such as the entrapments of academia and personal professional developments. This is not an easy thing to work with and we are, at times, guilty of it.

The question of knowledge is also much linked to space, place, and identity. So how do we open critical discursive spaces to articulate complex, multiple, and contesting epistemologies and ontologies? In my anti-colonial writings, I have called for an "epistemology of the colonized" (Dei, 2000, see also Dei and Asgharzadeh, 2001). I see this call and insistence as an important marker of critical anti-colonial scholarship. Implications of such intellectual stances for politics and for anti-racist and anti-colonial praxis. We should deploy critical Indigenous epistemologies for anti-racism and anti-colonial work like the ideas of reciprocity, relationality, humility, sharing, connections, and spiritual ontologies. There are intellectual and political conditions that make this possible. For instance, one is the space we create or come into. For example, the importance of creating spiritually centred spaces and sacred learning spaces, or what Garcia and Shirley (2012) call, "sacred learning landscape" (p. 77), or what Dei (2012) refers as, "*Suahunu*, the trialectic space of body, mind, soul, and spirit interface" (p. 86). For Black and Indigenous peoples, learning spaces are productive when they are also spiritually centred. Hence there is much work required to ensure that multicentric learning spaces exist within our institutions like the Land and Earth teaching. I will return to this fully as I reframe the "anti-colonial". As Black scholars, our approach to theorizing must also engage the task of pioneering Indigenous, and new analytical concepts steeped in "home-grown culture perspectives" (Yankah, 2004, p. 25) and cultural knowings that help understand our communities. Such ideas of

"*Ubuntu*", "*Suahunu*", trialectic space and the knowledge of the Indigenous naming of Africa as "abibiriman" are significant.

The creation of safe learning spaces is usually seen as a prerequisite for decolonization. How do we theorize this connection of safe spaces and decolonization? When, and how, do safe spaces encourage learning? Can there ever be a safe space to teach about race, colonial violence, White privilege and oppressions? Whose safety are we talking about? And why are we talking about safety as a requirement in the first place? These questions are all extremely important. They demand honest discussions. As noted elsewhere, discussions on safety in the academy are often mired in the discursive space on "no person's Land of bureaucratic obfuscation" (Dei, 2014, p. 17) to the extent that a notion of academic freedom simply protects those benefiting from positions of power and privilege (see Leonardo & Porter, 2010; Shore & Halliday-Waynes, 2006; Di Angelo & Sensory, 2009; all cited in Townsend-Cross, 2017, p. 160). It is important for us to focus on a different kind of space, the spiritually centred space which welcomes the uncertainty of knowing. In this space safety does not become a concern since we are there because we feel emotional sincerity and the freedom to be human. There is no fear not to know. It only brings us humility. As many have argued, there are certain things we may "never know" (Aveling, 2006, p. 268) as much as there is certainty of knowledge. Our knowing (like coding) can be inductive (i.e., data/experience driven) or deductive (theory driven). But even these are not strict boundaries that do not always hold. It is a relation between theory and practice, real and the metaphor, the abstract and the concrete. Both data and theory-driven coding can be thematic coding. The important point is that our data analysis must be flexible. We will revisit these themes again as we talk of the principles of anti-colonial solidarity.

This is all about the goal and purpose of our scholarship. Our anti-racist and anti-colonial scholarship and work must not just be about lofty intellectual and academic engagement or positions on race, racism, colonialisms, and oppressions. In fact, first and foremost, we need to pursue a definitive, politicized, action-oriented commitment to oppressed communities. The same can be said of that which we take up as Black or Indigenous Studies. Studies of Blackness or Indigeneity should not simply be about Black/African and Indigenous peoples' lives. We must engage this scholarship as a study and inquiry for and in service of us (see Nakata, 2004, 2015 in another context). If one does not know what that "us" means it is their problem. This is not an us/them distinction, but an awareness of the severity of issues affecting Black and Indigenous people. Our scholarship must have community relevance.

It is important to bring a reflexive understanding of the "logics of possession" (Moreton-Robinson, 2004, p. 192, see also Wolfe, 2006) in our anti-racism and anti-colonial scholarship, discourse, and work? Such understandings of imperial conquest, property, colonial ownership, claims of *terra nullius* are that of a barren land discovered by Christopher Columbus, Captain Cook or David Livingstone. We can no longer allow reactionary scholarship to colonize our anti-colonial work. Post-colonial scholarship, notwithstanding its merits around the question of voice, difference, and identity has the tendency to universalize the colonial experience and encounter for all colonized and oppressed peoples. It also tends to discount or downplay Indigenous knowledges and spiritual ontologies. Elsewhere, I have referred to this as a need for the epistemology of the colonized subject and Indigene (Dei, 1999, 2000).

It is necessary to ensure that we work with critical constructions of race and racism and to bring an anti-colonial lens to the study of race. Race is a powerful social construction that "shapes and informs racist structures and systems of domination" (Townsend-Cross, 2017, p. 218). Racism is neither natural nor inevitable and yet, it has become endemic in society. An essentializing nature of racialization had been presented in the ways, "ideological racial knowledges" (Townsend-Cross, 201, p. 237) tend to defend and/or rationalize racism. We must examine how racial ideologies continue to perpetuate racism. Such ideologies emphasize White dominance and the rationality of power and must be subverted. We cannot fight racism while reasserting racial power at the same time.

The seduction of liberal anti-racism and the nation state's domestication of anti-racism have worked to make us complicit in our oppressions. We need a structural historical analysis of racism, social oppression, and colonization to understand the nature of politics required to bring about needed change. While it is important to understand the causes and effects of oppressions, we must fundamentally understand the very conditions and processes under which racism and oppressions are created and sustained. This may require sustained critical analysis of the historical foundations of structural domination, and the conditions under which global white supremacy has flourished and continues to prevail (see Mills, 1997). To engage in conversations about the possibilities of colonialism is to deny the basic humanity of many Indigenous and colonized peoples. Anti-racism and anti-colonialism constitute a challenge to anti-human systems. These oppressions destroy our humanity and bring a "human face to structural domination" and its impacts (see Townsend-Cross, 2017). We can only accomplish this by bringing "our theorizing to the ground" to connect with the real needs of our people and communities (Dei, 2014, p. 27).

A liberalized discourse of anti-racism often presumes we can know about racism and in fact succeed in eradicating the problem simply through having "more knowledge", that is, through education (see Ahmed, 2004). A pointed focus on Whiteness and White privilege is relevant and required. Our intellectual practice must not lead to a re-centering of Whiteness through White pedagogies. White pedagogies that claim to speak about power and privilege often have limits. We need critical discourse that seeks to strengthen the dispossessed, resistor, and marginalized. This understanding and changing of conditions, along with a "retooling" (Dei & McDermott, 2014, p. 1) of anti-racism, can resist the power of repressive ideological discursive mechanisms.

Creating conditions for such possibilities require dialogue across our differences. The spaces for such dialogues are going to be contentious and often resisted. The pursuit of critical anti-racism like any anti-colonial and decolonial studies usher us in the space of "difficult knowledge" (Britzman, 1998) with uncomfortable and destabilizing pedagogies. We must work with the effective dimensions of engaging, "difficult knowledge and uncomfortable pedagogies", to ensure effective learning and educational outcomes for all (see Townsend-Cross, 2017). We must not only shed the privileging of knowledges, but also, cultural deficit discourses which are Eurocentric, racist, feed on pathologies, victim blaming, making false charges of oppressed peoples always claiming victimhood, and embarking upon obfuscation of the structural dimension of oppression.

Similarly, we must cast a gaze of *cultural appropriation discourse* as it tends to fetishize, romanticize, and over-mythicize the Indigenous, colonized, and oppressed experiences, worldviews, philosophies, and standpoints. A fascination to know about the "other" passed on knowledge sharing and yet intended to serve the dominants' own interests. We must also deal with our own awakenings and insecurities (Hollingsworth, 2015, p. 15) in subversive work. Lastly, we need to consider the pedagogical aspirations and anxieties we share and bring to our learning and teaching about race, racism and anti-racism, colonialism, and decolonization.

In reframing Whiteness as coloniality, how we study the who, how, when and why of Whiteness in very complementary ways is important (see Levine-Rasky, 2000, pp. 285–287). Particularly for dominant bodies, this requires interrogating White privilege objectively, subjectively and with intersectionality, to see how Whiteness functions as an analytical tool of critical race theory, anti-colonial analysis, and the subversion of power and unearned privileges (see Townsend-Cross, 2017, pp. 240–263). Any counter-theorizing must examine Whiteness as a problem. Many scholars argue Whiteness is a racial category, speaking to a structure, and as an oppressive system. Whiteness is also constitutive in the oppression of others. White identity as a subject body is separate and yet connected to Whiteness because it facilitates easy access to Whiteness. Whiteness as a propertied system affords underserved privileges and advances to White bodies. This access to wealth is about unearned privilege reserved mostly for White bodies (Levine-Rasky, 2000).

Gabriel (2002, p. 13) writes about "exonmination", that is, "the power not to be named". This is the privilege of the dominant (see Townsend-Cross, 2017, p. 242), and this power is further compounded by the ability to racialize Others, to claim innocence and to exonerate the dominant self (see Dei, 2008). When we fail to separate Whiteness and White identity as distinct and separate, the intellectual and political capabilities of dominant bodies to interrogate and subvert Whiteness as an oppressive structure is impeded (see Solomon, Daniel, & Campbell, 2005; Levine-Rasky, 2000). In light of the desire for seduction and fascination of Whiteness, we must consider Whiteness beyond our own subjectivities. We need to be critical of the essentializing tendencies of racialization. We must identify and understand how we become implicated, and complicit, within the axis of privilege in which we are represented or not represented. Intersectional analysis must speak to sites of oppression, as well as sites of privilege. Our anti-racist and anti-colonial intellectual analysis must always reveal intersectional privilege as "intersectional axes of privilege" (Townsend-Cross, 2017; see Crenshaw, 1989, 1991).

The question of power and resistance is integral to subversive praxis. I deploy Foucault's (1987, p. 114) distinction of "relationships of power" and power that are "states of domination". Speaking about power per se is not the problem. Relations of power must not necessarily lead to a system of domination but unfortunately, in our White dominated society they often do. Therefore, it is important we insist that although power can be diffused, there is always an anti-colonial take on power which always recognizes the power of the colonial dominant. Nonetheless, Foucault's distinction is useful in speaking about the possibilities of educational and social change. It also helps us to understand the relations of identity and subjectivity. There is always the possibility of resistance in each relationship of power (Foucault, 1987, p. 123).

The political interplay of identity and subjectivity is also critical to our understanding of subversive, decolonial praxis. Identity is conceptualized as knowledge about self, while subjectivity is about positionality or selfhood and the ways this self is placed in the context of relations of structural identities and thus constitutive of personal intersections such as race, class, gender, sexuality, [dis]ability and so forth. Our subjective identity is always historically, socially, and politically inherited. The individual understanding and societal interpretations of the self is always in relation to others.

It is important for us to continue to work with the categories of "oppressor" and "resistor" notwithstanding asymmetrical power relations. And, for us also to understand the moments when our struggles must contend with dominant attempts to shift debates beyond power, privilege and wealth.

Coming to Theory

The journey of "coming to theory" has at times been perilous for Black and African bodies. One of the issues that confront the Black scholar in the Western academy is how we come to theory and the meaning of theory for our practice. An important area of focus for me is to expand on colonialism and enslavement ontologies to understand the complexity of the Black, African, Indigenous, and colonized experience. While colonialism is not our only story, if we take the "colonial" as anything imposed, the colonial is a marked feature of every social life, regulating and dominating. This means we start theory where we are at using our history, culture, identity, and politics as significant entry points to discursive practices. This begins by situating Indigeneity and the complex complications of Land and space in the politics of knowledge. Cesaire (1972) asserted colonialism is barbaric and it has not been swept to the dustbin of history as some would think. Today, colonialism circulates through ideas and practices, in the orthodox and rigid orthodoxies, and mythologies of the dominant. A resulting effect is the denial of our own knowing and much more. Colonialism is more than White mythology (Derrida, 1982). Colonialism is also more than mental incarceration (Mazama, 2003). Colonialism is about physical, cultural, structural, and symbolic violence. Hence, a need to re-conceptualize the colonial as unending, nothing about it a "post" or "after thought" but a conscious, complex, and on-going configuration of power that has at its core White supremacist and capitalist logics.

We note that there is no uniform trajectory of colonialism. We tell a story of colonialism pointing to the divergences and convergences in the colonial and colonizing experiences for different bodies, not as a celebration of difference and voices, but a call to hear the power of different voices. Personally, I cannot talk about anti-colonial theorizing without reclaiming my Black, African Indigeneity in the Euro-colonial space. In such reading, it is also crucial to bring a complicated understanding to Blackness and Africanness. There are multiple stories to be told of Black Indigeneity and the Diasporic context that gestures to implications, complicities, erasures, denials.

There is a story of race, colonization, Indigeneity and coming into new spaces. There are Black peoples Indigenous to Lands outside of Africa. For African bodies, if we take race and coming into new spaces, we may, for example, see Black immigration scholarship has tended to separate race from ethnicity. While we acknowledge that ethnicity helps break down the racial umbrella, it must also be noted that ethnicity is a racializing project. While we may want to disaggregate race from ethnicity there is also a conundrum. Ethnicity is racialized in ways that punish some bodies (African ancestry) and rewards others (e.g., Anglo ancestry). Ethnicity has always been a trope used in the road to Euro consolidated Whiteness. Thus, there are intellectual and political limits of separating ethnicity from race. Ethnicities are not raceless. So, what accounts for the supposed racelessness of ethnicity? It is a denial of white ancestry privilege. What we need to do is to see the process of racialization in far more complex ways that engage simultaneously with different processes of colonization, imperialism, globalization, and immigration. This also calls for understanding rhetorical solidarity as beyond obligated Blackness to a realization of the political and economic materiality of Blackness in Euro-America contexts and global contexts. As Africans and Black bodies, we are still racialized outside of North American geopolitical boundaries. Race does exist outside the America, North American and European context. A "pigmentary passport of privilege" reveals itself in a racial a sanctity of Whiteness (Johal, 2005), as well as a pigmentary passport of punishment lodged in dominant imaginations of Black criminality.

So, we need to complicate the ways we speak about Blackness and insist on the power of extending ideas and understandings of Blackness beyond enslavement ontologies. For sure White supremacists' logics are rooted in anti-Blackness and anti-Indigeneity. Yet Blackness has different conceptions in African and Indigenous thought. We must come to understand global racialization and the African Diaspora and how Black immigrant ethnic identities, and identifications converge with racial and racialized identities. It means the same and different to talk of race in Africa and in North America and it is important for us to go beyond race as premised solely on enslaved ontologies. What this entails is that new forms and understandings of racialization [beyond political economy questions] are called for. Similarly, we need different frameworks for rethinking Blackness. There is the global coloniality of Blackness. One example is the socio-cultural homogenization and erasure of complexities of Blackness by global white supremacy. We must address the limited constructs and constructions of Blackness and begin to ask uncomfortable questions. Can we search for joy in these moments of global turmoil on racism and Black Lives Matter? How can our knowledge help us decolonize by adding to critical conversations about new global futurity? Clearly, Black scholars and Black scholarship must interrupt everyday conversations and deeply held assumptions that serve to maintain current social order. We have collective complications, implications, and responsibilities and unless we act on these, we have all failed. We need critical Black theorizing to combat White supremacy in all its forms, as well as Islamophobia, anti-Blackness, xenophobic hate, and violence.

Anchoring Black Theorizing

In the anchoring of Black theorizing, I want to highlight some particular social thoughts.

Black and racialized scholars in the academy have raised the question of theory in different contexts. While "the Black radical tradition" has a specific meaning in the U.S. context, the truth is there has been a growing Black intellectual tradition and heritage for years (see Asante & Berry, 2000). This intellectual tradition saw the Black body as a knower, thinker, and an embodied Blackness as relevant for politics, resistance and agency.

Black theorizing has long emerged from Black radical intellectual traditions on the sociology of knowledge. Manning Marable (2000) defined Black Intellectual Tradition as "the critical thought and perspectives of intellectuals of African descent and scholars of black America, and Africa, and the Black diaspora" (p. 1). He enthused that this has always been arbitrary and dating back to the colonial era, Black intellectuals have sought to elevate the genuine state of Black people by amalgamating "scholarship and struggle…social analysis and social transformation" (p. 2). However, it should be noted that this very dedication to social advocacy did not, and has not, watered down the solemnity of Black intellectual work. Marable (2000) argued this by stating that the "common recognition of the broad social purpose of intellectual work did not mean that black scholarship must be...a partisan polemic with no genuine standards of objectivity" (p. 2).

Du Bois's stellar career was to prove Marable's point that Black scholars have consistently produced significant scholarship and advanced their academic disciplines even as they empowered their communities. Gordon (2009) argues that Black Intellectual Tradition(s) are intellectual movements that have come up in the "modern" world due to the formation of Black people. He noted that given "Black" people emerge from a vast and diverse set of ethnic groups, the origins of Black Intellectual Tradition(s) differ starting from the Atlantic region since about the 18th Century. This intellectual tradition focused a great deal of vitality on the subject matter of liberation from colonialism and enslavement by challenging and questioning what it means to be human. Gordon (2009) further noted that Black Intellectual Traditions have since been woven into the politics of the "modern" world and up to the 1980s, were severely rooted in various non-academic institutions such as churches, mosques, synagogues, unions, and political parties. In his work Gordon (2009) enthused that under "modern day" Black thought, six major traditions can be pointed out: 1) Black feminism, (2) Black religious thought, (2) Black pragmatism, (3) Black existentialism, (4) Black postmodernism, poststructuralism, postcolonialism, and cultural and queer studies, (5) Afrocentrism, Afrocentricity, and Africology, and (6) Africana thought. Each of these in one way or the other cuts across political lines like liberal, neoliberal, radical, conservative, nationalist.

Over the years, Black theorizing has come to revolve around contested understandings of Negritude Philosophy (e.g., Aime Cesaire), Pan Africanism and Black Nationalism (as in explorations of Africa and African Diasporic unity in the ideas of Marcus Garvey and the New African of Kwame Nkrumah), Fanonian and anti-Colonialism (e.g., Franz Fanon, Aime Cesaire, Leopold Senghor), Afrocentrism and African-centered Thought (e.g., Cheikh Anta Diop, Molefi Asante), Black Feminist Thought (Patricia Hill Collins), Intersectionality Theory (e.g., Kimberle Crenshaw), Critical Race Theory (e.g., Derrick Bell), Anti-Racism and Critical Anti-Racist Theory (e.g., Troyna, Lee, Dei), Black Crit Theory(Dumas) Black Marxism (e.g., C.L.R. James, Cedric Robinson), Black radical politics (e.g., Booker T Washington,

W. E. B. Du Bois, Carter G Woodson, Anna Julia Cooper, Manning Marable, Robin Kelley, etc.).

Many of these scholars utilized oral cultural narratives as a key component of Black identity. Contrary to some thinking these scholars have not been "obsessed" with race but the production of counter knowledge to Western/dominant knowledge. Enlightenment philosophers like Locke, Hume, Kant, and Hegel "fashioned the content and contours of modern White supremacist thinking and conduct" (Shore, 2003, p. 85) that denied the intellectual agency of Black peoples. It was a mindset that Black and African people cannot think of. We cannot conflate the "sociology of knowledge with epistemology" and I agree such conflation may well constitute a "genetic fallacy" (Ferguson, 2003, p. 78). We must understand the Black intellectual tradition as a philosophy born of struggle and resistance. There is a shared understanding that to know is to act and that knowledge must always be employed for the purpose of cultural criticism and social change (Shore, 2003, p. 83). In effect, Black scholarship and our intellectuality must be relevant to our communities. Black scholarship must always exhibit creative imagination in our thought processes (see Dei, 2020).

It is argued that Black lives constitutes, "a counter-white *episteme*, a mode of knowing and being that [is] deconstructive, reconstructive, and transformative of what it meant to be Black (Yancy, 2003, p. 51). Similarly, there is some significance in working with "facticity and possibility" (Yancy, 2003; p. 51) and the understanding that the pursuit of knowledge [scholarship] "should make a "material" difference in the lives of ordinary folk" (Yancy, 2003, p. 56). An important question has always been how do we bring a "sense of social and deep personal existential accountability" to our work as Black scholars and to move from "knowledge-getting [to] knowledge-doing" (Yancy, 2003, p. 56)? This is putting our knowledge to the benefit of our peoples and our communities (Dei, 2020).

For example, Garveyites philosophical thought centered around developing an anti-colonial Black social and political movement for a "viable means for economic development, cultural exchange and enrichment, the development of ethnic pride and love, self-esteem, self-respect and worldwide cooperation" (Spady & Wright, 2003, p. 58). These objectives were expressed in Garvey's ideas of "Africa for the Africans" and the establishment of the "Black Star Steamship Line."

In the two generational thinking of Pan Africanism as expressed in Marcus Garvey and Kwame Nkrumah we see the "confraternity of people of

African descent and the freedom and unification of the African continent" (Spady & Wright, 2003, p. 60). There was Garvey's pursuit of the unity of peoples of African descent globally after the Trans-Atlantic slave trade had falsely portrayed Africans as "intellectual[ly] inferiority to the remainder of humankind" (Spady & Wright, 2003, p. 59). Kwame Nkrumah challenged this thinking and extended the thought of black and African agency with the idea of a "politically free and unified African continent, one divested of all traces of Europe's political economic, social, and psychological domination" (Spady & Wright, 2003, p. 60).

Later scholars will come to interrogate both of these thoughts about African redemption (Garvey) and African traditionalism (Nkrumah). For example, Garvey's was perceived as an "Eurocentric conception of African traditionalism" in which he "envisions an African diasporan leadership paving the way to the redemption of Africa, advancing the continent out of cultural backwardness to Western (bourgeois) modernity" (McClendon, 2003, p. 61). On the other hand, Nkrumah's was viewed as "the affirmative view of African traditionalism and political reaffirmation of Indigenous African leadership" (McClendon, 2003, p. 62). Notwithstanding their divergent interpretations these views on Pan Africanism have passed the merit of time. Nkrumah's belief in the African humanity and African spirituality as an anti-imperialist ideological force was not limited to Africa and the "belief that Africa had a golden past and that the people of the Diaspora were destined to help 'redeem' it and 'regenerate'" (McClendon, 2003, p. 63) shaped much of contemporary politics of African-centred thought as counterpoint to Western Eurocentric thinking.

For example, Black theorists are advancing scholarship focused on African education and philosophies that serve African anti-colonial aspirations. The "cultural paradigm" of an African anti-colonialism "can only start from Africa's Indigenous culture" (McClendon, 2003, p. 68). This cultural paradigm must be anti-capitalist and anti-imperialist embracing cultural, spiritual and racial politics. In fact, this was an idea C.L.R. James, as a Marxist philosopher, long interpreted very well. C.L.R. James saw the power of spontaneous rebellion from the proletariat, strategically organized by the Vanguard. He challenged the Marx, Engels and Lenin alignment with the Hegelian dialectical logic of ideas propelling change, arguing these ideas are stepped in material conditions offering "a dialectical guide to political practice and organization" while insisting that "philosophy was an instrument in the proletariat's struggle for scientific socialism" (Ferguson, 2003, p. 73). James' ideas centred on the dialectics of freedom that sought to address the "question of what should be the organizational form that the proletariat adopts in fighting against capitalist exploitation (Ferguson, 2003, p. 73)? To him "the emancipation of the proletariat rests not in the formation of new political organizations and political organizational structures but in the spontaneous activity of the proletariat" (Ferguson, 2003, p. 73).

While for Marx, "a social revolution is contingent upon the contradiction between the productive forces and relations of productions", James on the other hand, identified "spontaneous activity, upsurges and rebellions as the necessary and sufficient condition for a social revolution" (Ferguson, 2003, p. 73) and that "the spontaneous activity of the proletariat is seen as a self-generating, internal contradiction which gives rise to its own freedom" ....and it is "self-caused and independent of objective (material) conditions" (Ferguson, 2003, p. 74). Ferguson (2003) goes on to point out that James "neglected the importance of political organization, ideology, consciousness and, most importantly, human agency in determining the fate" (p. 77) arguing instead that "political leadership and organizations such as Lenin's vanguard party are an obstacle to the freedom of the proletariat" (Ferguson, 2003, p. 78). While James has been criticized for a failure to understand how "freedom is limited or determined by material forces such as social relations of production and bourgeois ideological hegemony" (Ferguson, 2003, p. 80), he nonetheless is significant for Black social thought for political action. Black, Indigenous and racialized scholars have to be part of this continuing struggle of our communities both in our theorizing and educational practices within our educational institutions.

C.L.R James' work connected with Cedric Robinson's thesis exploring racial capitalism and anti-capitalist stance has been influential in shaping Black radical politics. Today there is a central question to be asked for Black theorizing: What does it mean for colonized peoples, particularly Black peoples, to build a movement that works with Marxism and take these ideas to a new level in order to make sense to us and to suit our needs and concerns? Clearly politics is key to survival but we must also understand what self- determination concretely means on the ground (see Black Ink Info, 2020)?

The revolutionary thinking of what Black radical politics was to be about influenced Cedric Robinson's intervention on Black Marxism and the Black radical tradition, and what it means for colonized peoples, particularly Black peoples, to build a movement that works with and take the ideas of Marxism to a new level in order to make sense and to suit our needs and concerns.

Understanding the meaning and purpose of Blackness was key. Black philosopher George Yancy's work on the place of the Black body in White modernity focused on the "ethico-onto-epistemic implications for Blackness" (Headley, 2018, p. 1220).

Later Robin Kelley's work has been about "deepening [our] awareness of the responsibilities of the subject formation, to recognize and cultivate new forms of agency that are comprehensive, that are informed by [our] collective [not individual] dreams of freedom" (Black Ink Info, 2020, p. 27). The task of Black theorizing is to ask hard questions: "what kind of world are we trying to build"? Why turn to our institutions to give us things rather than demand and take the things we want? (Black Ink Info, 2020, p. 9). We have a shared responsibility for human freedom and must tactically and strategically theorize to educate and mobilize in ways that demonstrate and reinforce Black, Indigenous and racialized anti-colonial solidarities. But we must first grasp the full meaning of the anti-colonial space and moment.

Black Theorizing in Academia as a Contestation of Knowledge

As Black scholars we must contest knowledges from particular and multiple vantage points to explore the possibilities and challenges of Black theorizing in the [Western] academy. Black theorizing is both an intellectual and political act. It is located with a contest, history, and politics. It is intended to subvert and reject "Western modernist claims of neutrality, objectivity, rationality and universality" (Lynn, 1999, p. 610). I herald the power of anti-colonial philosophy and practice to advance critical scholarship and to upend mental and intellectual enslavement. We challenge the theoretical obfuscation in debates about what and who is included or excluded in conversations about what constitutes theory. We ask, how do Black/African learners theorize? It is conceded that such Black theorizations are not monolithic. Yet we proceed with the dialectics of theory, politics, and practices. We embrace an understanding of the body as a site of knowing, coming from a socio-political historical space. It is an appreciation of the embodiment of knowing and the fact that we have "somatic" or "bodily knowings" (Heshusius, 1994). The embodiment of self and knowledge is a political claim not a biological knowing. It alludes to the social, material, historical, intellectual, spiritual, and cultural legitimacy of Black and African peoples in the matrix of knowing.

A key question is the intellectual agency and power of claiming an African Indigeneity that is anchored on the reverence to Land and its teachings, as well as the interface of culture, society, and Nature. Such theorizing of Black/African identities as sites of knowing seek to validate African peoples' own understandings of our worlds. Embedded in the African Indigeneity is the spiritual, as ontology and epistemology, that espouse particular understandings of culture, and the principles of connections, relationships, interdependence, co-operation, sharing, reciprocity, generosity, mutuality, and the idea of "connected knowings" as critical to knowledge about self, groups and communities. We further contend that Black theorizing is particularly meaningful if it leads to a re-theorizing Blackness as a search for self and collective determination to give Black and African peoples' intellectual and political agency to fight anti-Blackness and anti-Africanness. This is an assertion of a locus of control over the story and how we tell these stories about ourselves, identities, histories, cultures and lived experiences. The telling of the story must include a theory of Blackness, empowering ourselves as Black and African scholars and learners to define the problems and challenges afflicting our communities. We must think through our own solutions.

In the focus on Black theorizing, Indigeneity, and resistance in academia our intellectual practice is not so much on Black canons or the canonization of particular Black scholars. Rather, we must seek to engage the intellectual. Next, we consider how some of us theorized and have sought to theorize about our Black scholarly experiences raising key issues of Indigeneity and resistance in academia. I will opine that we must understand the ways of sense making, knowledge production, interrogation, validation, and dissemination in both political and intellectual exercises. There is the need to simultaneously investigate the nature of colonialist and anti-colonialist philosophy and practice as developed to advance scholarship and politics. For example, we ask, how has the study of the "science of race and anti-Black racism", incorporating the logic of Western scholarship failed to fully engage with a more global consideration of Indigenous knowledges and sciences, political practice, and the interface between multiple worldviews, "world senses" (Oyewumi, 1997, p. 3)?

I have espoused the dialectic of theory and social practice elsewhere (Dei, 2020) where we should note the continuing struggles for Black, racialized, and Indigenous scholars to shed ourselves from the enduring legacies of colonial and imperial thinking. It is important that we do not conflate the sociology of knowledge with epistemology, a practice termed as a "genetic fallacy" (Ferguson, 2003, p. 78). I reiterate the idea that "to know is to act in good conscience" (Shore 2003, p. 83) and knowledge must be employed for the purpose of cultural criticism and social change. As a Black scholar, such a thinking process can lead to the path of academic radicalism with its urgency to couple academic intellectuality with social responsibility. Theory must be a weapon of change and transformation. Theorizing outside the box means we ask: How do we, in our theorizing, begin to trouble our deeply held convictions, racialized assumptions, or even, everyday sense understandings that merely serve to maintain and sustain the current socio-political order and system? How do our theories, epistemological frameworks, and ideologies we chose to engage with truly become weapons of change? The theories we develop and engage with in the academy are intellectual and political choices. Black theorizing and our intellectuality must be relevant to our communities.

Black life constitutes an episteme, a counter way of knowing and practice. As noted repeatedly, we must measure the social worth of a theory on two fronts: first, the fundamental principles of the said theory, and second, the ability of theory to offer a social and political corrective (Dei, 1999). Black theorizing must emerge from more theoretically generative research about schooling guided by community educational practice. This calls for both historicizing and contemporizing understandings of Black, Indigenous, and racialized education, nurtured in long standing and perhaps to some newer, epistemologies. For example, there is a need for a meta-framing of Black education from the local specificities of challenges that face Black youth in schooling. Such meta-framing is significant because issues affecting Black learners have very striking similarities and convergences across different geographies.

There are different ways of making meaning. Our sense-making must always tie the threads and create new spaces of learning outside the conventional school system. We must promote what Warner (2003) calls a "cacophony of opinions and reflections" of the Black experience. It is not enough "to learn to be Black or African", but more importantly, we must learn to think through and to act on one's Blackness and Africanness. It is a thinking process that has led and convinced me on the path of radicalism and academic and social responsibility. We cannot accept White Eurocentric cultural norms, ideals and social values in defining African humanity and, in general, what it means to be human.

We have still not resolved the question of what and who is the human and what has historically been left out. If the current fascination on posthumanism is to be appealing and transformative to many of us, the focus must be on a critique of the Eurocentric construction of the human and humanism lodged in the ideological tenets of individualism, freedom, liberty, choice. Notwithstanding our successes and struggles, we must be concerned with the high extent of Black nihilism that has resulted from a deep sense of anguish, fear, despair, a sense of living a deadened existence, as well as the perceived failure of Black leadership, including Black scholarship to lead the path for change in our communities (see Hayes, 2003, p. 83). To reiterate, such nihilism does not mean the absence of Black resistance. It constitutes a sort of Black existential crisis. As argued in Dei (2022), we need Black theorization to affirm and recognize young learners as the future, the vanguard for change and the capacity of knowledge for decolonization. For example, in Euro-colonial contexts it is important to recognize that white supremacy and anti-Black racism trump class and economics. There is some uniqueness to existential experiences of Black peoples that cannot be resolved strictly through class-based policies. White supremacy, anti-Blackness and anti-Black racism have succeeded in denying Black humanity. Instead, these ideas present Black people to wider society as a problem people/population (see Hayes, 2003, p. 85).

Theory must be a weapon of change and social transformation. Theory must be planted on the ground. Theory must give hope. Theory must be fulfilling to the soul, heart and desires of the Black academic and community worker. But this theory must also make sense to our lives. If Black, and by extension Indigenous and racialized scholars, see our roles in the academy as activist-scholars, it starts with how we navigate theory and the production, use and dissemination of theory/theories. Those we propose and those we engage, must be weapons of change. Our theorizing must offer a prism to understand Black pain, resistance and calls for redemption. Our theorizing must offer a way out to our communities in these difficult times of our collective dispensability. Our theorizing must affirm critical dialogues and political action. Righting Black wrongs for colonialism, enslavement, capitalist, and imperialist appropriations call for apologies, reparations, and the replacement of loss. Forgiveness will be a critical part of the equation, but only after these recognitions and acknowledgments of pain and suffering. We must be willing to give forgiveness, but the conditions must be right. Forgiveness can only come from the oppressed and not the colonial dominant, for "the wrongdoer does not have the power to bring about forgiveness" (Zack, 2003, p. 88).

Our counter hegemonic critiques cannot be guided or instructed by White Eurocentric perspectives (see Leonardo, 2002). The urgency of understanding the Black and African experience calls for a resurgence of groundbreaking subversive Black thinking and practice.

We must challenge our continual exclusions for decolonial theorizing, except the occasional reference to Fanon, and to a limited extent, Aime Cesaire and Amilcal Cabral. For the decolonial practice to be effective it must necessarily have an anti-colonial stance.

The Western academy is both a physical, social, political, visual, and now virtual space. Race and visuality work together. Notions of visuality and domination work within the tropes of Whiteness. The pervasiveness of Whiteness in our academic institutions also encounters Black visuality as informing understanding of Blackness. The struggle of Black theorizing then is for visual sovereignty, that is arresting images of ourselves as Black and Indigenous bodies from colonial representations.

Our radical critiques must confront the culture of anti-Blackness in our educational institutions (Gillborn, 2018). Just as Whiteness is everywhere, so is anti-Blackness which functions as the invisible weather, a climate (Sharpe, 2016) and the air we breathe. Sharpe (2016) writes, "The weather is the totality of our environments. The weather is the total climate; and that climate is anti-Black" (p. 104). Anti- Blackness as a system privileges all non-Black peoples to varying degrees (Hudson, 2018). Anti- Blackness is the denial of Black and African humanity, and the revealing of the totality of the Black and African experience in a cloak of criminality. The violence of the Western academy reveals itself in anti-Blackness. Blackness is an absent presence in White dominant spaces. Black life and agency should mean disrupting or subverting all ways that further White supremacist projects. When it comes to the critical study of Blackness, rather than nurture progressive discourses and practices, it is still lacking as a social and academic field of inquiry in our educational institutions.

White supremacy needs anti-Blackness to thrive everywhere. Whiteness makes itself invisible through a process of normalization that we see in our academies. Whiteness maintains its full effects on society by seducing "allies" believing in its fantasies. Black bodies have a largely absent presence in the Western academy. Our institutions fail to credit our past and the reading of history leaves us out. The past is constructed as a mythology characterized by absent histories. Some of the very powerful Canadian mythologies is the idea that Blacks and African peoples are all immigrants; that we have no history and no Land. Our colonial histories are often denied through such a discursive process and Black and African people are not always seen as colonized peoples whose Lands have historically been dispossessed (see Hudson, 2018).

For Black and African learners surviving the hostile environment of the Western academy can be attributed in part to our indomitable spirit. It is this same spirit that we can utilize to challenge the colonial mythologies that Black people are landless, without a history and can be perpetually enslaved. Clearly, the past is still with us but can be reclaimed only in a solution-oriented way offering lessons for a path forward. Our history has lessons that can never be forgotten or erased in knowledge production. In Canada we cannot conceptualize the history of colonized peoples that leave out Black and African peoples. Our African Indigeneity can also not be denied without resistance. Notwithstanding contestations on the applicability of the "settler" for all Black bodies we must still challenge the reading of what it means for the settler to "cease to exist" (Veracini, 2011, 2014) irrespective of the location and geography. By taking genocide, land dispossession, enslavement, and colonization simultaneously and as historically contingent upon different populations, we create the space for dialogue.

We must mobilize history to serve anti-colonial projects and causes that subvert claims of White settler nationalism, class nationalism and hetero-patriarchy, as well as settler colonial national power and White supremacy. Within the academy the concept of Canadian benevolence makes it difficult to argue anti-Blackness from within. But Black bodies experience this anti-Blackness every day in subtle and open ways. It is through Black theorizing that we can hope to challenge national social imaginaries of Black existence. Thus, we must locate and think through our Blackness as we continually subvert the on-going legacies of colonial thinking. Black theorizing must speak of the "Middle Passage" as a separation, dislocation and a knowledge generation gap in corresponding ways residential schooling separated Indigenous bodies from their communities and Elders. We must use the conceptual grammar of the Empire as subversive language and practice and begin to authentically invite ourselves into new anti-colonial spaces. We must use the power of our Indigenous intellectualism, going beyond "repairing" the colonial relationship to working with the dialectics of body, mind, spirit, and soul as complex ontologies. We must reclaim our moral-ethical sensibilities of love and engage this in our learning, teaching, and doing the work within our communities. An anti-colonial education is Land-based education stressing the importance of heart knowledge. While decolonization is violent, it is also a dynamic process.

Colonized peoples and our communities' relations to the Land differ. Such relations usually evoke spiritual, psychic, and emotional connections and attachments that are necessarily exploitative. The Land is also about the sky, seas, and water. But it is also beyond the physical and when in Toronto, for example, African Elders visit the sea to pour libations, the connection is to the underwater seas, where our dead ancestors might still be lying from being through overboard slave ships. Therefore Black diasporic relations to Turtle Island have to be looked at broadly rather than simply in terms of exploitations and settler hood.

But coming to Black theorizing is also to interrogate further the very questions we have been asking. For example, the whole idea of schooling and its underlying assumptions further a national project under the very terms set by the state. Why should schooling support the national project? Can we rely on a system set up to oppress us and free our minds? We must be prepared to confront the fact that the current school environment is hostile to critical and oppositional ideas. There are social, political, and theoretical implications and underpinnings of counter-visioning schooling for Black learners. Our rich intellectual traditions of Black life and histories offer learning moments to think through new educational possibilities for our Generation Z and millennials working with the overlapping diasporas. Black learning, schooling and education must be informed by our anti-Black experiences in society. There are many subtle ways Black concerns and issues get pushed to the background as we purportedly seek to be inclusive, to be accepted, and validated in academia. Hence, we must be authentic in affirming our lived realities and experiences. The value of schooling and education does not rest solely in participating in the job market.

We also need to understand the "human" outside of Western Eurocentric constructions of relations to capital, individual freedom, and liberty. The human is beyond a tangible reality and existence. The "human" implies an emotional, psychic, and spiritual connection and an "Other" not always definable. The human is a conception of life and values. As Perry and Delpit (1998, p. 106) note, drawing from the Egyptian principles of MAAT, the African conception of the "human" and "humanness" is about "righteousness, truth, honesty, propriety, harmony, order, and reciprocity" (see Lynn, 1999, p. 608). Embarking on such virtues in our daily actions ensure life and the indomitable human spirit of resistance and struggle for success. It is for this reason that a deliberate attempt was made by European colonizers to debase, devalue, and deny the African humanity and the values that would ensure strong spiritual backbone needed for resistance. There have been many accounts of the attempts made by early European ideological formations masqueraded under the guise of theory and civilizational thought to animalize, devalue, and debase African humanity and humanness (see Ani, 1994; Lynn, 1999). Consequently, it should be noted that Black theorizing has long stressed the necessity of inculcating in African learners an African cultural foundation from which to view other global cultures (Lynn, 1999, p. 618). Such theorizing has a long and rich intellectual tradition and grounding.

References Cited:

Ahmed, S. (2004). Declarations of whiteness: The non-performativity of anti-racism. *Borderlands e-Journal*, 3(2).

Ani, M. (1994). *Yurugu: An African-Centered critique of European cultural thought and behavior*. Africa World Press.

Asante, M., & Berry, S. (2000). *African intellectual heritage: A book of sources*. Temple University Press.

Ashcroft, B., Griffiths, G., & Tiffin, H. (2007). *Post-Colonial studies: The key concepts*. Routledge.

Aveling, N. (2006). "Hacking at our very roots": Rearticulating white racial identity within the context of teacher education. *Race Ethnicity and Education*, 9(3), 261–274.

Black Ink Info. (2020). "Solidarity Is Not a Market Exchange:" An interview with Robin D. G. Kelley. Black Ink Info. https://black-ink.info/author/blcknk/

Britzman, D. (1998). *Lost subjects, contested objects: Toward a psychoanalytic inquiry of learning*. University of New York Press.

Césaire, A. (1972). *Discourse on colonialism*. Monthly Review Press.

Cesaire, A. (2010). Culture and Colonization. *Social Text*, 28(2 103), pp. 127–144.

Crotty, M. (1998). *The foundations of social research: Meaning and perspective in the research process*. Sage.

Dei, G. J. S. (2014). A prism of educational research and policy: Anti-Racism and multiplex oppressions. In G. J. S. Dei & M. McDermott (Eds.), *Politics of Anti-Racism education: In Search of strategies for transformative learning* (pp. 15–28). Springer.

Dei, G. J. S., & Vasquez, M. (2017). The Foundations of Transformative Anti-Racism: A conversation with George J. Sefa Dei and Andrea Vásquez Jiménez. EdCanNetwork. https://www.edcan.ca/articles/foundations-transformative-anti-racism/

Dei, G. J. S., (2022). Black theorising: Indigeneity and resistance in Academia. In S. Styres & A. Kempf (Eds.), *Troubling the truth and reconciliation in Canadian Education*.

Dei, G. J. S., & Atweneboah, N. S. (2014). The African Scholar in the Western Academy. *Journal of Black Studies*, 45(3), 167– 179. http:// www.jstor.org/ sta ble/ 24572 948

Dei, G. J. S., & McDermott, M. (2014). Introduction to the politics of Anti-Racism education: In Search of strategies for transformative learning. In G. Dei & M. McDermott (Eds.), *Politics of Anti-Racism education: In search of strategies for transformative learning* (pp. 1–11). Springer.

Delpit, L. (1993). The silenced dialogue: Power and pedagogy in educating other People's children. In: M. Fine & L. Weis (Eds.), *Beyond silenced voices: Class, race and gender in the United States*. State University Press of New York.

Derrida, J. (1982). *Margins of philosophy* (A. Bass, Trans.). Chicago University Press.

Foucault, M. (1987). The ethic of care for the self practice of freedom: An interview with Michel Foucault on January 20, 1984. *Philosophy and Social Criticism*, 12(2–3), 112–131.

Gabriel, J. (2002). *Whitewash: Racialized politics and the media*. Routledge.

Garcia, J., & Shirley, V. (2012). Performing decolonization: Lessons learned from indigenous youth, teachers and leaders' engagement with critical Indigenous pedagogy. *Journal of Curriculum Theorizing*, 28(2), 76–91.

Gillborn, D. (2018). Heads I win, tails you lose: Anti-Black racism as fluid, relentless, individual and systemic. *Peabody Journal of Education*, 93(1), 66–77. doi: 10.1080/0161956X.2017.1403178

Gordon, L. (2009). Black intellectual tradition. In M. Orvell (Ed.), *Encyclopedia of American Studies*. John Hopkins University Press.

Handler, R. (1986). Authenticity. *Anthropology Today*, 2(1), 2–4.

Harding, V. (1974). The vocation of the Black scholar and the struggles of the Black community. In Institute of the Black World, *Education and Black struggle: Notes from the colonized world*. Harvard Educational Review (Monograph no. 2), 3–29.

Hayes, F. (2003). Review of: Clarence Shole Johnson, 2003 Cornet west & philosophy: The quest for social justice. In McClendon & G. Yancy (Eds.), *Newsletter on Philosophy and the Black Experience*. Routledge.

Headley, C. (2018). Reading George Yancy's backlash: Afro-pessimism and the conundrums of liberalism. *Philosophy Today*, 62(4), 1219–1241.

Hickling-Hudson, A., Matthews, J., & Woods, A. (2004). Education, postcolonialism and disruptions. In A. Hickling-Hudson, J. Matthews, & A. Woods (Eds.), *Disrupting preconceptions: Postcolonialism and education*. Brisbane: Post Pressed.

Hollinsworth, D. (2014). Unsettling Australian settler supremacy: Combating resistance in university Aboriginal studies. *Race Ethnicity and Education*, 19(2), 412–432. doi: 10.1080/13613324.2014.911166

Hudson, S. (2018). [Unpublished MA Thesis]. University of Toronto.

Kelley, R. D. (2016, March 7). *Black study, Black struggle*. Boston Review. http://bostonreview.net/forum/robin-d-g-kelley-black-study-black-struggle

Leonardo, Z. (2002). The souls of White folk: Critical pedagogy, whiteness studies, and globalization discourse. *Race Ethnicity and Education*, 5(1), 1–50.

Levine-Rasky, C. (2000). Framing Whiteness: Working through the tensions in introducing whiteness to educators. *Race, Ethnicity & Education*, 3(3), 271–292.

Loomba, A. (2015). *Colonialism/Postcolonialism*. Routledge.

Lynn, M. (1999). Toward a critical race pedagogy: A research note. *Urban Education*, 33(5), 606–626.

Marable, M. (2000). *Dispatches from the Ebony Tower: Intellectuals confront the African American Experience*. Columbia University Press.

Mazama, A. (2003). *The Afrocentric paradigm*. Africa World Press.

Memmi, A. (1967). *The Colonizer and the Colonized*. Beacon Press.
Mills, C. W. (1997). *The racial contract*. Cornell University Press.
Mills, C. W. (2009). Critical race theory: A reply to Mike Cole. *Ethnicities*, 9(2), 270–281.
Moreton-Robinson, A. (2004a). Whiteness, epistemology and Indigenous representation. In A. Moreton-Robinson (Ed.), *Whitening race: Essays in social and cultural criticism* (pp. 75–88). Aboriginal Studies Press.
Moreton-Robinson, A. (2004b). Whiteness matters: Australian studies and Indigenous studies. In D. Carter, K. Darien-Smith, & G. Worby (Eds.), *Thinking Australian studies: Teaching across cultures* (pp. 136–146). University of Queensland Press.
Nakata, M. (2002). Indigenous knowledge and the cultural interface: Underlying issues at the intersection of knowledge and information systems. *IFLA Journal*, 28(5–6), 281–291.
Nakata, M. (2007). The cultural interface. *The Australian Journal of Indigenous Education*, 36, 7–14.
Nakata, M. (2007a). *Disciplining the savages, savaging the disciplines*. Aboriginal Studies Press.
Oyewumi, Oyeronke. (1997). *The invention of women: The making of African sense of western gender*. University of Minnesota Press.
Perry, T., & Delpit, L. (1998). *The real ebonics debate: Power, language and the education of African-American children*. Beacon Press.
Rizvi, F., Lingard, B., & Lavia, J. (2006). Postcolonialism and education: Negotiating a contested terrain. *Pedagogy, Culture & Society*, 14(3), 249–262.
Said, E.W. (1995). *Orientalism: Western conceptions of the orient*. Penguin.
Senghor, L. (2001). Negritude and modernity or negritude as a humanism for the twentieth century. In R. Bernasconi (Ed.), *Race* (pp. 143–166). Blackwell Publishers.
Sethi, R. (2011). *Politics of postcolonialism: Empire, nation and resistance*. Pluto Press.
Sharpe, C. (2016). *In the wake: On Blackness and being*. Duke University Press.
Shore, S., & Halliday-Wynes, S. (2006). *Preparing for the professions: Practicalities and politics of teaching in higher education – Discussion paper developed for the project "Reflecting on Privilege in the Teaching Professions."* University of South Australia.
Simpson, L. (2011). *Dancing on our Turtle Back: Stories of Nishnaaberg recreation, resurgence and a new emergence*. Arbeiter King Publishers.
Solomona, R. P. (2005). The discourse of denial: How white teacher candidates construct race, racism and "White privilege." *Race Ethnicity and Education*, 8(2), 147–169, DOI: 10.1080/13613320500110519
Townsend-Cross, M. (2017). *Difficult knowledge and uncomfortable pedagogies: student perceptions and experiences of teaching and learning in critical Indigenous Australian studies* [Unpublished doctoral dissertation]. University of Technology.
Veracini, L. (2014). Defending settler colonial studies. *Australian Historical Studies*, 45(3), 311–316.
Veracini, L. (2011). Introducing settler colonial studies. *Settler Colonial Studies*, 1(1), 1–12.
Warner, D. (2003). Review of George Yancy The Philosophical i: Personal reflections on life in philosophy". Rowman & Littlefield Publishers. In "Newsletter on Philosophy and the Black Experience." *APA Newsletters*, 2(2).

Wolfe, P. (2006). Settler colonialism and the elimination of the native. *Journal of Genocide Research*, 8(4), 387–409.

Yancy, G. (2018). *Backlash: What happens when we talk honestly about racism in America*. Rowman & Littlefield.

Zack, N. (2003). "Review of Rodney C. Roberts (ed). 2003. *'Injustice and rectification'*". New York, NY: Peter Lang. In "Newsletter on philosophy and the black experience". (McClendon and George Yancy, eds.). *APA Newsletters*. Volume 2, Number 2, Spring 2003

· 3 ·

FRAMING THE ANTI-COLONIAL FOR BLACKCENTRICTY

In this chapter, I push forward "anti-colonial discourse", building on the pioneering scholarship that already exists on colonialism and decolonization. Later, I touch on the intersecting theme of Black scholars' responsibility for advancing a path of Blackcentricity wedded in Black and African Indigeneities to address global anti-Black racism and anti-Blackness. I believe any "coming to know" must be matched with a desire to "knowing differently". This is what an anti-colonial prism brings to the critical process of knowledge creation.

Throughout this chapter, I work with conceptual framings that link colonialisms, including settler colonialism, and the understanding that Land occupation and settlerhood as produced through the twin processes of Indigenous genocide and African enslavement. It is noted that colonialism and settler colonialism, while requiring separate analytical distinctions are both cut from the same cloth: racism, slavery, and capitalism (Smith, 2012). Any attempt at decoloniality cannot happen solely through a Western scientific knowledge. An anti-colonial pursuit engages decolonization as starting in the mind and beginning with the self (see also Alfred & Corntassel, 2005, p. 611). Coloniality is understood as the "continuity of colonial forms of domination after the end of colonial administration" (Grosfoguel, 2002, p. 205). Coloniality exercised as an on-going process ensures and sustains a coloniality of power. And coloniality operates on a world scale establishing Europe's "undisputed hegemonies over non-European peoples"; and, as a process, coloniality is facilitated by the "globalization of the capitalist world economy" (Grosfoguel, 2002, p. 205). Thus, showing the power of coloniality from this perspective.

Alongside this vein, I see White supremacy as a concept, process, and ideology that serves the central organizing logics of Euro-colonial modernity, legitimizing both Euro-colonization and on-going settler projects (Bonds & Inwood, 2015, p. 720). White supremacy is not "a relic of the past or an ideology of extremists" (e.g., slavery, Jim Crow, KKK, but an "on-going colonial project" that maintains "the presumed superiority of White racial identities in support of the cultural, political and economic domination" of racialized peoples (Bonds & Inwood, 2015, p. 719). It is a materially grounded set of practices with profound economic, political and social impacts on marginalized peoples.

White supremacy works to sustain material advantages of Whiteness falsely justifying entitlements of White bodies globally. White bodies are "implicated in the reproduction of White supremacy" and the "White anti-racist subject [is not] disaffiliated from White supremacy" (Bonds & Inwood, 2015, p. 728). Andrea Smith's (2010) three pillars of White supremacist logics are – (i) slavery/capitalism, (ii) genocide/colonialism, and (iii) Orientalism/war which reveal intricate understandings of how we are each complicit and implicated in each other's oppressions through White supremacy. In a society that rewards a closer proximity to Whiteness while conversely punishing a proximity to Blackness, we stand to find ourselves easily made complicit in the logics of White supremacist thinking. Thus, an anti-colonial praxis will entail shifting from a "Black/White" binary to a "Black/White" prism (Dei & Vasquez, 2017), complicating the "Indigenous/Settler" binary, and further troubling the ways social hierarchies have been naturalized through colonial patriarchy and heteronormativity (Smith, 2010).

Similarly, Euro-modernity marks a supposed shift to a more rational human existence characterized by a particular mode of thinking and operation defined/informed by ideas and values of West/Europe. It is seen as a phase in human development characterized by the imposition of European norms and ideas (e.g., Christian, secular West; [neo]liberalism; Western democracy, views of cosmopolitanism, and the spirit of corporate American/Western consumerist culture). It is a period marked by the foundations of the Empire (e.g., Europe's colonial conquest of Africa and the Americas; control of the Atlantic after 1492; C17th Northern Europe and the Age of Reformation/Restoration; Age of Enlightenment; aftermath of the French Revolution; and the C18th Industrial Revolution). The problem with Euro-modernity is it leaves other communities behind and maintains a Western hegemonic understanding of history and human progress.

Notwithstanding the contestation of "Indigenous" it is contended that it is only Indigenous subjects who can define what "Indigenous" means to them. Indigenous peoples globally see Land as about resource, identity, relationship and spirituality. The Land is used physically, socially and metaphysically as a relation to place, territory, air, water, seas and sky. The teachings around such conception of the Land engenders the values of reciprocity, sharing, interdependence, relationality, mutuality, respect and responsibilities (see also Alfred & Corntassel, 2005, p. 605). Today, Euro-modernity has validated neo-liberalism as a cultural-ideological and socio-economic system with the imposition of Western ideas, solutions to prevailing human ecological, social, political, cultural and economic crises. In neo-liberal climate questions of responsibility, complicity and implications, they are usually skirted around for the force of markets and privatization of resources. The values associated with both Euro-modernity and neo-liberalism have become so entrenched in our daily lives that we are not able to imagine outside (not beyond) our current context and predicament. As argued elsewhere (Dei, 2019a), neo-liberalism has been a modernist discourse determining lives and death of global communities.

The anti-colonial challenge is to construct and deconstruct the rhetoric of [Western] modernity as rational, reasonable, logical, and abstract universals and to problematize how modernity is grounded on Europe's "theoretical or cultural achievements" and contributions to humankind (Maldonado-Torres, 2004, p. 32). The rhetoric of neo-liberalism obfuscates different truths and facts and there is a mythology of positivism and science that relates what is deemed development and human progress (see also Mignolo, 2007, p. 469). The modern/colonial world system represented by neo-liberalism universalizes the experiences of Europe for the whole world. A continuing dialectic of coloniality and Euro-modernity leaves no room for thinking through counter futures (Mignolo, 2007, p. 466) and it is through an insistence of subaltern and sub-intern knowledges of the Global South that the potentialities of the anti-colonial can be unleashed. The relationship between knowledge, power, identity, subjectivity, history, and politics must be framed differently for people. For colonized, Indigenous, and racialized scholars we must strive to put on the table our counter and oppositional knowledge of both the challenge and subvert Western epistemic domination. Again, as noted in Dei (2019) for Black, Indigenous, and racialized subjects and communities, we must insist upon having an authorial control of our authentic voices well beyond any assertion of the "pedagogical codifications of difference" (Mohanty, 1990, p. 194). We must challenge abstract universals of Western modernity by cultivating diverse voices, ideas, experiences, and stories in the spaces of pluriversality and multicentricity (Dei, 1996).

And so, I ask: How do we counter-hegemonic knowledge production in the academy to ensure that we come to know and produce knowing differently to challenge the particular Western science knowledge that masquerades as universal knowledge in academia? We can engage this question from a stance examining the coloniality of knowledge in the academy and finding ways to centre Indigenous knowledge systems to disrupt Euro-colonial hegemonic knowledge. This requires us to challenge the "grammar of coloniality" of Western knowledge and affirm the possibilities of a re-imagining of "new geographies" and cartographies of knowledge (Raghuram, personal communication, 2017) as varied and intersecting ontologies and epistemologies that inform our human condition as "learning experiences, research and knowledge generation" practices (see Lebakeng, 2010; p. 28, citing Teffo, 2002)? It is also imperative that we address some epistemic challenges, including the challenge of going beyond "epistemic provincialism" (see Ahenakew, Andreotti, Cooper, & Hireme, 2014) while insisting on the multi-centricity (Dei, 1996), that is, ways of knowledge as critical to understanding the complete history of ideas and events that shaped and continue to shape human growth and development. Throughout this book, I have argued for "cartographies of Indigenous and Indigeneities", to centre the importance of African Indigeneity. Reclaiming African Indigeneity is a counterpoint to the colonial appellation and apparition of the "Indigenous", while it also takes the "Indigenous" salient entry point to produce counter-hegemonic knowledge.

Colonialism has been barbaric and violent in its exploitation of Land, space, place, and resources. This practice has historically fed Western capitalism and its consumption impulses. Through the colonial process, justice and futures have been denied. But there has also been strength, courage and solidarity through the colonial process and encounters. The critical study of colonialism continues to raise questions for learners, teachers, educators, practitioners, development workers, social policy officials, as well as our institutions, the places we inhabit, including our diverse communities and broader global society. Colonialism is about life and living things. It is about the lives and dreams that are cut short or stolen. Colonialism is not just about a past, but a present and future. It is about impositions and dominating influences, relations and experiences that continue to script lives. There have been differentiated effects of the colonial encounter just as there have been different colonialisms.

Black and Indigenous feminist scholars have unmasked the different levels of colonization in history and contemporary times which are worth reiterating, as we seek ways to articulate the key principles of anti-colonial theory and practice. Long ago, Collins (2002) taught us the gendered effects of a system built on the oppression historically sustained through colonialism and the impact on women's lives and knowledge production. In her writing, she states:

> Taken together, the supposedly seamless web of economy, polity, and ideology function as a highly effective system of social control designed to keep African American women in an assigned, subordinate place. This larger system of oppression works to suppress the ideas of Black women intellectuals and to protect elite White male interests and worldviews. Denying African American women, the credentials to become literate certainly excluded most African-American women from positions as scholars, teachers, authors, poets, and critics. Moreover, while Black women historians, writers, and social scientists have long existed, until recently these women have not held leadership positions in universities, professional associations, publishing concerns, broadcast media, and other social institutions of knowledge validation. Black women's exclusion from positions of power within mainstream institutions has led to the elevation of elite White male ideas and interests and the corresponding suppression of Black women's ideas and interests in traditional scholarship (Higginbotham, 1989; Morton, 1991; Collins, 1998a, 95–123) (p. 5).

Collins (2002) goes further to show how women can collectively produce critical foundational knowledge from their experiences and stories of resistance that is layered in multiple contexts of colonial oppressions, both within and outside academic spaces:

> Because clarifying Black women's experiences and ideas lies at the core of Black feminist thought, interpreting them requires collaborative leadership among those who participate in the diverse forms that Black women's communities now take. This requires acknowledging not only how African American women outside of academia have long functioned as intellectuals by representing the interests of Black women as a group, but how this continues to be the case. For example, rap singer Sister Souljah's music as well as her autobiography No Disrespect (1994) certainly can be seen as contributing to Black feminist thought as critical social theory (p. 6).

Such knowledge Collins (2002) will argue is generated through research on the lived experiences of Black women, including those in leadership positions to ensure the transformation of structures and institutions:

> Research on Black women community leaders reinforces this notion that Black women work for institutional transformation in characteristic ways (Gilkes, 1983b, 1988). In one study, Black women leaders used their positions as heads of social service agencies to change the rules by which those agencies operated. One agency director commented, "You will never eliminate discrimination through complaints. … The thing that you've got to do is to get into those institutions and work from top to bottom: how they set policies; who's setting policies; why this is the policy" (1983b, p. 129). Even though their agencies were funded and controlled by Whites, in the same way, that Black women domestic workers used their positions to deliver material goods and skills to their children, these women used their institutions to empower African- Americans. They "saw the black community as a group of relatives and other friends whose interests should be advanced and promoted at all times, under all conditions, and by almost any means" (1983b, p. 117).

This speaks to the agency and power of Black women which is often unacknowledged when we speak about resistance to colonization. But such agency has also been used collectively to bring people along to see their potential in carving their own futures. Furthermore, Collins (2002, p. 227) in her epigraph quotes anti-colonial feminist scholaractivist, Angela Davis, to show how anti-colonial struggles must be waged with communities in mind to bring all people along. In her work, Angela Davis (1989, p. 5) counsels, "We must strive to 'lift as we climb.'… We must climb in such a way as to guarantee that all our sisters, regardless of social class, and indeed all of our brothers climb with us. This must be the essential dynamic of our quest for power." This aligns with the myriad ways in which bell hooks (2006) notes how exploitation works with images and representational practices of a consumerist culture engendered by colonial practices of Otherness:

> The world of fashion has also come to understand that selling products is heightened by the exploitation of Otherness. The success of Benneton ads, which with their racially diverse images have become a model for various advertising strategies, epitomizes this trend. Many ads that focus on Otherness make no explicit comments, or rely solely on visual messages, but the recent fall *Tweeds* catalogue provides an excellent example of the way contemporary culture exploits notions of Otherness with both visual images and text (p. 28).

These are racist colonial practices that are speaking of relations of domination and subordination that cannot be reduced to mere acts of fantasy, desires and taste. They highlight the commodification of difference which continues to operate in society from the dominant understandings of colonial differences which are about power and domination and denial of people's histories. As noted by hooks, "Mutual recognition of racism, its impact both on those who are dominated and those who dominate, is the only standpoint that makes possible an encounter between races that is not based on denial and fantasy" (2006, p. 28).

Colonial practices usually twin race and Indigeneity and roots the subjectification of human lives in a consumerist capitalist culture that not only represents Indigenous peoples in the colonial imagery and imaginations but also, caricatures the histories and lives of colonized peoples, which ends up dehumanizing us. hooks (2006) also notes media representation has been a powerful force of colonization, stereotyping and denying Indigenous humanity and further justifying our Otherization for exploitation. One of the least discussed aspects of colonization is its power to silence the critical narrative and talk on its horrors. We cannot discuss genocide and African enslavement without charges of reopening old wounds and creating the desire to speak of our shared commonalities rather the pain and suffering that is still being endured under the legacies of Euro-colonization. There is regulation of the unspeakable colonial horrors from human extermination whether that is among Indigenous, African peoples or Jews, as well as the right of the Palestinian people to self-determination. Again, as hooks (2006) reflected:

> Globally, survivors of the holocaust (whether it be the Japanese who suffered nuclear attack, Jews and Gypsies in the Nazi concentration camps, or African slaves in the Middle Passage) found it difficult, if not downright impossible, to speak about the horrors they had experienced. While there is current interest in the way children of Jewish survivors are affected by the torture and persecution of their ancestors, there have been few attempts to understand how the horrors of slavery and the genocidal assault on Native Americans has affected the children of survivors. Since much racialized genocidal assault against both these groups continues in less aggressive forms than all-out massacre, it is easy for everyone in this society to act as though red and black people do not suffer ongoing trauma. No one speaks of how the pain that our ancestors endured is carried in our hearts and psyches, shaping our contemporary worldview and social behaviour (p. 220).

In articulating an anti-colonial discursive framework and practice it is important to connect histories of colonization and to understand the significance of bringing the past and present in dialogue on colonial oppression and resistance. Anti-colonial praxis is about creating and working for decolonial solidarities explored by this important observation by hooks (2006):

> Celebration of shared history between African American and Native American will have lasting impact only if it is linked to efforts to construct and maintain ongoing political solidarity. We affirm the ties of the past, the bonds of the present, when we relearn our history, nurture the shared sensibility that has been retained in the present, linking these gestures to resistance struggle, to liberation movement that seeks to eradicate domination and transform society (p. 194).

To pursue anti-colonial change we must not only understand history and local struggles but be able to connect these in a way that furthers global resistance as well as our collective complicities and responsibilities in each other's oppressions. This is the only forward for social justice work and anti-colonial futurity. Slavery like colonialism extracted human tools and enriched the capital of Europe. Slavery as a form of colonial exploitation played out differently in geo-spaces but the colonial processes have much in common in terms of the assault on Black and Indigenous peoples' dignity, self-worth, and humanity highlighting the significance of the intersections of race and Indigeneity in anti-colonial analysis. As McKittrick (2006) writes:

> Transatlantic slavery profited from black enslavement by exacting material and philosophical black subordinations. A vast project, the practice of slavery differently impacted upon black diaspora populations in Africa, the Caribbean, South America, Canada, the United States, and various parts of Europe, between the seventeenth and nineteenth centuries. Slavery differed markedly in different locations. For example, periods of institution and abolishment, the scale of the trade, and uses of slave labor all produce unique time-space differentiations. At the same time, the particularity of slaves' lives and selves — gender, age, labour tasks, phenotype, ethnicity, language, time, place — fractures the meanings of slavery even further. As histories, recollections, and narratives of slavery clearly demonstrate, different slaves negotiated bondage in very different ways (p. xvi).

McKittrick also instructs us on anti-colonial epistemology as a new discursive formation uncovering the messiness, nuances, and complexities of colonization as connected with different Lands, spaces and subject identities:

> The historical and contemporary geographies of Canada are colonial. Critical theories in Canadian native studies importantly highlight the ways in which exploration and conquest resulted in the violent displacement and genocide of First Nations communities. Indeed, this "making" of Canada situates a struggle that enmeshes

race, whiteness, and the soil as they are attached to the nation's legal, political, and ideological claims of colonial superiority. Bonita Lawrence argues, for example, that claims to the land were deeply connected to human "exterminationist" practices, in effect "vanishing" native identities and communities through genocide and cultural imperialism (p. 95).

We cannot deny nor erase colonial domination on different Lands and how local resistances were shaped in the pursuit of freedom and justice. This brings us to the importance of the re-conceptualization of Land and its teachings for anti-colonial practice. The colonialists did their dirty job on Indigenous lands. This includes Land dispossession, privatization and prioritization of communal Lands, bringing diseases into Indigenous spaces, and also devaluing their teachings of Land and Earth [environmental] degradation. The confluence of colonial politics and Land plays out very clearly in the settler colonial practices on Indigenous communities with significant impacts on both the materiality and pedagogy of Land, especially the spiritual, emotional, cultural, and political aspects. Tuck and McKenzie (2014) point to a "second aspect of problematic relationships between dominant political systems and the land [that characterize] the historical and ongoing land-based practices of colonialism and, in particular, settler colonialism". This included "the legacies of the spatial practices of European colonization over the past 500 years in many parts of the globe continue to be supported by governments, but also social practices more generally, which establish and reify hierarchies of settlers over Indigenous" (p. 4).

The true intention of Euro-colonizers was clear, they were meant to seize, appropriate, or steal. Tuck and McKenzie (2014) again citing Wolfe (2006) insist "settler colonialism wants Indigenous land, not Indigenous peoples, so Indigenous peoples are cleared out of the way of colonial expansion, first via genocide and destruction, and later through incorporation and assimilation" (p. 66). It is through a discourse of colonialism that we can look for critical articulations of new futurity, to repair, replace, and restore what was stolen in terms of social, cultural, material, physical and spiritual wealth Tuck and McKenzie (2014) argues, "replacement is invested in settler futurity; in our use, futurity is more than the future, it is how human narratives and perceptions of the past, future, and present inform current practices and framings in a way that (over) determines what registers as the (possible) future" (pp. 69–70).

Anti-colonial conceptions of Indigenous Land have implications for how we view settler-futurities. It calls for "a relational ethics to future generations would decenter a settler futurity because settler futurities depend on the remaking of land and life into property and because settler futurities foreclose all others. There are other futurities to consider and enact. There are also very present concerns related to the futurities of (drinkable) water, water salinization, and temperature, soil contamination, and overproduction, shrinking shorelines, and the reduction of important pollinating species (such as honeybees) and species of cultural significance. These imminent concerns require immediate and sustained action" (Tuck & McKenzie, 2014, p. 164).

TOWARDS ANTI-COLONIAL PRINCIPLES

How does the foregoing discussion contribute to the framing of anti-colonial theory and educational practice? How do we pursue a culture of learning sustainable, meaningful, educational and grounding spiritually attuned pedagogies to enhance anti-colonial practice? We need to be disruptive and subversive because this is what is urgently required. There are varied conceptions of anti-colonial theorizing that embrace Indigenous struggles for independence, transhistorical discursive analysis of re-colonial relations, and the discourse of "coloniality", i.e., the knowledge of colonialism as unending/ongoing in multiple geographies; and subverting the periodization of colonial histories (see Dei, 2000).

Anti-colonial theorizing is not about creating definitions in and of itself, but rather an explanation of relationships, and exercise of power embedded within an anti-capitalist critique. Anti-Colonial Theory (ACT) is a critical tool to work with, rather than a normative statement [i.e., an interrogation of how bodies, knowledges, experiences, and histories are positioned hierarchically and in relationalities]. For example, ACT perceives the "school" not as a neutral space—with implications for what is internalized and what becomes a learned disposition; violence can be concealed or embedded in "common sense knowledge" of the dominant (see also Bourdieu & Passeron, 1977).

As articulated in multiple places (Dei, 2000, 2006; Dei & Asgharzadeh, 2001) we can spell out 10 inter-related intellectual and political principles of Anti-Colonial Theory (ACT):

First: ACT is about the mechanics and operations of colonial and re-colonial relations and the implications of imperial projects on three objectives of knowledge and social action: (a) processes of knowledge production, interrogation, validation, and dissemination; (b) the understanding of Indigeneity and local Indigenousness; and (c) the pursuit of agency, resistance, and subjective politics. It is maintained that knowledge is power and that colonial relations are sustained through dominant discourses. To interrupt colonial and colonizing relations, we need to produce, interrogate, validate, and disseminate counter, oppositional and alter/knowledge forms informed by local people's cultures, cultural histories, life experiences, and myriad identities. Such knowledges would represent a cultural resource base for local peoples and communities to resist their domination. Uncovering and asserting such knowledge by local peoples help in the evocation of local intellectual agencies for politics and resistance. So, by its nature, anti-colonial knowledge is counter and Alter knowledge.

Second: the "colonial" in ACT is not simply defined as "foreign" and "alien". Rather, it is seen as anything that is "imposed" and "dominating". Knowledge can be imposed from several sites and sources to seek dominance and oppression. We need counter knowledge to purposely serve to challenge the such colonial imposition of dominant ideas and practices and, particularly, help all learners to decolonize. The value and relevance of such an expansive understanding of the "colonial" is that it allows us to see colonizing relations in every aspect of social life, including how social identities and differences (e.g., race, gender, class, sexuality, ability, religion, culture, identity, language etc.) can themselves become sites of colonial domination. This key principle of ACT is intended to admit to our collective complicities and implications in oppressions and the necessity to use knowledge to resist or fight colonial imposition. Hence ACT must entail an action-oriented process and engagement of knowledge to ensure the centrality of all learners to pursue education from our myriad identities and lived experiences to counter-hegemonic practices.

Third: ACT must constitute a discursive shift and an inclusive understanding of colonialism from variegated forms of territorial imperialism and state/cultural control of resources (including subjects) to other direct and indirect mechanisms and processes of power within communities to subjugate and resist (e.g., the way technologies, education, knowledge, and ideologies reveal power saturated practices that can dominate and subvert). To understand variegated forms of knowledge we must connect sociality and polity and embrace Land as a site of Earthly teachings offering counter knowledges of sharing, reciprocity, mutual interdependence, connections, and relativity. An embedded meaning is the relevance of coming to know in a given space which entails bringing responsibility and relationality to knowledge in the pursuit of social justice.

Fourth: ACT must be employed as a cultural criticism interrogating the complicated nature and extent of social domination and, particularly, the multiple places, power and relations of power that work to establish dominant-subordinate relations. ACT as a prism requires we examine social existence not only in terms of our relations to history, social context, identities, and politics but also, to understand local and global events through the interplay of colonial and colonizing narratives consciously put in place to define the terms and rules of social communication. To interrupt these terms and rules which are usually set by the dominant in society we must call on the power of local histories, cultural memories, identity formation,s and the cultural politics of education as necessary entry points of critical conversations and dialogues for change.

Fifth: ACT brings a transhistorical read on the "coloniality of power", such coloniality transcends geo-spaces in interconnected practices. These practices converge in the force of an imperial power beyond which must be distinguished from the power and agency of the subordinated. For example, while power can be diffused in the Foucaultian sense, ACT recognizes the power of the colonial dominant as salient and different. The power of the colonial dominant culminates in the making of the Empire. Therefore, any analysis that uses ACT as a framework would have to extend beyond the asymmetrical power relations as expressed in multiple geographies to point to how, within all spaces, the power of the colonial dominant has real consequences beyond the individual agency. For example, ACT offers a different analysis of racism and colonialism that focuses on systems and structures of exploitation and the conflation of institutionalized power.

Sixth: ACT reiterates the significance of understanding the colonial encounter as violent, destabilizing and inherently destructive, harmful, and inhumane. To resist is to reclaim our humanity from the evil forces of colonialism and oppression. There are no redeeming qualities of colonialism. The engagement of ACT, therefore, requires a continual process of the regeneration of self and the collective through a nurturing of a "literacy of resistance". This literacy is a politics of coming to know differently, and in particular what decolonization, power, agency and resistance all mean in the context of Indigenous authenticity and authentication of local voices as an exercise of the intellectual agency of colonized peoples. The "literacy of resistance" is important if colonized peoples are to part ways with colonial vestiges, colonial inheritances, and break away from hierarchical relations and practices.

Seventh: ACT is about critically examining "coloniality of knowledge" in an educational setting purposely aimed at disrupting Euro-colonial/Western hegemony. Decolonization cannot seek legitimacy from the eyes of the colonizer. Decolonization also can be accomplished through an emphasis on "multicentricity" (Dei, 1996), or "multi-epistemes" (Cajete, 1994) to challenge the idea of a dominant narrative or a knowledge system as the standard bearer to which everything else is measured. ACT is a prism working with multiple ways of knowing, doing, and acting. But most importantly, ACT "is not just de-Westernizing, but rather a total re-assertion of (the Indigene) at the centre of knowledge discovery, interrogation, validation, and dissemination" (see Asante, 2013, p. 12 in another context).

Eighth: ACT emphasizes the central place of spirituality and spiritual knowledge as constitutive of the embodiment of knowledge of local peoples. Local peoples embody their knowledges through spirituality as a relation of self and the collective to a physical, metaphysical, and supernatural realm of existence. The spiritual ontologies and epistemologies that ACT speak to include making relations of body, mind, soul, and spirit in the process of coming to know about self, others, and communities, understanding the nexus of society, culture and Nature, as well as the linkage of the physical and metaphysical worlds. While ACT embraces the certainty of knowledge it also accepts the uncertainty of knowing which is beyond the capacity of the human senses and explanations. Inquiry into knowledge in an ongoing process with no end and there is no knower of everything. Science is the subject of continuing search for knowledge. The oppressor can be complicit (both consciously and subconsciously) in the very things they seek to contest.

Ninth: the "anti-colonial" as an epistemology of the oppressed and colonized, anchored in the Indigenous sense of collective and common colonial consciousness. In effect, ACT centres the power of Indigenous (as a dynamic moment in time and place) and Indigeneity (as identity and process of knowing self and others) as well as the authenticity of Indigene (in terms of the voice and narration of experience). The "Indigenous" is engaged as a subversive educational approach, not a superficial add-on, requiring direct actions to dismantle and rebuild the social order (see also Taiaiake, Mihesuah, & Wilson, 2004; Hewitt, 2016). The "Indigenous" as a site and source of knowing help the learner to develop a critical consciousness of oneself, as an educator/learner/development practitioner located with/in place, context, history, and with an identity, culture, and ancestral memories (see also wa Thiong'o, 1986; Afful-Broni, Anamuah-Mensah, Raheem, & Dei, 2020).

Lastly: a central gaze of ACT is White supremacist logics and the way it functions or operates in society to normalize oppressive practices. ACT is a prism to understand the myriad faces of White/colonial privilege and power as crucial to pursuing anti-colonial practice. This includes understanding the ways White colonial privilege can be denied, and how privilege conceals itself or seduces even the colonized while refusing to admit to acts of complicities, responsibilities, and accountability of all bodies. Within the ACT prism, there must be a powerful link made between race, Indigeneity, and decolonization. This is primarily because colonization was/is a process that knew/knows its targets in terms of the bodies, identities, places, and Lands to colonize.

Let me go back to some significant quotes to capture words that constitute the essence of this last principle of ACT for me. Tuck and McKenzie's (2014) contention that "place is not adequately described.... [and] places are not always named, and not always justly named. They do not always appear on maps; they do not have agreed-upon boundaries. They are not fixed. Places are not more readily understood by objective accounts" (p. 14). How we name the places colonizers occupied/occupy and oppressed/occupy is significant to ACT. Land is an integral part of anti-colonial resistance. Although McKittrick (2006) also writes with a particular gaze of Black bodies and Black geographies, her works give deep meanings to anti-colonial theorizing of oppressions, colonialism, and colonization. Drawing on the history of Transatlantic slavery, McKittrick (2006) "illustrate[s] that black women are both shaped by, and challenge, traditional geographic arrangements [and] this history heightens the meanings of traditional arrangements, which rest on a crucial geographic paradigm, human captivity" (p. xvi). She continues,

> I want to suggest that space and place give Black lives meaning in a world that has, for the most part, incorrectly deemed Black populations and their attendant geographies as "un-geographic" and/or philosophically undeveloped. That Black lives are necessarily geographic, but also struggle with discourses that erase and de-spatialize their sense of place, is where I begin to conceptualize geography (p. xiii).

Geography is an interesting concept. It is more than physical markers and landscapes. It is about who belongs, who is allowed to belong, who experiences and what is experienced. However, geography is also fundamentally about Lands and the meanings we bring to land as places and spaces. For colonized and oppressed peoples, the social and physical geographies of Land give us memory, identity, spiritual and cultural meanings relating to our lived experiences, histories, resistance, and survival. The geography of Land is also about a desire to see ourselves, a yearning to define our realities and to begin to re-imagine new humanity. Subsequently, it is fitting that I now turn to the lived experiences of Blackness and anti-Blackness, as viewed from the perspective of what I have called "Blackcentricity".

The enduring intellectual significance "Blackcentricity"

The "decolonial" is a path to travel to an "anti-colonial" end. For Black scholars how do we travel the decolonial path? In this section, I am pushing for Black scholarship to be anti-colonial using a paradigmatic lens of "Blackcentricity". In the current climate of anti-Black racism and its culture of Black disposables and dispensable, I seek a paradigmatic path to specifically address global anti-Blackness and the colonial violence perpetrated onto Black lives. Elsewhere (Dei, 2020a), borrowing from our pioneering scholars such as Molefi Asante, Maulana Karenga, Jawanza Kunjufu, Ama Mazama, and Cheikh Anta Diop, I frame "Blackcentricity" as an approach to study and research anchored Black and African Indigeneities and making connections with race and decolonization. I claim African/Black "Indigeneity" to signal a deep shift in thinking and political work, and not merely an intellectual ploy to replace words. It is the Cabralian sense of a "return to the source" or the proverbial bird in the lexicon of the Akan of Ghana, *Sankofa* (i.e., go back and fetch that which is of great value).

Blackcentricity is a discursive and philosophical prism for the construction of Black narratives, and stories of our lived experiences as lodged in culture, history, politics, and identity. Blackcentricity is about Black, African, and African diasporic peoples pursuing research scholarship and training informed by our Indigeneities for our own collective and transnational welfare. It is a philosophical and political perspective to center Black, Africa, Blackness and Africanness in the intellectual praxis of shared Indigeneities. Black and African Indigeneities are continually under assault. They are often denied as if we lost everything about ourselves with Euro-colonialism. But there was Africa (*Abibiman*) before Europe. The teachings of the Land, Earth, sky, waters etc. continue to guide Black and African peoples differently and globally. For example, many of us still have a veneration of our ancestors and Elders. We have spiritual communion with the dead. We maintain connections with the spiritual, material, and metaphysical worlds to inform the ways Black and African peoples understand our surroundings. I caution that this stance does not mean every Black or African body or learner uses this prism or will find it appealing in fighting anti-Blackness and anti-Black racism. However, what I am arguing for is that there is a philosophical standpoint/worldview that informs a coming to know that cannot be dismissed as untenable in the era of cosmopolitanism, post-modernism or post-coloniality. Blackcentricity is also "the idea of unashamed Blackness, a desire to speak with a distinctive Black voice with a discursive politics affirming the Black soul and spirit soul in a moment in history when our Blackness and Africanness are under assault from state-sanctioned violence (Dei, 2020a). Blackcentricity is about the African Indigenous ontological existence and claims African and Black Indigeneities as decolonial resistance. Just as there are multi geo-spaces of African and Black Indigeneities and Blackness itself is heterogenous and multi-dimensional, there will also be class, gender, sexual and dis/ability perspectives that inform any articulation of Blackcentricity.

As opined in Dei (2020) and Dei, Odozor, and Vasquez (2020) we need to recover Black/African cultural knowledges and locate the onto-epistemologies of Black subjects in our understanding of Black life, social existence, and the pursuit of political activism. Drawing an anchorage in Molefi Asante's (2003) framing of Afrocentricity, I posit a form of trans-local Black African episteme, "Blackcentricity" which through the variety of our diverse and yet connected histories as Black peoples, offers a counter-reading of Black and African life as an intellectual reference point to global White historicity and supremacist logics. The insistence on our African Indigenous epistemologies and ontologies is more than an intellectual act. It is very political. It has increasingly become a "matter of life and death for the victims of colonial domination" to find a frame of reference to organize for our survival and a way forward for our collective existence in a hostile, violent world (see also "Black Ink Info", 2020, p. 29).

In a previous chapter, I alluded to the importance of rooting the Black theorizing in our rich intellectual heritage as African peoples. Black and African peoples have to claim our Indigeneity as a necessary exercise in our decolonization. The prism of Blackcentricity fundamentally informs debates about how to view Blackness and Africanness in multiple geographical spaces, drawing on their synergies and convergences, as well as offering a political discursive stance to challenge imperial, colonial and racist constructions of African identities and Black lived experiences. As Black, African, and African diasporic scholars, students, and educators, we must be the key theorists of

African Indigeneity for contemporary anti-colonial praxis. We need Black research and education to operate from the position of Blackcentricity to give a historical anchorage to our shared ancestries irrespective of where we may be today. A Blackcentric approach can help create space for learners to interrogate the reproduction of oppressive, colonial, and White supremacist logics within our communities and across multi geo-spaces. Thus, for example "Black Lives Matter" will have as much meaning in Africa as it does in North America, Asia, Europe, Latin America, and the Caribbean. Notwithstanding our differences, our issues connect and intersect when it comes to global racism, colonial and imperial violence. Black lives matter in Africa when local elected officials and the leadership of the nation-state blatantly ignore the hardships facing their own communities by pursuing a development agenda that serves the interests of global capital and the international financial community.

In our global dispersals, Black and African peoples have been systematically and disproportionately excluded from the sharing of wealth, resources, and property. We need to come together to develop and do transformative Blackcentric, anti-colonial practices to challenge colonial oppressions both from within, amongst and outside ourselves. Blackcentricity offers a discursive approach to tie anti-Black racism and anti-African racism that is internalized by even some diasporic Blacks and racialized groups further placing Africa and African peoples at the bottom of racial strata or "epidermal schemata".

A Blackcentric educational research agenda is about the relevance and responsibility of Black scholarship and politics. It is developing an anti-colonial educational agenda to re-orient the institutional structures of schooling and education in myriad settings, to advance Black and African peoples' social and political causes. The Blackcentric agenda can be accomplished through research, writing, teaching, and community work informed by a global Blackcentric prism. Black scholarship continues to assist local and global scholars to think more robustly about, and to challenge the idea of knowledge, to ask what and whose knowledge, and more importantly, to trouble the structural configurations that limit Black peoples from truly (co)creating liberatory/emancipatory knowledge for social change (Dei & Vasquez, 2020).

The Blackcentric anti-colonial educational agenda can be pursued from multiple levels. We can think through counter and alter/visions of schooling as Afrocentric initiatives have long pursued. The Blackcentric educational agenda is to provide support and healing to our communities to deal with the spiritual and emotional consequences of racism and oppression, and to be able to map and triangulate power as it is manifested in racist acts, beliefs, microaggressions as well as the systemic and structural practices of colonial violence. This agenda includes not only critically teaching Blackness and anti-Blackness, but to facilitate anti-colonial conversations to build communities and strong caregiver relations by leveraging the African cultural knowledges within our communities. We need Black and African learners to see themselves reflected and their voices represented and heard within educational curricular programming in all subject areas. We need local Black and African families included in debates and strategies for their Black and African youth educational outcomes (i.e., key decision-making processes that promote a greater sense of belonging for students and their families). A Blackcentric educational agenda is to engage Black and African learners in leadership roles and within their own communities and politics.

Blackcentricity calls for an openness to critiques and interrogations of Black scholarship for its own professional development, but most importantly, for the advancement of our local communities. The prism and approach require that as Black scholars we position our work more clearly to clarify, elaborate, and identify the problems in our communities we are addressing and how our scholarly and political work is advancing and contributing to critical Black knowledge. It will require that we dig deeper, ask bold questions, and address the profound issues identified by our communities themselves. These questions include: How do we write ourselves and our communities into our own histories? How do we make learning an embodied encounter for our students? How do resistance and resilience become a self-generating encounter? How do we respond to the tensions of the de/colonial? How do we understand relational responsibilities and relational investments in our communities? How do we internalize Whiteness regardless of how anti-colonial we become? What does it mean to be with and within communities, and to always engage in our intellectuality/scholarship with love and care?

To reiterate, there are implications of the Blackcentricity for the Black scholar today in the current climate of anti-Black racism and ongoing coloniality of Black existence. Not every Black scholar adheres to Blackcentricity, and I do not recommend this as a measure of the scholarly worth of the Black scholar. Elsewhere, I allude to resisting any "forced compliance" when discussing Black scholar responsibilities, and our particular practices ought to be (see Dei, 2019b). I am, however, expressing the Black scholar's anti-colonial politics to be strived for. As raised earlier the Black Scholar everywhere must exhibit the power of our own onto-epistemologies. To do so we must understand both the analytical distinction and the necessary intellectual and political linkage between the "scholar" and our "scholarship". Who and what the "Black Scholar" and "Black Scholarship" are, is not always the same thing. Therefore, it is necessary to make the analytical distinction between the "body" and "knowledge" produced by the body even when there could be a clear linkage. The "Black Scholar" is foremost a body, an identity, subject positionality, and a location in academia. "Black scholarship", on the other hand, is about knowledge produced by the body and the purposes of such knowledge for anti-colonial change. The case I am making is for Black knowledge (as anti-colonial Black scholarship) to be related to the lived experiences of Black, Indigenous, and colonized bodies. So anti-colonial Black scholarship is not just any knowledge produced by a Black body. We cannot simply conflate the "Black scholar" to a necessary requirement that states their production of knowledge by their body has to be related to the social realities of Black, Indigenous, and colonized peoples (anti-colonial Black scholarship). What is clear is that through history when we allude to Black intellectual traditions there is a significant correlation of the scholar and their scholarship in a way that shows a dialectics of theory and social change for the community's advancement. For example, I have already alluded to how Black scholarship is tied to a rich intellectual heritage, i.e., the Black Radical/Intellectual Tradition of pioneering thinkers and activists (e.g., CLR James, Cedric Robinson, W.E.B. Du Bois, Marcus Garvey, Julia Anna Cooper, Claudia Jones, Kwame Nkrumah).

I advance a few contentions and the relevance of seeking the linkage as well as awareness of the important analytical distinction between the "Black scholar" and "Black scholarship". Who is a "Black" academic/scholar who chooses not to do his/her research on "social realities of Black people"? There will be different answers to this question. For me, this body is merely a scholar/intellectual. But in this day and age with all the "crises" (some manufactured) our communities are confronted with; can we as Black scholars afford to be simply scholars/intellectuals? I contend therefore that the Black scholar is one Black scholarship in a dialectic way for social and political change in our communities. The problems confronting our communities require that whatever scholarship we engage in must have relevance to our communities and beyond. Hence, we must focus on building the concept of critical, anti-colonial "Black scholarship" as a meaningful part of the "Black scholar" identity in the academy. The issues anti-Black racism, violence against Black communities, glaring health, employment, media, judicial, and education disparities etc.

must motivate a form of Black intellectual and political activism to become "academic warriors" with an anti-colonial attitude (see Dei, 2014).

The search for the legitimacy of our [Black] scholarship is a constant struggle. We see the epistemic injustice as quite often scholarship that is based on the social realities of Black, Indigenous, and colonized peoples, only gains legitimacy when White and dominant scholars begin to do research on the topic. We also note the resulting consequences when as Black scholars we search for legitimacy in the Western academy. We can be "intellectual imposters" (Nyamhjoh, 2012) in the academy, sometimes not true to our own authentic selves and souls as we mimic theories, experiences and epistemologies that hardly speak to our communities. This problem of "colonial mimicry" (Bhabha, 1994) as we pursue the path of searching for validation, acceptance and legitimation in White/colonial spaces has attendant psychic, spiritual and emotional injuries (see also Fanon, 1963).

We always must contend with the problem of neo-liberal accommodation that positions Black learners as needing remedial attention and help to be successful. And this is not just in the global diasporic space. We see it even in African academies when African scholars wanting to be recognized as "world class scholars" would rather team with Western "international collaborators" and not with our own colleagues on the continent. Even debates about the intellectual (not the political) merits of what constitutes our scholarship, coupled with the general suppression of knowledge grounded in the social realities of Black/Indigenous and colonized peoples globally, present many challenges and hurdles to overcome.

Black scholars also have to maintain a critical gaze of White supremacist logics that can easily find its way into academic work. This is the power of White supremacy as more than a problem of conceptualization. It is a pervasive thought/thinking machine, a framework, a structure, about action and systemic practice of education broadly defined outside schooling. White supremacy implicates both our work as Black scholars and Black scholarship. Hence there is a need to engage with White supremacy as a core feature of the manifestation of Black academic life. This requires the advancement of anti-colonial Black scholarship focused on undoing the coloniality of power and Being. Progressive scholars can be caught in the tentacles of White supremacist logics. In fact, White supremacy has a long human history. It predates capitalism and this is why the failure of Marx to account for the exigencies of race has been painful for anti-colonial Black scholars. What we need to do is to treat White supremacy as "a cultural and material export good [and cultural resource knowledge] that accompanied all trade, conquest, and appropriation [of knowledge and cultural materials]" which continues to this day (Black Ink Info, 2020, p. 25).

There is also the use of language that can itself be colonizing. Language use points to the complexities of the Western academy and needs anti-colonial reads. Anti-colonial Black scholarship must be careful not to fall into the trap of using language that further marginalizes Black subjects, including our contributions to knowledge. For Black scholars our language use must always be anti-colonial and Blackcentric. There is a need even to ensure the language and framing of the "Black Scholar" and "Black Scholarship" does not reinforce deficit thinking and, thereby, contribute to epistemic injustice. For example, I have a few times heard even Black learners buy into the old trick of devaluing Black theorists when we say "anti-racist practice needs deeper theoretical analysis." Never mind the fact that Black communities including Black educators and activists have been at the forefront of advancing anti-racist thought and practice. There is a reification of theory that can be a form of coloniality of Black scholarship and Black bodies. Also, what does it really mean to say blanket- wise the problem of hegemony or even race/racism etc. have not been addressed in academia?

While it may be true given the culture of the academy, it is equally important for us to always specify who and what we are talking about. This way we do not erase the efforts and contributions of those Black, Indigenous, and racialized scholar-activists who have historically been and continue to be deeply committed to challenging epistemic injustice, race and racism in academia. Black intellectual and political agency must not be diminished because it has been a struggle of life and death in the Western academy. We know that not all Black scholars have been part of the mainstream academic culture to its full extent. Many of us resist even as we work with the tools and rules of academia. But it seems to me it is discounting Black struggles in academics when it is claimed simply that our presence in the academy makes us "mainstream". Also, we should be careful when we make the distinction between "Black" and "mainstream actors" in the academy. It could imply that there are no Black scholars who have become part of the mainstream although also in solution-oriented ways.

An anti-colonial Black Scholar's responsibilities include exploring Blackness as the everyday experiences of Black peoples and how we live and resist our Blackness globally/transnationally. We can never escape our Blackness. This goes for those who see Blackness as a problem. What this entails, therefore, is that we accept and work with our Blackness. We must understand what it means to wear Black skin/body today (see Dei, 2018). Blackness must be content with its past, present and future. Blackness must be freedom. The (in)visibility and hypervisibility of the Black experience in the Western academy is such that we can be under the gaze of the dominant and yet never be validated nor recognized for our scholarly worth. Within the academy we are prone to the hypervisibility to violence sometimes given our physical formidability.

So then, what should our responsibilities be? Part of Black scholars responsibilities is speaking truth to power and having the courage to stand up and to speak about our experiences. This means developing the courage to speak about race, difference and social oppression. We must become part of the intellectual struggle for our own epistemic survival. In my intellectual praxis, this means becoming anti/colonial, Afrocentric and Blackcentric. Our knowledge base must be lodged in the social and physical contexts of our Indigeneities and multiple geographies to challenge and subvert the exclusion of knowledge from our varied communities, including the Global South. We must match our intellectuality with politeness and become a distinctive "Black Voice". As the saying goes, "silence will not keep the Black scholar safe!". Our silence may offer some protective functions (e.g., minimize retaliation) but can still pose larger threats and dangers (e.g., continued microaggressions/mistreatment; guilt/self-blame; etc.).

We must bring moral and ethical issues to the table, that is to trouble the ways through which we have come to objectivity and negate subjectivity. We must not only understand Blackness as an intellectual, political, and epistemological framing, but also, as moral/justice/ethical framing. If Blackness is an episteme, it is important then in evoking our Blackness (through Blackcentricity prism) in the search for understanding and knowledge of our problems. In fact, there are serious ethical and moral issues of negating our Black knowings. There is the necessity to take intellectual and political stances (violence of schooling, the epidemic of mass incarceration of Black peoples) cannot be responded to with a mere "search for knowledge". It must be a search for knowledge with an anti-colonial purpose. We must become aware of the extent our work can assist in the dehumanization Black people and contribute to the commodification of Blackness. Vincent Harding (1974) long ago enthused, we need a sort of "critical repositioning" (p. 6) of ourselves in the Western academy, that is to link "Black intellectual radicalization" and political activism by responding to the community relevance of our scholarship.

Black scholar anti-colonial radicalization is also understanding our challenges as the "predicament of Blackness" to borrow the phrasing of Pierre (2006). We acknowledge the complexities and heterogeneities of Blackness and the politics of resistance, and liberation in particular moments, time and spaces. The fact of the matter though is that the predicament of Blackness has remained through time; it has largely been a question of how we contend with the past.

We need to draw a distinction such that Blackness is either read as an obstacle to achieving Whiteness or pursued for Blackness as politics of liberation. We can draw lessons from the "predicament of Blackness" in postcolonial Africa. Achille Mbembe's (1992, 2002) work is most influential in understanding the role of the postcolonial Black nation-state in Africa in the oppression of its peoples. Blackness has been contained in the postcolonial state and in Western modernity. There is a failure to grasp the true meaning of Fanon's (1963) words that decolonization is fundamentally about the politics of space and body. Decolonization has maintained the spaces of privilege (see Gibson, 2001, p. 12) and the failure of Black decolonization (e.g., formal independence does not meet the aspirations and dreams of Black masses). We have also come to realize with time that Black leadership is not necessarily Black power and that the search for Black unity is incomplete if the goal is not Black power.

We need to challenge an emerging Black consciousness lodged in Western thought, liberalism, and humanism. For example, an idea of Blackness is affirmed within the context of capitalism and imperialism. Capitalism has worked to maintain the internal racial power structures embedded in Blackness that sustain White economic hegemony. There has also been the liberalization of the decolonization project and "post-colonial" politics for elitist and puritanism ends. Through all this, there emerged [and continues to exist] a nationalist narrative that is not produced on the understandings of the Black oppression from the oppressed peoples themselves, but rather, from a desire to claim a named space [in reaction or response to the Euro-colonial space]. As noted, the Black body continues to search for legitimation, acceptance, and validation in White colonial spaces. An elite version of freedom has been developed which reveals itself in false versions of anti-colonial nationalism that simply sees itself within a White image/mirror (e.g., Black Independence of nation states in Africa, Caribbean).

We continue to reproduce a very problematic understanding of "re-humanizing Black body" as becoming "human" just like the White body. Embedded in this practice has been a form of Black anti-Blackness and a failure to acknowledge that Blackness has strong racial, cultural, political, and spiritual dimensions beyond the skin and body image. There is an anti-Black space where through internalized colonialisms and racisms African elites can oppress their own kind. There is also the appropriation of Blackness to achieve Black political sovereignty which is far from any semblance of anti-colonial resistance. I attribute all of this to the failed attempts to understand Blackness as an identity, a set of practices, a social condition, a state of being, politics and geography (see Dei, 2018).

A key question is how does anti-colonial Blackness redeem itself from the standpoint of the Black scholar? I contend that through Blackcentricity we could allow for a re-claiming of Blackness from our Earthiness (i.e.: Indigeneity), not our nothingness. When Fanon (1963) said "Africa is the future" I took the meaning to be reclaiming Africa in terms of her Indigeneities for articulating a new anti-colonial Blackness. In rooting Black theorizing through the Black radical tradition and the influence of Leftists and Marxist ideas, one contemporary thinker that I have found worth engaging is Robin Kelley. I see him as a critical thinker influenced by Marxian tradition and Cedric Robinson's intervention on Black Marxism and the Black radical tradition. Robin Kelley brings an understanding of diaspora that will help us connect the relevance of Blackcentricity across multi-geo-spaces of peoples of African descent globally. To him diaspora is an "analytical framework and a metaphor for understanding Black world experience" (Black Ink Info, 2020, p. 30). Diaspora evokes culture, politics, knowledge, and geographies and "a political and historical community rooted in resistance" (Black Ink Info, 2020, p. 30). While there are differences in time, space and place, diaspora is a concept worth fleshing out in claiming cultural knowledges from multiple geo-spaces. We need current conceptions of the "diaspora" that do not "erect boundaries [but] rather than topple them" (Black Ink Info, 2020, p. 30). We must begin to think of Africa beyond the real and imagined to be inclusive of an anti-colonial new internationalism and/from the perspective of Blackcentricity.

I would like to see "Diaspora" put forward more as an anti-colonial framework that "account[s] for the full range of Black identities and transnational histories…. especially those that do not fit within a Pan-African imaginary" (Black Ink Info, 2020, p. 30). The Black scholar using a Blackcentricity prism should be making broader alliances and political identifications across national and international borders, as well as from the geo-boundaries of Blacknesses. These alliances make it possible for us to "discern the contingent, malleable nature of identities and the limits of a diasporic framework that centers primarily on Africa and African dispersal" (Black Ink Info, 2020, p. 30). Rather than "limits", I see "potential" to extend the reading of Africa as a global dispersal of Blacknesses. It is, in fact, such anti-colonial reading, that will allow us to think through and "construct a new global [anti-colonial] history, [and to open up] new possibilities for writing a world [anti-colonial] history [of Blacknesses] from below" (Black Ink Info, 2020, p. 30). This is the enduring significance of Blackcentricity that I am hoping for.

Decolonization is a path to getting back, to recreate/resurrect the past for an anti-colonial future. We must understand the emergence, development and decline of European modernity and the consequences of the exclusion of African and Indigenous peoples in constructions of Euro-colonial modernity. To articulate an African/Indigenous modernity as a specific form we need an anti-colonial Blackcentric perspective. The intellectual and political exercise is "not to despair or embrace cynicism but to see the impossibility of the present as a symptom" of the problem and a shared element of those [Black scholar] activists who have gone before us (Black Ink Info, 2020, p. 26). The challenge is how we turn the despair and cynicism of "impossibility into the seeds of possibility" of anti-colonial Black futurity through the power of ideas (Black Ink Info, 2020, p. 26)? It is not enough to imagine an anti-colonial world without oppression (e.g., anti-Black racism, capitalist exploitation or even the overthrow of capitalism), but also to "understand the mechanisms or processes that not only reproduce structural inequity but make them common sense and render these processes natural or invisible" (Black Ink Info, 2020, p. 26). Our work as Black scholars must be to reclaim the past to transform society or create new anti-colonial Black futures.

References Cited

Afful-Broni, A., Anamuah-Mensah, J., Raheem, K., & Dei, G. J. S. (2020). Introduction. In A. Afful-Broni, J. Anamuah-Mensah, K. Raheem, & G. J. S. Dei (Eds.), *Africanizing the school curriculum: Promoting an inclusive, decolonial education in African contexts*. Myers Educational Press.

Ahenakew, C., de Oliveira Andreotti, V., Cooper, G., & Hireme, H. (2014). "Beyond epistemic provincialism: De-provincializing indigenous resistance." *Alternative, 10*(3), 216–231.

Alfred, T., & Corntassel, J. (2005). "Being Indigenous: Resurgences against contemporary colonialism." Government and Opposition Ltd. http://web.uvic.ca/igov/uploads/pdf/Being%20Indigenous%20GOOP.pdf.

Asante, M. K. (2013, August 7). *Decolonizing the Universities in Africa: An approach to transformation*, [Keynote Address]. Conference of African Scholars Promoting Critical Consciousness: Deconstructing Colonial Knowledge Legacies in the Academy, Port Elizabeth, South Africa.

Bhabha, Homi K. (1994). *The location of culture*. Routledge.

Black Ink Info. (2020). "Solidarity Is Not a Market Exchange:" An interview with Robin D. G. Kelley. Black Ink Info. https://black-ink.info/author/blcknk/

Bourdieu, P., & Passeron, J. C. (1977). *Reproduction in education, society and culture*. Sage Publications.

Bonds, A., & Inwood, J. (2015). Beyond White Privilege: Geographies of white supremacy and settler colonialism. *Progress in Human Geography*, 40(6), 715–733.

Cajete, G. (1994). *Look to the mountain: An ecology of Indigenous education*. Kivaki Press.

Collins, P. H. (2002). *Black feminist thought: Knowledge, consciousness, and the politics of empowerment*. Routledge.

Dei, G. J. S. (1996). *Anti-racism education in theory and practice*. Fernwood Publishing.

Dei, G. J. S. (2000). Rethinking the role of Indigenous knowledge in the Academy. *International Journal of Inclusive Education*, 4(2), 111–132.

Dei, G. J. S. (2006). Mapping the terrain: Anti-colonial thought and politics of resistance. In G. Dei & A. Kempf (Eds.), *Anti-Colonialism and education: The Politics of Resistance*. Sense Publishers.

Dei, G. J. S. (2014). The African Scholar in the Western Academy. *Journal of Black Studies*, 45(3), 167–179.

Dei, G. J. S. (2018). Black like me: Reframing Blackness and decolonial politics. *Educational Studies*, 54(2), 117–142.

Dei, G. J. S. (2019a). "Neoliberalism as a New Form of Colonialism in Education". In. Stephanie Chitpin & John Portelli (Eds.), *Educational policy in Neoliberal Times: Issues, challenges and possibilities an international perspective* (pp. 40–58). New York: Routledge.

Dei, G. J. S. (2019b). "An Indigenous Africentric perspective on Black Leadership: The African Scholar Today". In T. Kitossa, P. Howard, & E. Lawson (Eds.), *African-Canadian leadership: Continuity, transformation and change* (pp. 355–369). University of Toronto Press.

Dei, G. J. S. (2020a). "Teaching Race, Anti-Blackness and [African] Indigeneity: Personal Reflections of a Black Scholar." In G. Dei, A. Vasquez, & E. Odozor (Eds.), *Cartographies of Blackness and Black Indigeneities* (pp. 1–22). Myers Educational Press.

Dei, G. J. S., & Asgharzadeh, A. (2001). The power of social theory: Towards an Anti-Colonial discursive framework. *Journal of Educational Thought*, 35(3), 297–323.

Dei, G. J. S., & Vasquez, A. (2017). The foundations of transformative anti-racism: A conversation with George J. Sefa Dei and Andrea Vasquez Jimenez. *Canada Education*, 57(3), 50–52.

Dei, G. J. S., Odozor, E., & Vasquez, A. (2020). *Cartographies of Blackness and Black Indigeneities*. Myers Educational Press.

Fanon, F. (1963). *The wretched of the Earth*. Grove Press.

Hooks, b. (2006). *Black looks: Race and representation*. Academic Internet Pub Inc.

Gibson, N. (2001). Transition from Apartheid. *African and Asian Studies*, 36(1), 65–85.

Grosfoguel, R. (2002). Colonial Difference, Geopolitics of Knowledge, and Global Coloniality in the Modern/Colonial Capitalist World-System. *Review - Fernand Braudel Center for the Study of Economies, Historical Systems, and Civilizations*, 25(3), 203–224.

Harding, V. (1974). The vocation of the Black scholar and the struggles of the Black community. In Institute of the Black World (Eds.), *Education and Black struggle: Notes from the colonized world*. Harvard Educational Review (Monograph no. 2), 3–29.

Latty, S., Scribe, M., Peters, A., & Morgan, A. (2016). Not enough human: At the scenes of Indigenous and Black dispossession. *Critical Ethnic Studies*, 2(2), 129–158.

Lebakeng, T. (2010). Discourse on Indigenous knowledge systems; sustainable socio-economic development and the challenge of the Academy in Africa. *CODESRIA Bulletin*, 2010, pp. 24–29.

Maldonado-Torres, N. (2004). The topology of being and the geopolitics of knowledge: Modernity, empire, coloniality. *City*, 8(1), 29–56.

Mbembe, J. A. (1992). Provisional notes on the postcolony. *Africa*, 62(1), 3–37.

Mbembe, J. A. (2003). Necropolitics. *Public Culture*, 15(1), 11–40.

Mbembe, J.A. (2002). The power of the archive and its limits. In Refiguring the archive. Hamilton, C., Harris, V., Pickover, M., Reid, G., Saleh, R., & Taylor, J. (Eds.).Springer Netherlands.

McKittrick, K. (2006). *Demonic grounds: Black women and the cartographies of struggle*. University of Minnesota Press.

Mignolo, W. (2007). Delinking: The rhetoric of modernity, the logic of coloniality and the grammar of decoloniality. *Cultural Studies*, 21(2–3), 449–514.

Mohanty, C. (1990). On race and voice: Challenges for liberal education in the 90's. *Cultural Critique*, (14), 179–208.

Nyamnjoh, F. B. (2012). 'Potted plants in greenhouses': A critical reflection on the resilience of colonial education in Africa. *Journal of Asian and African Studies*, 47(2), 129–154. https://doi.org/10.1177/0021909611417240

Pierre, J. (2006). *Predicament of Blackness: Postcolonial Ghana and the politics of race*. University of Chicago Press.

Simpson, L. (2004). "Anticolonial strategies for the recovery and maintenance of Indigenous knowledge". *American Indian Quarterly*, 28(3/4), Special Issue: The Recovery of Indigenous Knowledge, pp. 373–384.

Simpson, L. (2014). Land as pedagogy: Nishnaabeg intelligence in rebellious transformation. *Decolonization: Indigeneity, Education and Society*, 3(3), 1–25.

Smith, A. (2010). Indigeneity, settler colonialism and White supremacy. *Global Dialogue*, 12(2). http://www.worlddialogue.org/content.php?id=488.

Smith, A. (2012). Indigeneity, Settler Colonialism, White Supremacy. In Racial Formation in the Twenty-First Century. University of California Press. https://doi.org/10.1525/california/9780520273436.003.0005

Smith, L. T. (1999). *Decolonizing methodologies: Research and Indigenous peoples*. London: Zed Books.

Taiaiake, A., Mihesuah, D., & Cavender Wilson, A. (2004). *Indigenizing the Academy: Transforming scholarship and empowering communities*. University of Nebraska Press.

Tuck, E., & McKenzie, M. (2014). *Place in research: Theory, methodology, and methods*. Routledge.

wa Thiong'o, N. (1986). *Decolonising the mind*. Oxford.

Wolfe, P. (2006). Settler colonialism and the elimination of the native. *Journal of Genocide Research*, 8(4).

· 4 ·

BLACK LIVES MATTER: FINDING MY BLACK AFRICAN VOICE

Black life *is* and *must* be worth living. This is worth saying, not just because of the growing mass incarceration of Black youth, but the easy disposable Black life. How do I rediscover the African self and the African voice in the reframing, re-writing, and re-storying of the Black scholar identity and Black scholarship? How do we reclaim a collective notion of Black and African identity and narrative? These questions have become more significant in recent years with the continuing colonial and imperial influences on Black and African identities and experiences.

We live in an era of unprecedented exploitation of White fear and grievance. Calling out systemic racism, racist vigilante violence and police brutality is often met with White resistance. Numerous people reject race as a useful social and cultural concept, deny the existence of racism, and even insist the assumption of White privilege is false. At best, they dispute racism is "normal", insisting that it is only aberrant. They reject the tenets and assumptions of Critical Race Theory and anti-racist scholarship. White supremacists are bent on inflating their Whiteness through brutal force and vitriol of dog whistles, dog barks, and racial animus. The crude ethnonationalism of White supremacists is on full display daily. Fortunately, there is growing resistance from Black, Indigenous, and racialized communities with the support of critical White friends and allies. More than ever before we seek to assert all humanity and to take control over our lives, including the narratives and stories told about us.

In this chapter, I dwell on recent events of White supremacist violence using concepts and intellectual framings to expose the reach and effects of such practices on the life and death of Black peoples. I further illuminate some conceptual framings to emphasize their transmutative quality. I then raise pencil-sharpened questions to add momentum and strength to the work required for our collective survival. I am reminded of the perseverance, persistence, the indefatigable imagination, and defiant hopes of our mothers and fathers, our mentors, community activists, spiritual activists, our visionary leaders, our unselfish teachers, our loving families, and our critical-thinking scholarly communities across the globe. I am also reminded that although the difference can be posed as a threat and fear, working with the right approach and right spirit we have a chance to kindle, excite, and strengthen the work we do to bring about change.

As noted, events of the recent months (e.g., the Buffalo massacre, George Floyd's murder by Derek Chauvin and, in fact, the murder of many others, including Breonna Taylor, Elijah McClain, Ahmaud Arbery, and more) and ongoing historical trajectories manifest horizons where our understanding of anti-Blackness cannot proceed without seeing it as poetic, as aesthetic, and as drawing upon myriad synergies and convergences both between and before all our experiential realities of myriad racisms and oppressions. The Empire building work of White supremacy devours life-supporting systems and lives of Black, Indigenous, and racialized peoples and our communities through the capitalist project of material consumption. White supremacy depends on death for life. Unfortunately, it does not see this as a problem; it is simply how the system works! Former President Donald Trump and his elected officials in the US government, with the backing of conservative right-wing media, especially FOX TV, argue Critical Race Theory is a threat to world civilization and that teaching White privilege in federal agencies is divisive (Metzger & Lahut, 2021). They are banning diversity and sensitivity training in all federal workplaces! They have consistently denied the existence of systemic racism and been very hostile to the Black Lives Matter movement calling it a "symbol of hate."

In previous discussions, we explored what anti-Blackness means and how it plays out in everyday society. Anti-Blackness is alien in its meaning and incomprehensible in human decency. And the future anti-Blackness and anti-Black racism seeks to create can be unimaginable. Terror and rage are possible reactions to anti-Blackness. For Black youth and local communities who extol the poetic virtues and aesthetic expressions of Blackness, the hope of the "Blackness" in anti-Blackness must be reclaimed to restore love, spirit, health, hope and energy to the self, group, and the collective. There are chords, discords, synergies, convergences, and divergences in the inhumanity of anti-Blackness and the accompanying resistance of progressive politics. In our resistance, we need to think about different ways to structure, install, and evaluate a critical learning forum on which Black, Indigenous, and racialized youth (and, indeed all youth) will occupy. The disgust of anti-Blackness is the axis in working for change. For Black peoples the various permutations, visible and invisible, of anti-Blackness are palpable in the tissues of our bodies and lives. We must infuse resistance in everyday living as refusals, hate and violence.

Anti-Blackness offers Black life up as a sacrifice. It instantiates Black life with Black death, always acting perniciously and deleteriously on and through every moment of living for us. There are material, spiritual and political expressions of this order. There is also a "forgetfulness" or "forgetting" of Black values. In this forgetting and forgetfulness, we act out hate and violence both at the surface and deeper levels. We fail to do the work required of us despite imagining ourselves as "free" and "sovereign" beings. We are stimulated by the wider socio-economic, and political structure to which notwithstanding this forgetting of Black value and humanity we remain deeply attached by strings. The forgetting, the internalizing of it, as well as the Pavlovian strings of desire, continually ready the subject for discipleship within the institutions we occupy, with their Whiteness and to some extent for some, White supremacy serving as a protecting army. The institution, and its disciplining, that I speak of resonate at incrementally higher and higher frequencies. They galvanize the great apparatus of tagging, flagging, claiming, naming, sorting, monitoring, evaluating, categorizing, prioritizing, segregating, reducing, refusing, denaturing, and detonating Black life and value. Curiously, it has never quite succeeded to extinguish Blackness. Perhaps this is where "forgetting" is also useful. That, however naive we may claim the Black body, it is what keeps Whiteness supreme. It is that Black body, not fully human, a subspecies, that needs White fetching to keep the White body clean, pure, bored, entertained, wanting, and to imagine what is not here yet, but soon coming, consuming hungrily and distractedly more than is ever needed. This is the privilege of

White skin. Consuming without fetching. It is also the social and spiritual death of the Black body – to be fetched and consumed.

Through acts of White privilege and through Black bodies being fetched and consumed, it becomes the "hard problem" for all Blackness and the diversity of Black life to assert our collective humanity. It is only by understanding such nuances of Blackness and its nexus with anti-Blackness that we can do our work better and deepen our analysis for social change. We can begin by listening to one another, encouraging one another, and respectfully challenging one another to act decisively. Let us do these politics as the Civil Rights generation before we have at least tried to do. We are here now because they were there then. We cannot forget history. We must expect the work to continue in this vein. While we know some things have changed, unfortunately, some things remain the same. Ant-Black racism work although mobilizing also gives us the opportunity to pause and think thoroughly, reverentially, and collectively about our next move, our next turn.

The desire for social transformation can stir critical conversations and dialogues over the existential realities of Blacknesses to reach deeper, skillfully nuanced understandings that point to complexity and thoroughness. I reflect and bring forward a few understandings and frame these with present time events. I do so to establish a foundation of critical understanding for the entry or returning reader, a kind of perspective tuning, for the resonance and depth of our personal reflections of the moment now and here. Consequently, I locate the chapter on how current events of anti-Blackness, anti-Black racism, Whiteness and White supremacy all implicate us. And, also how the work we do whether as community leaders, scholars, and workers place enormous responsibilities on broad shoulders.

Underneath all the bluster we can easily begin to unravel, fray, become brittle, wobble, and slow down to expose what is beneath the neat covering. Under current conditions, we must look at ourselves under the eyes and gaze of, and into, all of humanity. The movement of Black thought the "paraontology" of Blackness is the constant escape of Blackness from the fixity of racial ontology that structures White supremacy. In 1985, Black sociologist Orlando Patterson used the phrase "social death" to examine the various iterations in which Black bodies were not accepted as fully human by society, thus resulting in their disposability. Ryland (2013) has described hypervisibility as "scrutiny based on perceived difference, which is usually (mis)interpreted as deviance" (para. 2). It is the result of an individual being recognized for their "Otherness" or deviance from the norm. This is necessary for the development and (re)translation of ideas and concepts that underpin dominant paradigms, to destabilize, and change them. As we continue to build upon knowledge and create new frameworks for action, this work is going to be scrutinized differently for legitimacy and relevance. Blackness and anti-Blackness are lenses and practices that secure power and wealth for a dominant few. These concepts also reveal the global debt and the responsibility to work for social change. The change we want and eventually arrive at will be determined by our vision of humanity, given that our collective existence has depended so much on the insatiability of the "consuming human." For some, social wealth has depended on proximity to Whiteness, and, because they will conveniently claim "at least they are not Black." And yet, they utilize the Black body to sustain the status quo working for their material interests while sustaining a global position of anti-Blackness.

Blackness conditions the placement of Black bodies in spaces and determines work and worth. Dominant society situates bodies in places and spaces and opens and closes various gates. Movement and mobilization in life serve special interests and conditions with material outcomes for the powerful. There is a reason why "essential workers" are overrepresented by Black, Indigenous, and racialized bodies, and why the sub-humanity of the Black and Indigenous body and life is advanced. The Black body is hyper-visible and, simultaneously, it is emptied of its subjectivity, to become fungible, one of many, not fully human. This obfuscates the real threat of resistance and subversion as elite powers continue to advance an unsustainable regime of economic injustice, epistemic injustice, aesthetic injustice and grotesque hyper-consumption and exploitation. Of no small additional note is the fact that the level of change anti-Blackness work demands is massive, and the scale-up for this change is incomprehensible. Where it is comprehensible and understood, one can only imagine a kind of outrage or terror that has emerged and the unassuaged activities or enlists of an iteration of the anti-Blackness regime.

This is the reality for our scholarship and activism communities. We must be clear about this as we mobilize for change. We also must be ready. This will need to be part of the anti-Blackness curriculum, a political and educational text for the readiness for action. State institutions will not support this curriculum, and we must be ready to continue anyway, to advance change and to reconstruct Black futures no matter what the circumstance. We can draw the legacies of inspiration. I remind myself, and all of us, that our own work and our interdisciplinary scholarship emerge from a critical and vast body of work that includes centuries of Black activism, Black art, Black music, Black spoken word, Black dance, Black oral history, Black story, Black study, and more recently Black scholarship. I remind myself as well that our persistence and insistence in doing this work and supporting each other as what we do is necessary especially when anti-Blackness is dismissed. Our defiant hope and collective engagement will kindle, excite, and strengthen our work as well as our action

Blackness is a series of negotiations that have occurred between the myriad synergies and convergences that structure and elicit the poetics and the aesthetics that inspire and are the spirit of the Black body. Blackness is contoured by the tensile forces that exist between the Black body, Black being and Black becoming, as it confronts the bludgeoning force of anti-Blackness. Anti-Blackness shows us the epistemic, ideological, material, and spiritual hyper-violence that seeks the Black body. Anti-Blackness presses through the existential realities of Black life at their respective sites to enslave Black Life. And it does so by seeking precision and always seeking power. This is an ordinary experience in an ordinary Black Life.

Anti-Blackness is a force that seeks and surrounds the Black body. It is silent, always present, ready to spark and ignite any moment during every encounter. It seeks out and is ferried through historical, psychological, ecological, social, and political structures. Where it suffuses them and tempers them anti-Blackness confidently bends environments, cultures, words, forms, and diverse expressions of Black life into space and place to hail Whiteness, to emplace it, proclaim it and thoroughly ratify White life, leaving Black bodies as fodder in its wake. Anti-blackness is additionally produced, reproduced, and sustained by individuals who, through internalization of the external historical-psychological-ecological-social-political order, come to forget it. Through this process, anti-Blackness becomes implicit, efficient, reflexive and more dangerous and less accountable.

I have been convinced of anti-Blackness is a problem of a racist structure and system. Anti-Blackness is about the climate, weather, environment, culture (Sharpe, 2016), and the socio-organizational life of our institutions produced and supported by particular practices (Dei, 2020c; Dumas, 2015). Anti-Blackness is institutionalized, violent oppression against Black and African peoples/bodies as a systematic practice on the basis of our culture, values, knowledge system, histories, identities, and social locations. Anti-Blackness is propelled by the interpellation ideologies of assumed Black inferiority and White superiority, rationalized in the Western capitalist and racist logics of reason, normal, respectability and acceptability. At the core of anti-Blackness is the sub-humanity of the African and Black body. The "anti" in Blackness is against anything about Black life, the totality of our experiences and our expressions (cultural, political, arts, beauty, aesthetics, literature, etc.). We can fathom anything that is anti-Black which is not racist and oppressive, and it is here the link between anti-Blackness and anti-racism is anchored. Within schools, anti-Blackness brings to the fore questions of power, knowledge, representation (curriculum/texts/pedagogies), bodies and leadership, discipline and punishment (like suspensions and streaming) as issues reflective of the processes of educational delivery, that is teaching, learning and administration of education in the school curriculum for Black, African, Indigenous and other racialized learners (see Dei, 2020c).

Anti-Black oppressions manifest themselves in institutional practices like everyday schooling practices, curriculum, classroom pedagogies, and texts, that negate, denigrate, deny, exclude, devalue, and discredit Black presence, contributions and lived experiences. They play out in everyday microaggressions beyond racist name-calling, language, and accents. It means a lot to wear a Black body/skin in school or at work. Our lives as Black learners must ensure a firm political, material, symbolic, and spiritual presence in all spaces. We must challenge the contradictory experiences of Blackness as hypocritically desired, valorized, and fetishized, but simply to serve the interests of capital, and the curiosity of the dominant.

I purposely titled this chapter *Black Lives Matter Too* to narrate a couple of incidents that have etched in memories of late. These are memories which must justifiably question our conscience if we truly believe "all lives matter." I also want to find my voice of courage and speak in no uncertain terms about how I feel in a way that says to my soul, "I have found my African voice." There is a geopolitical response to Black life that continues to enslave and torture the fungible Black body, to extinguish the intelligence, the spirit, the creativity, the aesthetic, and the poetics of Blackness and Black life, and the Black livelihood.

I know to say, "Black Lives Matter" (BLM) one must acknowledge the work of the three Black women behind the creation of the #Blacklivesmatter hashtag that transformed into a collective rights and cultural movement. Alicia Garza, Opal Tometi, and Patrisse Khan-Cullors (and many unsung others) founded the hashtag, #Blacklivesmatter, as a direct response to the killing of Trayvon Martin in 2012, and subsequently have their names etched in history. The objective of #Blacklivesmatter was to spark a conversation locally and internationally around systems of power that allow Black lives and communities to be disproportionately victims of over-surveillance, police brutality, daily microaggressions and racial profiling. #Blacklivesmatter has made us more aware of the global fights for Black life, the treatment of Blackness in global communities, erasures and slippages in Black experiences, the bio-politics of Blackness, the undesirability of Black citizens and bodies in communities, and the social control of Black bodies and perceived Black transgressions.

In truth though, the idea and politics of BLM have a long history and constituted a global cause. BLM has been at the forefront of all Black struggles, including civil rights movements, that demanded the global community to begin to re-imagine Black humanity differently. Anti-Black racism was brought to our consciousness in political struggles over schooling and education, the criminal justice system and the courts, housing, media, health care, income, and wealth distribution. Today, we recall the role of Black activists in advocating for environmental justice, and economic justice, working in solidarity with Indigenous communities for Indigenous sovereignty (e.g.: BLM support for Land and water defenders in Wet'suwet'en), and solidarity with other oppressed peoples. We know they are standing on the shoulders of those activists gone before. In effect, BLM is built on the long-standing struggles of Black peoples against social injustice.

Yet, it is heartening to note that since 2013 #Blacklivesmatter has cemented the Black struggle as a global movement with a rallying cry for solidarity for Black lives. Contending slogans like "All Lives Matter" and "Blue Lives Matter" are fake, attention-seeking moves, hypocritically intended as distractions from the harsh realities of Black living. To be for Black lives, one must be for all lives in the first place. One cannot help reading about the murders of George Floyd, Regis Korchinski-Paquet, D'Andre Campbell, Breonna Taylor, Ahmaud Arbery, Abdirahman Abdi, Philando Castile, Alton Sterling, Andrew Loku, Kwasi Skene-Peters, Jermain Carby, Freddie Gray, Sandra Bland, Eric Garner, Laquan McDonald, Michael Brown, Tamir Rice, and Trayvon Martin, that some lives have not mattered. These people, and many countless others, are people killed for who they are as Black and African peoples. These killings must impact one's work as a Black scholar. What is equally frightening is that these will not be the last Black killings or death.

But it is not just these deaths, killings, or murders that pain. It is how some in our communities respond to Black death. After George Floyd's murder, you may think we will reflect more critically on the implications for our collective humanity. On June 12, 2020, a young Black man, Rayshard Brooks, 27, was murdered by Atlanta police Officer, Garrett Rolfe. Video footage shows the Black man initially struggling with the officers and then fleeing from the police, after being arrested for sleeping in his car. Why are we surprised about a Black man resisting a police arrest, after recent incidents show the death of Black men, even when it appears they have or can be easily subdued by officers? In the struggle leading to the flight, Brooks gets hold of the taser of one of the police officers. He runs from the officers only to see them chase him, and he then turns the taser on them. He is shot and killed by an officer. The police officer had information on the man's identity, the car he drives, presumably his driver's license, and likely where he lives.

The whole situation leaves many unanswered questions: Why couldn't the police officers de-escalate the situation? Is a taser a violent weapon (like a gun or knife) to justify killing a man? Haven't the police long argued in their defence that a taser is not a violent weapon? What threat are these officers wearing bulletproof vests under? And truly, will this happen to a White man fleeing the police? But for me, what was equally disturbing was the incident happening so close to the unprecedented global uproar over George Floyd. I ask those, who question why Rayshard was trying to flee from police, this simple question: Do we really understand why happening so close to George Floyd's case another Black man will attempt to flee from police when accosted? Saying, "Oh, he should not have resisted arrest!" does not cut it for me. A Black man who did not resist arrest was dead just a few months earlier. Hello!

Some community leaders and state elected officials are never shy about crying "Black responsibility." Part of that responsibility is asking us to eat well and exercise for good health. Right? Never mind the subtext that somehow Black people don't eat well, or even fail to acknowledge the income barrier to eating well. Yet, we have a Black man, Ahmaud Arbery, in Georgia who decides to exercise for good health and gets killed while jogging in a neighbourhood. Which is which? There comes a point when we say "Enough is enough!" Black people are human beings who also deserve to live. This calls for collective reflection. We can hope for a change of minds of those who defend such police killings. But we must work to challenge those who continue to excuse such murders. Black resistance and flight are for survival. Black radicalism is an epistemic and political survival strategy.

For those who deny there is systemic racism, think of the significance of the June 2020 incident in New York involving Amy Cooper, a White woman walking her dog without a leash in the Ramble (an area of Central Park, where leashing is required) when she is confronted by a Black man, Christian Cooper, who was bird watching. Amy Cooper gives us a lesson when she tells Christian Cooper so shamefully that she will call the police and tell them an African American man is threatening her. She is not saying, I will call any particular policeman who is bigoted or racist. She is not saying, she will call one police officer she knows. She is saying "she will call the system." The Black man is deemed violent and a threat in North American culture. Amy Cooper knows it and she is using that knowledge to her White advantage and to address her unfounded White fears. Frankly, I am not surprised. Black bodies, especially Black men, have become easy prey.

We should devote the energies we spend defending police violence or rationalizing anti-Black hate to looking for effective ways to stop anti-Black violence and police brutality. There is no excuse for the excessive use of force to murder a defenceless human being or even someone who does not pose a serious threat to an officer's life. If we sanction or legitimize this behaviour it only serves to diminish certain lives, Black life. Black lives must matter to us.

Let us look at the two phrases, each with three words- "Law and Order" and "Black Lives Matter"- that matter of late to many of us. Based on the facts, which is more sincere honestly? These words register to Black people differently. One phrase, "Law and Order", is a racist dog whistle of White fears and anxieties, the other, "Black Lives Matter," registers with Black pain and suffering. "Law and order" but do not search for underlying causes of the violence. Resist "Black Lives Matter" with "All Lives Matter" as if they are both coming with the same sincerity. Which slogan started first, "Black Lives Matter" or "All Lives Matter?" Clearly, one has been a counter-response when it has not traditionally mattered for some. We cannot pit these words against each other, specifically, White fears and anxieties and Black pain and suffering. "Law and order" are meaningful words only if backed by justice. For a people who have been deprived of justice, equality, and freedom to claim "Law and order" is a privileged rant. It is deeply immoral to insist on law and order when justice is not being served. We need "law and order" to protect what and from whom? Are people simply prone to violence? Whose "law and order" are we protecting when throughout our history "law and order" have become code words for Black suppression? This is not a recommendation for violence but a clarion call to act on injustice.

When criticisms of systemic racism are lodged, we often get a response that the problem is with a few bad apples. How do we explain then when a group of police officers all stay silent and watch and/or assist when one of their own has his foot on a human neck, choking the life out of a Black man? Is it the blue wall of silence? In June 2020, in Buffalo, New York, two police officers are caught on video shoving a 75-year-old elderly man who hits his head on the ground. He received no assistance from other police officers present who clearly saw what had happened. They stood there doing nothing to help this elderly person. When the officers are charged their peers congregate at the court to cheer them on, upon their release by a judge, all in a show of solidarity for the police act! Police officers must be held accountable! For people who have received the brunt of police brutality, it should not be difficult for anyone to comprehend why an important cry of protestors is to defund the police.

To reiterate, if just a third of the attention paid to expressing outrage about the "destruction" of property, looting, and violence by protesters seeking justice for George Floyd, Breonna Taylor, and Jacob Blake, amongst others, was also paid to addressing the problem of structural anti-Blackness and anti-Black racism in North America, we will all be better for it. The narrative needs to change. When people come up in droves to protest in the middle of a pandemic that has taken several lives with no end in sight this must tell us something. We cannot lose the irony and hypocrisy of former Minnesota police officer, Derek Chauvin using his knee to murder George Floyd and former San Francisco 49ers quarterback, Colin Kaepernick getting so much flack and abuse for taking a knee to protest injustice.

If we are going to excuse a patrol cruiser plowing its way through protesters for social justice, implying the driver might have been left with no choice we must also ask questions about why people are protesting. Should we also excuse the "looters" and protesters who also might feel they have been left with no recourse other than to lash out? Martin Luther King Jr. (1967) once remarked, "…a riot is the language of the unheard." There is a language being spoken here. A language that is highlighting a disease we recognize as anti-Blackness. At no time should the sanctity of human life be measured against wealth or property. It seems that the pandemic of anti-Black racism was compounded by another global pandemic, Covid-19. The deaths in our communities captured a sense of literally a pandemic over a pandemic! But let us fancy this. I recently watched White nationalist protesters complaining about "shelter in place". His reasoning was that they do not want the government to keep them safe. This is when we know the nation-state has always protected its citizens, except sometimes, it feels like not all of its citizens.

In recent calls to tear down colonial monuments celebrating White oppression, a dominant response is we cannot rewrite or revise history. But I ask: What have we been doing all the time when we weed out Black and African people from history? How much African history do we teach our children in schools? So, teaching colonial history must be complete including preserving the history of those who fought to preserve slavery, but it is okay if that history does not include Black resistance and humanity?

How Do We Make Everyday Sense of All?

Like many each day I am trying to make sense of all this. Sense-making starts with reminding ourselves of the everyday sense misconceptions within a culture of denialism. For example, there is usually a misunderstanding that somehow claims of White privilege are a denial that White people also face hardships in life. Of course, White bodies do experience hardships based on class, gender, sexuality, and ability, amongst other factors. However, White identity can be a mitigating factor. In other words, White privilege means skin colour does not contribute to White hardship the way Black people have continually experienced oppressive conditions of existence based on our skin colour. Our system protects Whiteness and punishes Blackness. It is for this reason that we need to understand White privilege as a system and structure of unearned privileges. There is nothing like anti-Whiteness as oppressive because it is based on unearned privileges.

Admittedly, as Black, and African people we may also be privileged on the basis of our class, gender, sexuality, [dis]ability, etc. But we face different realities in terms of our privileges because of how race intersects for us. Our skin colour is responded to differently. We cannot have any false sense of entitlement that comes with our skin colour. Our skin cannot be a ticket or a passport or currency allowing us to enter freely into any space without accountability and responsibility. As Black and African peoples our potential is usually in doubt. We are not generally seen as individuals with the potential to do great things, unlike others. Black students need to work three times as hard to prove their worth. In other cases, Black students need to prove they are not like the other Black students, that they are not a threat, and that they are good students, all because of anti-Black racism. We are less likely to see ourselves reflected in books, movies, conversations, and public places. We must work extra hard for the world to value the things we; our families and our communities do. We are expected to adapt to the White world, not the other way around. We must struggle to have everyday conversations framed from our viewpoint as well. We must fight to dictate the terms of the conversation about us. We need to challenge who we are attaining success, worth, and recognition from and the consequent violence we inflict on our communities as a result. We need to challenge the denials of privilege. We do not have the luxury and power to consciously decide NOT to work for change if we do not want to.

The visceral reaction to assertions of anti-Black racism and anti-Blackness is part of the culture of denialism. Anti-Blackness does not simply mean one hates or dislikes Black people. Rather, anti-Blackness broadly means that one does not extend to Black people, and to Black life and our social existence the same attributes and characteristics that are cherished in White people, White life, and the social existence of Whiteness. We must act politically beyond the acknowledgement and mere validation of the existence of anti-Black racism.

At this moment, we should also make everyday sense of Covid-19. The current global Covid-19 pandemic is considered a disaster by researchers and clinicians. One might think of it as a different species of disaster because it is sourced more directly by human behaviour and can be controlled more directly by human behaviour. A flood or tsunami on the other hand are less proximal in their links to human behaviour and cannot be stopped by population health behavioural interventions, at least not in the short term. Our relationship with the environment and with life more broadly potentiates disasters. The current one is the largest global disaster for the Western world and the coming months will show us what the impact is on the south. The devaluation of life generally and Black, Indigenous, and racialized life specifically are evident during this pandemic.

One does not need statistics to convey the impact of Covid-19 in terms of its human death toll on Black and racialized communities. Racially and historically marginalized communities experience diverse forms of systemic oppression amounting to a lack of resources and opportunities, thus resulting in worse health outcomes. This is not new. These inequities have long been known and discussed, with a myriad of government reports highlighting outbreaks of violence and gross negligence within society experienced by Black bodies. Covid-19 has disproportionality affected Black bodies who are regularly subjected to inequitable access to health care, a greater likelihood to live in a densely populated neighbourhood crowded, a higher chance of working a front-line job that does not adhere to health and safety rules, providing job security, sick leave options and other basic workplace protections - all factors that have contributed to a higher infection and death rate. Anti-Blackness is the driver of these poor health outcomes and inequities.

There is another conversation that has been silenced in terms of why Covid-19 has impacted Black life so hard. Covid-19 reveals how anti-Blackness work writes its way into Black bodies and Black lives. The negation of Black as human is central or foundational to questions of agency, subjectivity, and relationship and are often not to be considered. When and where they are considered, it is at least in part often a performance. Anti-Blackness would not make sense if Black life mattered, if Black life was human life, if Black life was sovereign life, if Black life was equal and if dignity were allowed expression. And because it is core, Black life is the place from which anti-Blacknesses grow and take form. We must see Black life always in relationship with the climate, the conditions, the socio-politico- organization and organism through constant erasure, social death, and the fatigue of order that denies the human and in denying the human the chattel are ever more aware that they are human.

Covid-19 is directly linked to a larger global emergency - our environmental crisis. Our environmental crisis is at all scales an effect of, and continuously exacerbated by, the frank disregard and devaluation of life, because the social system is built for economic advancement, for wealth, and for the imperial project of white supremacy. There is the overvaluation of wealth. Zoonotic transmission, the transmission of a virus from animal to human, occurs when animals that would not be in contact are in contact because of the destruction and elimination of their natural habitat and supporting ecosystems. Animals are closer together in more desperate environmental conditions and so are humans, i.e.: non-White humans. Covid-19, like SARS and MERS, is a zoonotic virus. It moved from animals to humans. Environmental conditions are poor for many Black, Indigenous, and racialized bodies, and they are also poor for their animals.

There are also fewer species of animals so wet markets are places where trade of available animals occurs to support livelihood where environmental change and devastation occur. Most of the world's population is not White. They are Black, Indigenous, and racialized. The non-White majority experiences the greatest direct and cumulative effects of the environmental crisis, a crisis that is sourced by lifestyle and life practices of Whiteness in place. The loss of land, unworkable land in unworkable conditions, diminished and contaminated natural resources, poor health, disasters, and migration are all experienced as poverty, starvation, factory work, conflict, absence of schools and schooling, multiple health and disease conditions, absence of or inability to buy necessary treatments and therapeutics for these conditions and other contagious diseases, limited or inaccessible infrastructure for advancing health and well-being, and limited capacity to escape or change the conditions of their life.

Where Do We Start Moving Forward?

When someone complains about racism and our response is to say we stand by our actions or words, it means there has been no listening. The pain and hurt are still there. The pain is raw, the wound is still there, and there has been no healing or restoration. We must acknowledge the pain, harm and suffering caused if we are to heal and move forward. There is the denialism of structural racism and White privilege. Black, Indigenous, and racialized peoples must not be the first to speak out on these issues. This culture of speaking courage must change. To be privileged and not have the courage to speak out simply sustains/reproduces/maintains our privileges.

To reiterate we say, "Black lives matter", precisely because "All lives matter." The fact is that not all lives have really mattered. So, if we cannot say or act to affirm that Black lives matter, then it is a huge problem - complicity and failed responsibility - especially, in a society that has throughout history operated as if Black lives don't matter. We must acknowledge the mechanisms and structures of White privilege upon which our institutions have been built and continue to be sustained for other benefits.

There is specificity to anti-Black racism – skin, enslavement, colonization, property, and humanity.

We need our universities/institutions of higher learning to be proactive and lead the way to build and restore community trust and faith in our learners. Any betrayal must be questioned. Our communities are only as good as we collectively work to create or make them. For many of us, the time for the nice platitudes of solidarity statements while nice, comforting and perhaps needed may also be gone. We need immediate and concrete action NOW. We need to adopt a more comprehensive integrative anti-racism and anti-colonial lens that forces us to look seriously at race and the specificity of anti-Black racism. We need to have a lasting solution to the long-standing problems of anti-Black racism. For the most part, new policies and recent changes happening now at different levels, although granted are positive adjustments, sometimes end up being temporary flashes.

Our collective action cannot be directed just at the police and criminal justice system but at the entire institutional structures that uphold Whiteness and anti-Blackness, whether in schools, education, health, housing, employment, transportation, media, and courts where there are perceived systemic disparities and barriers hindering Black and African advancement. There is a younger generation demanding that as a society we seriously pay down on their futures rather than mortgage these futures. The youth also want to design their own futures because of failed leadership from elected officials and community leaders. For today's generation as Fanon, the anti-colonial theorist said long ago, we must discover our mission, fulfill or betray it. We speak because we have not been heard. And we will continue to speak for as long as we can breathe and only hope that we will be heard clearly in ways that acknowledge complicities and responsibilities.

It is very heartening to see many youths in the summer of 2020 taking to global streets with radical optimism as political hope, mobilizing collective cultural and political possibilities as revolutionary demanding anti-racism change. For all learners, educators, and community workers, I will concede that what we need is scholarly, intellectual, and political generosity which goes beyond empathy to think through "collaboration" and "solidarity" in concrete political terms for action. Empathy is an important starting point. While I see the place of empathy as a fundamental condition of practice within shared political struggles, creating solidarities among "people suffering through a particular set of circumstances/struggles," and developing an understanding that "we are all struggling with life and death questions" (Black Ink Info, 2020; p. 6), I contend that to be successful, empathy must be backed by concrete action. We cannot talk our way out of systemic racism and colonial oppression and violence. It demands messy hard work on the ground where we all accept our complications, implications, and responsibilities: taking out politics but making sure we are not hurtful to others in the process.

In doing decolonial and anti-colonial solidarity work, there are fundamentally political issues to be dealt with because once "these political issues are lost, then we are lost" (Black Ink Info, 2020, p. 7). These political issues are about how we navigate and proceed around power, privilege and resource sharing, how we are able to tell our own stories, listen to the stories and also be able to connect these stories to our shared and intertwined histories. We must collectively work through liberation together and not necessarily that we all agree but rather in the collective work create opportunities for dialogue as we wage a social and political "critique that is open and loving" (Black Ink Info, 2020, p. 8). Such dialogue should not seek to confirm what we already know, but to challenge what we know.

We must be political while thinking dialectically, meaning we must be prepared to ask some hard/tough questions that lead to change. For example, what kind of world are we trying to build? Why are we turning to our [educational] "institutions to give us things rather than demand and take the things we want?" (Black Ink Info, 2020, p. 9). Rather than impose ourselves, are we going to be decolonial and anti-colonial and instead step outside of ourselves and "move into different periods of history" Black Ink Info, 2020, p. 9)? In an era of anti-Blackness should we just be fighting just for our own? Are we Afro-pessimist or futurist? And what are the possibilities and the futility of White engagement or existentialism? (see also Black Ink Info, 2020, p. 9).

We must see the need to "engage in a constant struggle to create community, (i.e., not to stop fighting); and creating communities with those we do not like" (Black Ink Info, 2020, p. 9). We must still hold on to a commitment to the primacy of the Black material subjective experience recognizing authenticity as a construction and a political articulation (Black Ink Info, 2020, pp. 11–12). To be true to oneself as defined by that self, not Western liberal ideologies, and capitalism. As I alluded to in the last chapter, I referenced Robin Kelley's work about, "deepening [our] awareness of the responsibilities of the subject formation, to recognize and cultivate new forms of agency that are comprehensive, that are informed by [our] collective [not individual] dreams of freedom" (Black Ink Info, 2020, p. 27). There is a need for us to "search for a shared epistemological and ontological outlook and set of experiences from which [an African] collective values grow" (Black Ink Info, 2020, p. 28). This search for Indigenous epistemologies and ontologies is more than an intellectual practice; it is a matter of life and death for the victims of colonial domination (Black Ink Info, 2020, p. 29). It is also an awareness of the "historical dynamics [that generate] ideas and identities, anti-essentialism, and decentering Western epistemologies as the only way to see these processes" (Black Ink Info, 2020, p. 29).

References Cited:

Adjei, P. B. (2013). When Blackness shows up uninvited: Examining the murder of Trayvon Martin through Fanonian racial interpellation. In G. Dei & M. Lordan (Eds.), *Contemporary issues in the sociology of race and ethnicity: A critical reader*. Peter Lang.

Asante, M. (2003). *Afrocentricity: A theory of social change*. Africa World Press.

Black Ink Info. (2020). "Solidarity Is Not a Market Exchange:" An interview with Robin D. G. Kelley. Black Ink Info. https://black-ink.info/author/blcknk/

Burman, E. (2016). Fanon and the child: Pedagogies of subjectification and transformation. *Curriculum Inquiry*, 46(3), 265–285.

Collins, P. H. (2002). *Black feminist thought: Knowledge, consciousness, and the politics of empowerment*. Routledge.

Dei, G. J. S. (2014). The African Scholar in the Western Academy. *Journal of Black Studies*, 45(3), 167–179.

Dei, G. J. S. (2017). *Reframing Blackness and Black Solidarities through anti-colonial and decolonial prisms*. Springer Publishing.

Dei, G. J. S. (2020c). "Foreword". Curriculum inquiry, Special Issue on: *Curricular confrontations in the wake of Anti-Blackness and in the break of Black Possibilities* [Guest Editors: Esther O. Ohito, Justin A. Coles, Fahima Iffe, and Michael J. Dumas].

Dei, G. J. S., Odozor, E., & Vasquez, A. (2020). *Cartographies of Blackness and Black Indigeneities*. Myers Educational Press.

Dugassa, B. (2011). Colonialism of mind: Deterrent of social transformation: The experiences of Oromo people in Ethiopia. *Sociology Mind*, 1(2), 55–64.

Dumas, M. (2015). Against the Dark: Anti Blackness in education policy and discourse. *Theory Into Practice*, 55, 1–9.

hooks, b. (2006). *Black looks: Race and representation*. Academic Internet Pub Inc.

Latty, S., Scribe, M., Peters, A., & Morgan, A. (2016). Not enough human: At the scenes of Indigenous and Black dispossession. *Critical Ethnic Studies*, 2(2), 129–158.

McKittrick, K. (2006). *Demonic grounds: Black women and the cartographies of struggle*. University of Minnesota Press.

Metzer, B., & Lahut, J. (2021, December 7). Trump issued an executive order on Critical Race Theory after seeing a segment about it on Tucker Carlson's show: book. *The Insider*. Retrieved from Tucker Carlson's Show Inspired Trump's CRT Executive Order: Book (businessinsider.com)

Patterson, O. (1982). *Slavery and social death: Comparative study*. Harvard University.

Pierre, J. (2006). *Predicament of Blackness: Postcolonial Ghana and the politics of race*. University of Chicago Press.

Ryland, M. (2013, August 8). Hypervisibility: How scrutiny and surveillance makes you watched, but not seen. [Blog post]. Retrieved from Hypervisibility: How Scrutiny and Surveillance Make You Watched, but Not Seen | Beauty versus the Beast (wordpress.com)

Sharpe, C. (2016). *In the wake: On Blackness and being*. Duke University Press.

Sicherman, C. (1995). Ngugi's colonial education: The subversion of the African mind. *African Studies Review*, 38(3), 11–41.

Simpson, L. (2004). Anticolonial strategies for the recovery and maintenance of Indigenous knowledge. *American Indian Quarterly*, 28(3/4), 373–384.

Simpson, L. (2014). Land as pedagogy: Nishnaabeg intelligence in rebellious transformation. *Decolonization: Indigeneity, Education and Society*, 3(3), 1–25.

Smith, L. T. (1999). *Decolonizing methodologies: Research and Indigenous peoples*. Zed Books.

· 5 ·

INDIGENEITY, DECOLONIALITY AND THE ANTI-COLONIAL PARADIGMS: CONVERGENCES, DIVERGENCES AND SYNERGIES

Indigeneity is a word we have been hearing a lot about as of late. For some of us, it is nothing new as we articulated the Indigenous long ago before it became fashionable. I cannot think of a reaffirmation of my African Indigeneity which is not tied to anti-colonial subversive politics. I come to my consciousness as a Black scholar through the trace of my African Indigeneity. But I must confess a fascination with this question: Is anti-colonialism the path to a decolonial end, or is decolonialism the path to a decolonial end? This is not an intellectual play of words. It is a difficult question to discern. And, frankly, there are no easy or quick answers. I have been brooding over the question because it has significant implications for my work. I have always sought to work with both aspects of the question. On the one hand, I see decolonization as a process as Fanon and others would argue. But, I also see the anti-colonial to be a proactive stance in whatever we do to make it action-oriented practice. Whichever stance we take we must be working on the connections and dislocations of decoloniality and anti-colonial paradigms. I think those intersections/distinctions are important to think about. Situating anti-colonial theory, pedagogy and praxis as a pathway to realize the goal of decolonization, this book helps me think through the myriad interventions that are necessary to advance race and social justice work and to understand the destructive legacies of colonialism and racism that are felt globally.

We need to address the vicious pervasiveness and multiple forms of colonialisms through a combination of theoretical perspectives and paradigms. The distinction between "anticolonial" and the "decolonial" is not neat and dry. There are slippages and conjunctures between the two stances. The decolonial may reinforce questions of the Land, culture, subjectivities and subject formations, the resurgence of local communities, as well as "de/colonial tensions" and contingencies. The anti-colonial, on the other hand, marks a radical break or departure offering a clear oppositional stance in history, transhistoricity, and Euro-colonial modernity. The anti-colonial affirms the centrality of race and class identity in politics with an intense interrogation of the role of the modern [Independent] nation-state in ongoing coloniality and imperialist projects. But the "anti-colonial" and "decolonial" have more in common that distinguishes them. This becomes apparent when we flesh out the parallels and convergences of Indigeneity, decoloniality and the anti-colonial moment and colonial encounters as we [colonized peoples] begin to reclaim our Indigeneities as a necessary exercise in our collective decolonization.

There are many paths to decolonization (Smith, 2012), and it is particularly important for educators to begin by grounding our de/anti-colonial projects in Black and Indigenous ontologies and epistemes (see also Dei and Cacciavillani 2022). To reframe a decolonial curriculum for example is to ask questions about omissions, negations, absences in school curriculum, and how we provide critical comprehensive knowledge that account for the diversity of the human experiences and histories. Decolonization as many have noted begins by asking new questions grounded in non-Western epistemes and Indigenous philosophies (see Dei, 2022, Parry 1994). It should be a "subversive educational approach, not a superficial add-on, but requiring actions to dismantle and rebuild" (see also Mihesuah, Mihesuah, & Waziyatawin 2004; Hewitt, 2016).

We must be cautious when decolonization is mainstreamed and liberalized. In other words, a truly decolonial project cannot seek acceptance, legitimation and validation from the eyes of the dominant or the colonizer! Anything else makes the decolonial project highly suspect. Our decolonial educational practices must be in the open and a very clear engagement for all learners to see what subversive or abolitionist educational agenda is being pursued. Long ago, Linda Smith (2012) asked us to acknowledge, "the reach of imperialism into our heads" (Smith, 2012, cf. Jackson, 2019; p.109). What this also means is for us to recognize the metaphoricity of decolonization (see Garba and Sorentino, 2020; Dei 2022, 2023) as equally about developing the oppressor consciousness and an awareness of cultural invasion (Freire, 2000). This is what Ngugi wa Thiong'o long ago referred to when he posited that we must be aware of the severity of the problem of colonization, particularly as it has to do with the colonization of 'the mental universe' of the colonized worlds (wa Thiong'o, 1981, p.16).

Clearly, de/anti-colonization must be about Land, healing and the Land literacies including spiritual ontologies. As has been noted by many others, these are crucial components of a de/anti-colonial education (see Styres, 2019). As we engage de/anti-colonial educational practice we must also be continually vigilant of how a 'decolonization' can be domesticated or liberalized as to appear as a "re-arrangement of the colonial furniture" (see Lloyd-Henry, 2022). The power of knowing 'decolonization is not a metaphor' (Tuck and Yang, 2012) is critical in shaping educational practice grounded in the question of Land and the ontologies of rivers, water, seas, and sky. Yet decolonization is also about the mind and coming to a consciousness to act. It is about an understanding knowing is a political and responsible act. This is why is always significant for us to flesh out both convergences and divergences of 'decolonization' and 'settler decolonization' in our educational practice so as to embrace a discussion of decolonization literally and metaphorically (see also Garba and Sorentino, 2020; Dei 2022, 2023).

I reclaim my African Indigeneity as something not lost but has always been part of my spiritual embeddedness and cultural memory. My Indigeneity resides in me politically, spiritually, and culturally. Colonialism failed in taking it away from my identity and subject formation. Even when residing in other communities outside of my birthplace, I can recall my Indigeneity in a discursive relationality with other Indigenous peoples. What is also important to me is acknowledging the lands upon which I make such claims and honour the spiritual connection to the ancestors and the Elders in the community while paying homage to my presence. As Garba and Sorentino (2020) recently noted "Indigenous peoples remain Indigenous when they move or are forcibly moved because Indigeneity expresses relationality, not possession" (p. 773). This "relationality" is embedded in a definition of what we are and what we stand for working alongside others. It becomes part of our core Being as defining marker of Indigeneity for most of us. We do not possess something but we share it and are continually in relation with what we share about ourselves, our history, cultures and identities.

To bring clarity to this intellectual and political positionality, I will explore the question, what is Indigeneity and what does it mean to be Indigenous? These are two distinct but interrelated questions. We cannot broach these questions without making important synergies, convergences, as well as divergence between terms such as "Indigenous peoples", "Indigenous bodies", and "Indigenous identities". Embedded in these discursive formations are the issues of the place of Indigenous knowledges and Indigeneity in decolonial and anti-colonial projects. It is important to recognize there are no neat, rigorous and uncontested definitions when it comes to any of these terms. We can however proceed with working definitions. The "Indigenous" has a cultural, political, spiritual and educational agenda. As many would insist, "Indigenous" must be understood under the naming of the Indigene. Alfred and Corntassel (2005) recall Weaver's argument that Indigenous identity can only be confirmed by others "who share that identity" (Weaver, 2001, p. 245). I agree.

Indigenous peoples have long defined themselves as people with a place, Land and situatedness in a grounded location that demonstrate the permanence of the place as an "unbroken occupation" and "long-term occupancy" (Fals Borda, 1991). Indigenous peoples are not colonizers who go out to conquer other Lands claiming them as their own. They are "Indigenous to the Lands they inhabit in contrast and in contention with colonial societies and states that have spread out from Europe and other centres of Empire" (Alfred & Corntassel, 2005, p. 597). They are a people who have come to understand their collective "existence as formed around axes of Land, culture and community", including history, politics and spiritual ontologies and epistemes (Alfred & Corntassel, 2005, p. 608). In other words, Indigenous peoples have a knowledge base. We will return to this theme later.

The absence of colonial imposition makes the distinction between "Indigenous" and "Western" societies plausible. It also allows us to extend the meaning of "Indigenous" to multiple geographies with shared ideas of political, cultural, and spiritual memories and histories. As has been noted, histories and geographies provide the "foundation for Indigenous cultural identities and sense of self", an understanding of place, Land, as well as one's culture and language (Alfred & Corntassel, 2005, p. 598). The geo-spacing and differences of Indigeneities (including the differential relations to different colonialisms including settler colonialism) give rise to what can appropriately be termed "Cartographies of Indigenous and Indigeneities" (see also

Dei, 1997; Dei, Odozor, & Vasquez, 2019). But, it is also significant to adhere to this caution: "Not all Indigenous peoples were 'conquered'…. nor are all Indigenous peoples non-dominant" (Alfred & Corntassel, 2005; p. 607). This is a recognition of the multiple and diverse claims of being "Indigenous" and "Indigeneities" and their discursive relationalities.

Indigenous is about difference and it is not a homogenous category. Consequently, we must endeavour to engender new meanings that point to relations of power, including, for example, queering Indigenous and Indigeneity. This in itself is a subversion of colonial ways of thinking about Indigenous and Indigeneity. There are masculinized, gender supremacist and heteronormative Indigenous knowledges and Indigenous struggles which the nation-state continues to foster. We must therefore respond by opening up critical conversations on gender, sexuality and Indigenous knowledge and Indigenous identities, and challenging "the intrusion of Western heteropatriarchy into Indigenous cultures" (Wilson & Laing, 2019, p. 143). For example, Wilson and Laing (2019) show how Indigeneity, LGBTA1A+ and Two Spirit identities/2SLGBTQIA can be linked. It is argued that Indigenous studies "must queer itself up [to subvert] "entrenched binaries and hierarchies related to gender and sexuality (Wilson & Laing, 2019, p. 139). It is enthused that to validate "Indigenous cosmologies that recognize and accept gender fluidity, gender and sexuality diversity and queerness" (Wilson & Laing, 2019, pp. 139–140). Indigenous women are deeply involved in ongoing Indigenous relationalities and resurgences, as well as everyday community organizations fighting for Indigenous political sovereignty, control over Indigenous Lands, control and promotion of Indigenous education, culture, language and a collective Indigenous liberation (Sunseri, 2000). Any agenda of Indigenous decolonization must integrate Indigenous women, Two Spirit and queer issues (Wilson & Laing, 2019).

Indigenity is built on a notion of "a dynamic and interconnected concept of Indigenous identity constituted in history, ceremony, language and Land…. and embodied relationships [as] at the core of an authentic Indigenous identity" (Alfred & Corntassel, 2005, p. 609). While being "Indigenous" is about the occupancy of a "place" (a given Land) and belonging to this place, Indigeneity is primarily about subjectivity, identity, and politics. Put simply, "Indigeneity" is a cultural and spiritual process of subject identification and political formations, and being "Indigenous" is coming to psychic, cultural, spiritual and emotional understanding and attachment to a place we claim to be "our own" (through culture, history, politics and language). Indigeneity brings awareness and consciousness of belonging to a place and claims to ancestral Lands with long-term unbroken residence.

There are also multiple expressions of Indigeneities. As Alfred and Corntassel (2005) note "Indigenous identities are (re)constructed at multiple levels – global, state, community, individual" (p. 600) leading to myriad decolonial and anti-colonial resistance, struggles and resurgences to on-going coloniality. All people who claim "Indigeneity" and to be "Indigenous" have "unique heritages, attachments to their homelands and natural ways of life" (Alfred & Corntassel, 2005, p. 597) pursuing a politics resistance with this identity and identification claims. Consequently, "Indigenous" and "Indigeneity" have both become synonymous with anti-colonial and decolonial resistances. These are not innocent claims; they are purposeful to resist stolen histories, cultures, psychic and spiritual memories and most importantly, Lands.

Throughout these years, the claim of "Indigenous" and "Indigeneity" has been read as "oppositional, place-based existence, along with the consciousness of being in struggle" against the Land thefts, dispossession, and the "logics of elimination" and "logic of possession" in regards to colonialism and colonization (Alfred & Corntassel, 2005, p. 599 see also Wolfe, 2006). Indigenous and Indigeneity are about politics, identity and knowledge residing in cultural and spiritual memories. To be "Indigenous" means thinking, speaking, and acting "with the conscious intent of regenerating one's Indigeneity" (Alfred & Corntassel, 2005, p. 614). For many colonized peoples the claim of "Indigenous" and "Indigeneity" will always be political given the "colonial assaults" and violence on our very existence and our humanity. Part of the resistance of Indigeneity is also to resist the colonial/nation-state's imposed political, legal, and jurisdictional definitions and fictions on local cultural peoples' aspirations, dreams and futures. These colonial acts of violence are ingrained in our collective psyche, cultural, and spiritual memories and we cannot fail to resist and act for change.

This realization also brings some understanding of Indigenous knowledges and their place in educational, social and political transformation. It is argued that knowledges emanate from the ground (i.e., the Land), Earth, seas and sky, and the existence between humans and the physical and metaphysical worlds, including other inhabitants of the Universe, plants, animals, material and non-material objects. Indigenous knowledges are passed down from generation and have become sacred histories and the "spiritual and cultural heritage embedded in the [wisdom] left to us by our ancestors" (Alfred & Corntassel, 2005, p. 610). Understanding Indigenous knowledges, through time, has constituted "the wisdom of the teachings of our ancestors" and Elders (*ibid*; p. 612). Today we reclaim our Indigenous knowledge as cultural and spiritual strengths that "reverberate outward from the self to family, clan, community, and into all of the broader relationships that form an Indigenous existence" (*ibid*).

For the Indigenous scholar, we must promote an understanding of Indigenous knowledge and its importance to pursue decolonization and anti-colonial politics. Indigenous knowledges heralds a peculiar character of Indigenous resistance as a struggle for liberation, in the creation of a "symbolic order [and] a cultural worldview expressed in ancient rituals and customs" and working with a collective memory (Cusicanqui, n.d., p. 3). This Indigenous resistance is informed by a "sacred meaning of space as the site of ancestor shrines and tombs, as well as traditional territorial organization" (*ibid*; p. 4). The formation of new Indigenous identities, developed from oral traditions, local writings, stories, "cultural memories", ritual and symbolic relations, "anti-colonial rebellions" and "anti-liberal struggles", metaphors of Indigenous ancestry, blood relations, all as part of the re-invention of Indigenous histories and indigenous identity (*ibid*; p. 2).

These ideas constitute an Indigenist perspective as an anti-colonial theoretical framework that even the non-Indigenous learner can work with. But a study of Indigenous knowledges requires a critical analysis of colonialism and why the need to reclaim one's Indigeneity as an anti-colonial liberation strategy to revitalize and build communities. Such analysis must focus on both the context and dynamics of colonial power structure and the politics of decolonization and anti-colonialism. This constitutes a requisite for coming to work with Indigenous knowledge and Indigeneity. Furthermore, such analysis must also bring attention to the place and context of teaching, learning and disseminating such knowledge. One such context is the academy. I share Simpson's (2004) critique that the Western academic culture, including its scholars, has long participated in the colonial (political and intellectual) oppression of Indigenous knowledges. We cannot remove Indigenous knowledges from the "political sphere" (Simpson, 2004, p. 376). There is a problem in the practice of depoliticizing such knowledges while using it s in the service of [Western] capital rather than focusing on a critique of the colonial structure and its political economy itself. As Simpson (2004) writes "unless academics, researchers, institutions, and Indigenous nations are prepared to name the forces that have threatened Indigenous Knowledges and their holders and challenge the colonizing forces currently within the academy, our attempts to use Indigenous Knowledge as a tool for decolonization will certainly fail" (p. 378). The academy with its colonial hierarchies and propensity for the marketplace of ideas has a limiting capacity to seriously teach, learn and disseminate Indigenous knowledge.

Nonetheless, for the Black, Indigenous and racialized scholar, the spiritual ontologies of Indigenous communities constitute worldviews, and social, cultural and psychic values that can be mobilized as important sources of anti-colonial resistance. Writing specifically on Indigenous knowledge, Simpson (2004) exhorts that we "must be strategic about how we recover and where we focus our efforts to ensure that the foundations of the system are protected and the inherently Indigenous processes for the continuation of Indigenous Knowledge are maintained" (p. 376). It is affirmed that Land (in its entirety of Earth, seas, waters and Earthly teachings) constitutes the basis of Indigenous knowledges. Hence a need for Land-based pedagogies. Local peoples educate themselves from the Land, through everyday observations, experiencing and learning from the natural, physical and metaphysical worlds (Simpson, 2004, p. 379).

Elders are custodians of the knowledges acquired from the Land as passed down from generations. In seeking to sustain and regenerate Indigenous knowledges, we can only proceed from a priori protection of the Land, recognize the value of its teachings for destabilizing colonial relations and power hierarchies of schooling, and not from the position that we need to do so because "Elders are dying" (Simpson, 2004, p. 374). A realization that "our knowledge comes from the Land, and the destruction of the environment is a colonial manifestation and a direct attack on Indigenous Knowledge and Indigenous nationhood" is an important starting point (Simpson, 2004, p. 377)

Indigenous teachings of sharing, relationality, mutuality, community building, social responsibility, respect for Elders, Land, and the environment, as well as the validation of spiritual ontologies and epistemologies all constitute important liberatory pedagogies for anti-colonial work. Given the link of Indigeneity and decolonial politics, the recovery, sustaining and teaching of Indigenous knowledges is critical for educational transformation. Indigenous resurgence, regeneration and revival bring the question of Indigenous language and culture into sharp focus. Indigenous knowledges are "oral in nature" (Simpson, 2004, p. 374) as orality, oral culture, and storytelling is synonymous with the study of Indigenous knowledges. Therefore, we must put our efforts in maintaining, sustaining and revitalizing Indigenous languages rather than the colonizing academic practice of collection, digitizing, storage, codification and systemization of Indigenous knowledges. It is noted that oral knowledges have long "sustained complex social, cultural, spiritual and political system" of Indigenous communities (Simpson, 2004, p. 375). We need to retain and sustain Indigenous languages to reframe, re-tell and re-story the Indigenous experience and highlight contributions to the education of the learner. The critical reading of Indigeneity that locates questions of language and modernity amidst the contentions and contestations of history all point to the importance of reframing decolonization for educational practice.

While I will agree that "Indigenous knowledge will not be relevant or of any use to the process of liberation if it exists only in documenting Elders' interviews" (Simpson, 2004, p. 381), in my view this is also a question of what we are documenting, what questions are being asked and how we put the received knowledge into action. Elders have a living curriculum and we must learn from them for educational and political liberation.

It is not enough to learn from Elders' teachings. We must be able to bring Indigenous knowledge and Indigeneity into conversation with decolonization. Decolonization ought to be understood as more than a "thought or a discourse". Cusicanqui (2012) argues that "decolonization of our gestures and acts and the language with which we name the world" (pp. 105–106) and acting within our worlds. She asks us to think of the decolonial space as "an arena of resistance and conflict, a site of development of sweeping counterhegemonic strategies, and a space for the creation of new Indigenous languages and projects of modernity" [as well as] offering a "condition of possibility" (Cusicanqu, 2012, p. 95). This possibility can happen only through concrete actions backing up our discourse. This may mean first unravelling some of our thoughts and ideas about current circumstances and understanding what practices are called to transform our communities.

In the current context, we can begin by re-articulating the link of modernity and decolonization. Modernity is neither an attribute or a characteristic of European history. It is for all human history in that world history has never been static nor frozen in tradition and the past. The present itself is constitute of what it is not, i.e., the past (Lattas, 1993). The Indigenous "perform and display our commitment to modernity" (Cusicanqui, 2012, p. 96). In responding to what "decolonization [has] to do with modernity" (p. 97), Cusicanqui argues that "Indigenous world does not conceive history as linear, the past-future is contained in the present" (p. 96). There is an Indigenous "vision of history [as] not linear or teleological but rather moves in cycles and spirals and sets out a course without neglecting to return to the same point" (Cusicanqui,

2012, p. 96). Hence, a project of "Indigenous modernity can emerge from the present in a spiral whose movement as continuous feedback from the past to the future, a principle of hope or anticipatory consciousness that both discerns and realizes decolonization at the same time" (*ibid*).

The "colonial condition obscures a number of paradoxes" (Cusicanqui, 2012, p. 96). A "de/colonial tension" is revealed in the continued presence of colonizing acts in the decolonial practice itself making the "colonial", an unending practice that must be continually fought. If decolonization is a process it means, none of us ever thoroughly becomes decolonized as we witness the continual insertion of ourselves (i.e., Black, Indigenous, racialized) in the logic and implicit assumptions of the very things we are either contesting or interrogating (see Emiljanowicz, 2019). This insertion is highlighted in how epistemic sites position the retelling of the "history of humanity and knowledge" (Ndlovu-Gatsheni, 2015, p. 492), along with the multiple theoretical schools of thought about decoloniality, that examine the conditions necessary to shift toward a future not premised on coloniality (see Maldonado-Torres, 2011; Ndlovu-Gatsheni, 2015).

As I previously alluded, decolonization is also a collective undertaking of the colonizer and the colonized since we each play multiple roles in lieu of our myriad subjectivities and locations. There are always new forms of colonization within the Indigenous modernity itself such as when we attempt to introduce Indigenous knowledge in the current colonial hierarchy structure of the schooling system and power relations along with the absence of Indigenous Elders in most schools as teachers. What is revealed then, is the importance of analyzing the complex and "different historical moments of domination" (Cusicanqui, 2012, p. 97) to fully understand the nature of the work required that is part of the decolonial struggle for structural transformation. Such observation is more than simply arguing that we are all complicit in relations of domination. There is always a "colonial dominant" but we must seek out collective responsibilities in working to break down power hierarchies of colonial modernity and to bring about social changes built on discursive relationality, sharing, and reciprocity of ideas and creating communities in solidarity.

What I am getting at, is affirming that decolonization must be beyond discourse, theory, and process to concrete practice for change. As Cusicanqui (2012) argues "there can be no discourse of decolonization, no theory of decolonization, without a decolonizing practice" (p. 100). To disrupt what we do in our complex roles as "colonizers" and "colonials", we must understand decolonial politics as challenging and subverting all forms of imposed and dominating ideas and practices. For Black, Indigenous, and racialized scholars this means reflecting and re-assessing our roles as "radical intellectuals" or "public workers" in the academy. Our approach to decolonization must take a different route. We must let our scholarship make sense in the everyday life of our communities. This is not always easy since we can often be seduced by the trappings of academia and fail to see how we have become complicit in the coloniality of the Western academy itself with its merit badges.

Black, Indigenous, racialized "radical intellectuals" in the Western academy can and do contribute to domination in the empire and we have a "collective responsibility not to contribute to the reproduction of this domination" (Cusicanqui, 2012, p. 101). We have to address the "internalization of the practices of the dominant, including the internal colonialisms concerning the 'knowledge-power' dialectic and dynamic. We must be aware of the "internal dynamics of the subalterns" and sub-interns (Cusicanqui, 2012, p. 104), including co-optation into dominant frames of reference, mimicking of dominant theories and the colonial hierarchies of the academy, including its internal colonialisms and racisms embedded in everyday academic practice. We can often fail to acknowledge the learning and wisdom received from our local communities which constitutes the basis of our academic theorizations. We forget the historic sacrifices that paved our entry into academia. We may feel as though we occupy our positions simply because of our academic excellence. We know that our excellence is not in doubt, but we must understand the past struggles that brought us to where we are. While the pace is slow, we must remember the history of our pioneers and to know that our absences in academia in the past were not because those before us were "not smart". There has been a systematic gatekeeping process that has kept us at bay. While in the academy today there are other forms of imperial academic knowledge production that we may unwittingly and wittingly contribute to. How many times do we put our communities under the bus to seek validation, acceptance, and legitimation in the eyes of the dominant (Dei, 2012, p. 45)? How many times have we been distinct voices on race, racism, and Indigeneity in the past at a time when it was "not popular" for the Black, Indigenous or racialized academic?

We may take pride in our "intellectuality" simply by spewing dominant postmodern, post-structural, and postcolonial narratives, and in the process, we are pitted against each other. I have seen how in the academy, Black scholars who work within oppositional frames of references such as Afrocentric, Blackcentric, and anti-colonial theory are read as angry and not "scholarly enough". Even when academics believe they are in dialogue with Indigenous local intellectuals, we still construct or perpetuate ourselves (as academics) in new canons and gurus (Cusicanqui, 2012) which is all part of the colonial hierarchies in academic knowledge production. There are ensuing academic colonialisms such as "patron-client" relationships, patronage, canonization, and citation practices we pursue (e.g., who is cited, who cites whom) that all reveal the trappings and construction of academic hierarchies revealing complex forms of cultural domination. We can easily fall prey to these mechanizations in our work. It is part of the seduction of the political economy of the academy.

Decolonization is about asking questions. So, we ask: what is the place of Indigenous local intellectuals in our anti-colonial practice? How does our academic research and writing subvert the "colonization of the imaginary" and the possible (Cusicanqui, 2012, p. 106)? In what ways do our discursive practices shift from the coloniality of knowledge and power to a critique and transformation of the global "political economy of knowledge" (Cusicanqui, 2012, p. 102)? To decolonize academic practice, we must move from the appropriation to crediting ideas of our Indigenous, subaltern, and sub-intern intellectuals, and bringing a "spiritual and culturalist agenda" to our decolonial politics. We must interpret decolonial practice to mean working with our collective psychic and spiritual memories, and/with the politics of critical language to bring new meanings to Black, Indigenous radical alterity.

Decolonization is *Buen Vivir* (Living Well) (Gudynas, 2011). It is worth fighting for collectively. We cannot decolonize on our own and decolonization must be collectively pursued to be successful. Decolonization as an epistemology and practice of change must promote a "radical critique" and a "critical practice" bringing the "nostalgia with our ancestors" and our Indigeneities into effective political ends (Gago, 2016, p. 5). Decolonization must be imperative to help us move to a "collective moment of political radicalization" knowing that we may be "oppressed but not defeated" (*ibid*; p. 3). We must radicalize our Otherness and our differences for collective change.

For Black and Indigenous scholars, decolonization is finding our voices through reading, re-writing, and re-telling the stories that constitute an intellectual practice of knowledge as resistance and survival. In these moments of social movement struggles we must embrace our knowing as "political practice" that continually reminds us of the "living traces of colonialism" and the imperative for anti-colonial practice (*ibid*; pp. 7–8). In the academy we must see possibilities with our presence even amid the limitations, exclusions, and marginalization and ensure that we continually work through any redemptive qualities of academia for any "elusive and distant good" (*ibid*; p. 1). Of course, part of the struggle will be to "refuse the academy" in ways that mean subverting its coloniality. We can work without and form outside for change. It does not have to be "either/or". We can subvert the rules of the game. We can propose counter spaces for our education. We cannot demand purity, but rather, we must dream on the "condition of firmly believing in [our] dreams" that change is possible (*ibid*; pp. 7–8). We must also develop and nurture a curious "capacity to connect heterogeneous elements" (*ibid*; p. 3), our differences and to be able to figure out what is at stake for us (i.e., to follow clues and subtext, disturb the hidden and open rules and regulations, and to work for change). We must also be able to communicate, such as "speaking to others and speaking with others" and develop "a recognition of the authorial effect of listening" and using voices to advocate for change (*ibid*; p. 3).

The "postcolonial moment" encounters decolonial and anti-colonial spaces with different but connected understandings of knowledge, power, and political criticisms. The postcolonial "as a desire" (*ibid*; p. 4) and its discourses of hybridity is still essentialist, metaphorical and about fantasies with "historicist interpretations of the Indigenous question" (Cusicanqui, 2012, p. 100). The postcolonial moment can be engaged to point to our complicities in ongoing coloniality. The anti-colonial offers the possibility of "a struggle" (Gago, 2016, p. 4) even in the decolonial politics of "obnoxious fashionable neologism" and the search for trans modernity (Cusicanqui, 2012, p. 102).

What should be the focus of decolonial politics in moments of the so-called Indigenous recognition? The settler colonial state politics offers a clue and strategy. The recourse to Indigeneity and to Indigenous resistance, particularly, in settler colonial states has always been a struggle for sovereignty and self-determination. As the work of Coulthard (2007) shows, there are profound structural, economic, cultural and psychological realms of colonial domination. The colonial state in truth wants "work" and "resource" from the Indigene not "recognition" of our worth (p. 430). The subjectifying nature of colonial recognition is built on derogatory images of Indigenous peoples through settler benevolence and appropriations of definitions of reciprocity, freedom, and justice usually under terms dictated externally by the colonial nation-state. The colonial nation-state will only recognize Indigenous peoples' rights, collective identities, struggles for self-determination etc. in so far as these "do not throw into question the background legal, political and economic framework of the colonial relationship itself" (Coulthard, 2007, p. 451).

Indigenous decolonization must focus on addressing the impacts of the cultural, spiritual, psychic, and "psycho-affective" influences and complexes of colonial domination continually faced by Indigenous subjects globally. Indigenous sovereignty can only be achieved through struggle and conflict. Indigenous and colonized peoples "must struggle to critically reclaim and re-evaluate the worth of [our] own histories, traditions and cultures against the subjectifying gaze and assimilative lure of colonial recognition" (Coulthard, 2007, p. 453). In effect, Indigenous subjects must resist "always being interpellated by recognition, being constructed by colonial discourse or being assimilated by imperial power structures" (p. 453; referencing Ashcroft, 2001; p. 35). Our goal must be to reclaim the Indigenous socio-cultural values that will challenge Western liberalism, capitalism, and corporate modernity and offer more perfect relations between ourselves with humans and Nature/creation (see also Alfred, 1999; p. 60).

We must also reframe "Indigeneity, Land, race and decolonization links" upholding race as a central question in decolonial politics. In their recent essay, Garba and Sorentino (2020) present us with an important question relating to the "the truth of colonization and its relationship to metaphoricity" (p. 778). In arguing that slavery is a metaphor they enthuse that anti-Blackness cannot "theoretically [be] engulfed by the settler-colonial paradigm" (Garba & Sorentino, 2020, p. 765). The authors refer to Tuck and Yang's (2012) key thesis in "Decolonization is not a metaphor", which argues that decolonization requires the repatriation of Indigenous Land and life (Tuck & Yang, 2012, p. 9). Land is central to decolonial projects. But how are we to understand the use of the metaphor? To Tuck and Yang (2012), the application of "metaphor" for the decolonization project is limiting, liberal and it usually turns decolonization into a project easily domesticated by the colonial state leaving questions of state power and colonial exploitations on Indigenous Lands intact. It can rightly be asked whether when "metaphor" invades the decolonization discourse and project decolonization is necessarily subverted, muted or "destroyed" (Tuck & Yang, 2012, p. 3) or simply "transported into to the realm of semantic superabundance" (Garba & Sorentino, 2020, p. 765)? The real, symbolic and figurative are always consequential. The material and symbolic are intertwined, and the physical space is not separated from its symbols.

We must insist on race being a central thesis in Indigeneity and decolonization studies. The "logics of elimination and/or possession" (Wolfe, 2006) equally applies to Land dispossession and physical extermination of lives, as well as the appropriation of bodies and their labour. Colonial settlers do not only claim Indigenous Lands as their own, they also claim Black bodies as their property. Furthermore, slavery and the Middle Passage are about Land and human dispossession. As such we cannot subsume Blackness and slavery under settler decolonial politics (e.g., a reduction of slavery to forced labour, and Black life to capitalism). Anti-Blackness is not just "a structure alongside settler colonialism" (Garba & Sorentino, 2020, p. 765). Each has a life of its own beyond its distinct colonial logics. There are both material and symbolic consequences of the experiences of colonization and the pursuit of decolonial politics. In decolonization, we must speak of "time and space coherence" and the articulation [not disarticulation] of the "soul, the body, the group, the Land and the universe" (Garba & Sorentino, 2020, p. 764).

Simultaneously there are discursive links to be made between Blackness and Indigeneity. Indigeneity is a political, gendered, class and racialized category. Race and the question of Indigenous sovereignty cannot be taken as distinct issues (Harris, 2019). The contest for Land is also a contest for life and colonialism and genocide "have typically employed the organizing principle of race" (Wolfe, 2006, pp. 387–388). We need to bring an understanding of colonialism through history, revealing an awareness of how our historical amnesia has worked with race and Land as part of the myriad Indigenous conjuring and conjunctures of Land for "the perpetuation of [colonial] domination" (Harris, 2019, p. 221).

Black peoples have always had complicated histories globally beyond questions of capitalism and citizenship. Harris (2019) calls for a theorization of "Blackness and Indigeneity in radical relationality" (p. 215), pointing out that settler colonialism was "deployed in ways to implicate "race, genocide, dispossession, slavery, colonialism and extraction in inter-related ways (Harris, 2019, p. 215). Thus, theorizing settler colonialism must engage African Indigeneity (see also Dei, 2017; Harris, 2019; Byrd, 2019). Blackness and Indigeneity have always been central to the reproduction of White and Whiteness as property (Harris, 2019, p. 222).

The pain of Land dispossession is equally an issue for Black, Africans whether on the continent or dispersed through the Middle Passage and the violence. This has implications for how we speak of "Land" and African Indigeneity. We need to conceptualize Indigeneity broadly then as about Land, labour, and bodies, (e.g., appropriation of Land, labour, the extermination, elimination or genocide of Black and Indigenous bodies globally). Within the global diaspora and, in the context of transnational mobility, Black existence is always in question constituting a denial of Black life.

The question of Land is one of multiple geographies. There is a colonial tendency to fix Indigenous identities in place. But Indigeneity is articulated with geography, positionality, and political struggle as constitutive of living and livelihood. In her piece "Indigeneity, capitalism and the management of dispossession", Li (2010) shows how market pressures of colonial capitalism affected Indigenous collective landholding regimes through Land displacement, the commodification of Land, creation of landless populations all through ongoing processes of coloniality. Li (2010) brings an understanding of Indigenous Land dispossession in multiple and complex ways. For example, through outright Land dispossession from people, subverting Indigenous collective landholding through individualized land rights, putting other structures in place that corrupted Indigenous landholding patterns, as well as promoting a particular colonial thinking and Indigenous politics revealing of ways colonizers and "colonial regimes [re]invented collective tenures over customary Land", to suppress (and facilitate) the commodification of Land in colonized communities in Africa, Asia and part of Europe (Li, 2010, p. 390). Even in Africa, a colonial policy of "preserving land for collective African use" (Li, 2010, p. 391) was usurped by colonial capitalism.

In Dei (2017) I discussed African Indigeneity as an entry point to interrogating the "Black as settlers" position on Turtle Island. It is not in dispute that Blacks were crucial to the settler colonial nation project, as Black people were racially subordinated to White national citizenship (see also Harris, 2019). For Diasporic Black peoples who were enslaved, slavery did not mean "giving up of Africa" (e.g., becoming or belonging citizens of the colonial state) or erasing their "African Indigeneity" (Harris, 2019, p. 216; Kelley, 2017). Africans and Blacks in diaspora were historically displaced of Land and place. Therefore, caution must be exercised in how we impose the "settler" concept on Black people. European colonizers in Africa wanted African Land (not just in South Africa alone) and our labour. But the colonizers also despised the African person (Kelley, 2017). All this has implications for how we speak of settler colonialism and the connections with other colonialisms as distinct and yet interrelated processes (see also Smith, 2010).

Questioning imposing the "settler" tag on Black bodies does not mean we deny Black complicities in Indigenous peoples' erasure and dispossession through colonial projects of the Empire. There is a need for examining the "unique positioning of Blackness in settler colonialism" and the complicities of Indigenous and racialized peoples in anti-Blackness (Harris, 2019, p. 216; Byrd, 2019, p. 211). I share the reading that "anti-Blackness and settler colonialism are indivisible" (Byrd, 2019, p. 212) and that the discourse of settler colonialism must not centre Whiteness by erasing or displacing Black and African peoples, our Blacknesses and our Indigeneities (Harris, 2019, p. 216; Byrd, 2019). Indigenous peoples are racialized for the settler nation-building project similar to the processes of racializing of African and Black bodies.

In concluding this chapter, I will turn to Indigenous resistance, solidarity and futurity. What can be gleaned from the global Indigenous anti-colonial struggle for anti-colonial solidarities today? I broached the subject of anti-colonial solidarity in a later discussion in this book. For now, I bring a gaze to Indigenous solidarity that brings Black, African, and Indigenous peoples struggles into a global sphere. We need to reclaim and transform Indigenous politics of identity to begin to work with collective Indigenous identities that learn from our global colonial exclusions. We must foster a radical posture to ensure the non-existence of the colonizer (see Veracini, 2011). This will entail creating the "new Indigenisimo" as a "demand [for] a radical restructuring of society" (Cusicanqui, n.d., p. 4).

There is an ongoing global struggle for Indigenous autonomy (territorial, social, linguistic and political) everywhere. The lessons of these struggles must be "the starting point for building a new [world]" (Cusicanqui, n.d., p. 4). Collective awareness and consciousness – Indigeneities, ethnic, racial, gender, sexual, etc. – of inter and intra-group relations, and rivalries, including the "internecine power struggles" should urge a coming together for a global pan-Indigenous social movement (*ibid*; p. 2). We could also learn from our varied and innovative ways of organizing – cultural centers, urban movements, and political organizations for global action to fight new forms of colonialism and capitalist imperialisms. We must also learn to translate Indigenous concepts into collective dialogues of action, all as part of collective politics restoring a new cosmic order or future.

The urgency for a new social order was long ago captured in the words of Alfred and Corntassel (2005): "We do not need to wait for the colonizer to provide us with money or to validate our vision of a free future; we only need to start to use our [cultural knowledges, histories and experiences] to frame our thoughts, the ethical framework of *our* philosophies to make decisions and to use *our* laws and institutions to govern ourselves" (p. 614). Long ago, Niezen (2003) alluded to an "Indigenism" that must be extended to a politicized meaning of pan-Indigenism, constructed as "radical Indigenism" (Garroute, 2003, p. 114).

Within this radical pan-Indigenism, not only do we build solidarities among ourselves, but also, to ensure that we actualize the "strength of Indigenous resistance, unity [which is] constantly under attack as colonial powers erase community histories and senses of place to replace them with doctrines of individualism and predatory capitalism" (Alfred & Corntassel, 2005, p. 603).

Black and Indigenous solidarities can only grow with a collective recognition of our shared implications and responsibilities to fight a collective battle against colonialism and capitalism and how the structures continue to script indigenous lives globally.

References Cited:

Alfred, T. (1999). *Peace power righteousness: An Indigenous manifesto.* Don Mills: Oxford University Press.

Alfred, T. (2005). *Wasase: Indigenous pathways of action and freedom.* Peterborough: Broadview Press.

Ashcroft, B. (2001). *Post-Colonial transformations.* New York: Routledge.

Alfred, T., & Corntassel, J. (2005). Being Indigenous: Resurgences against contemporary colonialism. *Government and Opposition, 40*(4), 597–614.

Byrd, J. A. (2019). Weather with you: Settler colonialism, antiblackness, and the grounded relationalities of resistance. *Journal of the Critical Ethnic Studies Association, 5*(1–2), 207–213.

Cusicanqui, S. R. (2012). Ch'ixinakax utxiwa: A reflection on the practices and discourses of decolonization. *South Atlantic Quarterly, 111*(1), 95–109. doi: 10.1215/00382876-1472612.

Cusicanqui Silvia Rivera. (n.d.). "The historical horizons of internal colonialism". Retrieved from https://homepages.web.net/~bthomson/bobs_files/Cusicanqui_Historical_Memory.pdf

Dei, G. J. S. 2023. "Decolonizing Education". Panel remarks Department Colloquium, Emmanuel College, Victoria University of the University of Toronto, School of Theology, Toronto, Ontario. Virtual, March 1.

Dei, G. J. S., & Cacciavillani, A. (2022) "Language Acquisition or Actualizing Decolonization: A Case for Decolonizing and Indigenizing the Curriculum. The Journal of Philosophy of Education, (Special Issue).

Dei, J. S. S. (2017). *Reframing Blackness and Black Solidarities through anti-colonial and decolonial prisms.* New York: Springer Publishing.

Dei, G. J. S. 2022. Reframing Anti-Racist Education as Anti-Colonial Practice: Implications for Radical School Leadership. Keynote address at the 3rd Annual Conference of the Centre

for Leadership and Diversity [CLD], Achieving Equity Through Radical Leadership. Toronto, Ontario, October 15.
Dei, G. J. S., Ezinwanne Odozor, & Andrea Vasquez. (Eds.). (2020). *Cartographies of Blackness and Black Indigeneities*. Gorham, ME.: Myers Educational Press.
Dei, G. J. S. 2017 Reframing Blackness and Black Solidarities through Anti-Colonial and Decolonial Prisms. New York: Springer.
Fals-Borda, O. (1991). Some basic ingredients. In O. Fals-orda & M. A. Rahman (Eds.), *Action and knowledge: Breaking the monopoly with participatory action-research* (pp. 3–12). New York: The Apex Press.
Freire, P. (2000). Pedagogy of the Oppressed (30th anniversary ed.). London: Continuum.
Gago, V. (2016). Silvia Rivera Cusicanqui: Against Internal Colonialism. Retrieved from: https://www.viewpointmag.com/2016/10/25/silvia-rivera-cusicanqui-against-internal-colonialism
Garba, T., & Sorentino, S. M. (2020). Slavery is a metaphor: A critical commentary on Eve Tuck and K. Wayne Yang's "Decolonization is Not a Metaphor". *Antipode 52*(3), 764–782. doi: 10.1111/anti.12615
Garrouette, E. M. (2003). *Real Indians: Identity and the survival of Native America*, Berkeley, University of California Press, p. 144.
Gudynas, E. (2011). Buen Vivir: Today's tomorrow. *Development*, 54(4), 441–447. http://www.miqols.org/howb/wp-content/uploads/2016/06/Gudynas_BuenVivirTomorrowDevelopmen.pdf
Lattas, A. (1993). "Essentialism, memory and resistance: Aboriginality and the politics of authenticity". *Oceania*, 63(3), 240–267.
Li, T. (2010). Indigeneity, capitalism, and the management of dispossession. *Current Anthropology*, 51(3), 385–414.
Harris, C. I. (2019). Of Blackness and Indigeneity: Comments on Jodi A. Byrd's "Weather with you: Settler colonialism, antiblackness, and the grounded relationalities of resistance". *Journal of the Critical Ethnic Studies Association*, 5(1–2), 215–227.
Hewitt, J. (2016) Indigenous restorative justice: Approaches, meaning & possibility. University of New Brunswick Law Journal. November 27, 2022, https://journals.lib.unb.ca/index.php/unblj/article/view/29082
Jackson, M. (2019). "In the End 'The Hope of Decolonization." In Handbook of Indigenous Education (pp. 101–110). Springer Singapore. https://doi.org/10.1007/978-981-10-3899-0_59
Lloyd-Henry, P. (2022). "Personal Communication". Ontario Institute for Studies in Education of the University of Toronto. March 14.
Kelley, R. D. G. (2017). "The rest of us: Rethinking settler and native." *American Quarterly*, 69(2).
Maldonado-Torres, N. (2011). Thinking through the decolonial turn: Post-continental interventions in theory, philosophy, and critique: An introduction. Transmodernity: Journal of Peripheral Cultural Production of the Luso-Hispanic World, 1(2), 1–15.

Mihesuah, Waziyatawin., Mihesuah, Devon A., & Waziyatawin. (2004) Indigenizing the academy : transforming scholarship and empowering communities / edited by Devon Abbott Mihesuah and Angela Cavender Wilson. University of Nebraska Press.

Niezen, R. (2003). *The origins of Indigenism: Human rights and the politics of identity.* Berkeley: University of California Press, 2003.

Ndlovu-Gatsheni, S. J. (2015). "Decoloniality as the future of Africa." *History Compass, 13*(10), 485-496.

Parry, B. 1994. "Resistance Theory/Theorising Resistance, or Two Cheers for Nativism". In F. Barker, P. Hulme and M. Iversen eds. Colonial Discourse/Postcolonial Theory. Manchester University Press. pp. 172-196.

Robinson, Cedric. (2000). *Black Marxism: The making of the Black Radical Tradition.* Chapel Hill.

Smith, L. 2012. Decolonizing Methodologies. London: Zed Press.

Simpson, L. (2004). Anti-colonial strategies for the recovery and maintenance of Indigenous knowledge. *The American Indian Quarterly, 28*(3 & 4), 373–384.

Smith, A. (2010). Indigeneity, settler colonialism & White supremacy. *Global Dialogue, 12*(2). Retrieved from: http://www.worlddialogue.org/content.php?id=488

Styres, S. (2019). Literacies of Land: Decolonizing Narratives, Storying, and Literature. In L. T. Smith, E. Tuck, & K. W. Yang (Eds.). Indigenous and Decolonizing Studies in Education: Mapping the Long View (pp, 24-37). New York: Routledge. Retrieved from https://ebookcentral-proquest-com.myaccess.library.utoronto.ca

Sunseri, L. (2000). Moving beyond the feminism versus nationalism dichotomy: An anti-colonial feminist perspective on aboriginal liberation struggles. *Canadian Woman Studies, 20*(2), 143–148.

Taylor, C. (1994). 'The politics of recognition'. In A. Guttman (Ed.), *Re-examining the politics of recognition* (pp. 25–73). Princeton: Princeton University Press.

Tuck, E., & Yang, K. W. (2012). Decolonization is not a metaphor. *Decolonization: Indigeneity, Education & Society, 1*(1), 1–40.

Vásquez Jiménez, Odozor, E., & Dei, G. J. S. (2020). *Cartographies of Blackness and Black indigeneities* (Vásquez Jiménez, E. Odozor, & G. J. S. (George J. S. Dei, Eds.). Myers Education Press

Veracini. (2011). District 9 and Avatar: Science fiction and settler colonialism. *Journal of Intercultural Studies, 32*(4), 355–367. https://doi.org/10.1080/07256868.2011.584614

wa Thiong'o. N. 1981. Decolonizing the Mind. London: Heineman.

Weaver, H. N. (2001). 'Indigenous identity: What is it and who really has it?'. *American Indian Quarterly*, Volume 25.

Wilson, A., & Laing, M. (2019). Queering Indigenous education. In L. T. Smith, E. Tuck, & K. W. Yang (Eds.), *Indigenous and decolonizing studies in education: Mapping the long view* (pp. 131–145). New York: Routledge.

Wolfe, P. (2006). "Settler colonialism and the elimination of the native". *Journal of Genocide Research*, 8(4).

Wolfe, P. (2016). *Traces of history: Elementary structures of race.* London: Verso.

· 6 ·

A VIEW OF SOCIAL JUSTICE EDUCATION

I have learned over the years that to write a good story, one must be able to tell it. This chapter makes no bold claims to reinvent the way social justice education has been discussed or practiced. However, it does encourage us to rethink the way we practice and understand social justice as we move toward new futures. This chapter is my way of speaking differently about social justice, a way that promotes critical conversation and stimulates internal reflection about the nature of social justice work and the bodies who claim knowledge.

Interestingly, before delivering public lectures, I have often been asked "are you nervous?", and I quickly respond with "No". I say "no" with such swift certainty because I have come to the realization that many people are not listening! After all, if people were listening, why then do we witness the slow pace of change from where I sit? The Canadian Education Association (CEA) selected me as a co-recipient of the 2016 Whitworth Award for Education Research. The award noted: "The Selection Committee members were genuinely impressed with the originality, depth and relevance of your research, which they felt has had such an impact on education policy and practice in Canada". My discomfort rests on a paradoxical feeling that if our work is making such an impact on policy, how come we have not yet seen the change many of us have so passionately been advocating for? Something is clearly wrong somewhere and I do not think it is merely about changing the message or messenger.

What particular understandings of social justice education do we bring to our work as intellectuals and community activists that are working toward social change? How do we broach social justice education in an inclusive way that extends discussions of justice and equity to highlight key questions of power, resource sharing, implications, responsibilities, and complicities? In this chapter, I will articulate an understanding of social justice education that draws on some of my early theorizing in anti-racism education, sketching in stories, reflections, and experiences that aim to advance, intertwine, and unravel understandings of social justice, race, Indigeneity, and anti-colonial education.

There is the power of imagination and new imaginings (even in the aesthetic sense) to dream big. However, we need to reimagine a new humanism outside of Western corporatism and industrial capitalism (see also Nussbaum, 2007). Greed and an insatiable need for power have been the cornerstone of many of the prevailing challenges of social justice. I share such sentiments to begin to see the emergence of something new, something different, and the possibilities of going beyond. In thinking anew we have been told to question the "ontologies that hold us apart", but what about questioning the "ontologies of things that hold us together"? For example – questioning power and the asymmetrical relations of power, by asking questions such as why do we want "to go beyond" in the first place? What are we afraid of? Who constructs this new transitory space? How do we make space for others to co-exist when the dominant insists they must have all the space? The postmodern fascination with shiftiness, fluidity, and flux, conveyed in discourses of transitions, can lead to a situation where we (as colonized, oppressed, Indigenous and racialized bodies) are left with no space to stand. When we advance critiques of the static and frozen, we must be critical and remind ourselves where we come from. No space, identity, tradition, or culture is static or frozen. We cannot accept an argument of the colonial construct of static, frozen only to turn around later to use such constructions by way of interrogating claims of the colonized and oppressed. This is significant given that it is often the oppressed, colonized, racialized and the Indigene who have continually challenged colonial constructions of themselves, their lives, experiences, and their knowledge.

Many of us continually fight against dominant constructions of ourselves, what we know of ourselves, and how others know and construct us.

We must hold on to the possibilities of reading our world differently, for example through Indigenous cultural framings. In September 2016, I gave a keynote address to an audience in Winnipeg, Manitoba, Canada. A scholar remarked that he has been following my work over the years, after hearing me speak a few years back on "African Proverbs and Stories as Indigenous Philosophies" at the American Educational Research Association (AERA) conference. He was struck by the richness of the theory behind my arguments. Such testimony stands in stark contrast to the times when I had to defend myself against "academic scholars" in search of theory. I know many racialized scholars in the Western academy who have experienced and expressed similar concerns. It should not surprise anyone, since the Western academy can often brand individuals who advocate for counter and oppositional discourses such as Afrocentric, anti-colonialism, and anti-racism as being atheoretical, anti-intellectual, or angry. The tension I describe is what I call "convenient intellectual placement", and it has many angles to it. It is also surprising to hear someone remark: "George, your anti-racism is not really about anti-Black racism" when for so many years one has had to defend charges that their anti-racism is only about Black people!

Similarly, I have always been wary of charges of the "Indigenous" and "Indigeneity" as essentialist, romanticized and over-mythicized. As to who is doing such questioning is worthy of noting. I write neither in response nor in reaction to intellectual allegations but to interrogate these contentions in terms of how they speak to me. In reflecting on my own trajectory of teaching, researching, and writing on race, Indigeneity and anti-colonialism, I have come to the realization that the pursuit of social justice work is a daunting task. I have noticed that there are times a "take no prisoners" approach to disagreements is exercised. I have also noticed that some scholars may seek to malign or undermine one's intellectual credibility if not in agreement. Unfortunately, we do not all have the luxury to choose to discard social justice work. We can maintain our separate but interconnected approaches from different angles with a myriad of positionalities. However, the intellectual and emotional labor social justice work requires may also require that at times, we simply move away from responding to dominant critiques.

But I feel it is imperative to connect knowledge to bodies and our identities. The body is a site of knowing. Inhibiting a Black body in a White supremacist context, the responsibility is not just to claim to know, but the politics to act for social change. This is why there is an old African adage: "it is not what one is called that is important but more so what one responds to!"

There is the urgency of using the epistemic saliency of Black/African and Indigenous bodies to refute dominant claims to know about my/our [racialized/colonized/Indigenous] experiences. This is not a call to privilege the knowledge of the Black/colonized/racialized/Indigenous body. We are insisting that we have something to say about our lived experiences worth listening to and we must be at the table when we are on the menu. In fact, Semali and Kincheloe (1999) are right in insisting that "nothing about us without us" (p. 37). Our voices become a counterpoint, a counter stance, an oppositional voice to change the insulting idea that others know us more than we know ourselves (Prah, 1997). Our voice is and should be part of the debate and any contestations around social justice and social justice work are incomplete when our voices are missing in dialogue and action.

I situate these personal reflections in the discussion because of the persistent inter-twinning problems of Indigenous genocide/erasure and the exclusion of Black/African experiences in Euro-Canadian/American national imaginings and constructions of identities. Euro-American schooling allows for the silencing and erasure of the Black/African and Indigenous identities, knowledges and experience, presenting social justice questions. Colonialism has worked to "kill off' certain populations while sustaining the lives of the dominant. On-going processes of colonization, coupled with its new forms such as capitalism and globalization continue to foster individual and corporate greed, subjecting equity to the whims of the markets and capital. There are ongoing colonial practices that serve to create wealth, power, and privilege for certain segments of our global community and poverty for others.

To understand contemporary processes of global colonialism, we must ask: why are people risking their lives to cross borders? We must also ask: why do nations hire individuals to facilitate migratory trajectories to more dangerous landscapes? How do we explain the hypocrisy of the nation/colonial state and state responses to such developments when they claim their societies are founded on justice and freedom? We need to (re)imagine the problems of migrant labour patterns and experiences through the rubric of colonialism and recognize the ongoing (forced) movement of resources and people to satisfy the industries of the North.

Talking about social justice is also reflected in contemporary discourse. The phrase "implicit bias" and SJW or "social justice warrior" have become mainstream mantras used to delegitimize critical thought and commentary. The term "implicit bias" is an attempt to implicate everyone, liberalize our critiques, and dodge the saliency of race. It is a way of shifting the gaze away from interrogations of structures toward individual prejudices and discrimination. An understanding of bias does require an acknowledgement of race, systemic racism, or oppression. It is an apolitical term that can be applied to everyone. The de facto understanding of "bias" is that we all have it within us. And if we all are implicitly biased, there is no need to even speak of systems, structures, and institutions. Bias is rendered an individualized problem of attitude, preference, and prejudice. Well folks, if the fight for social justice was simply a case of individual bias, the SJWs of the world would have won by now.

Connecting Race, Indigeneity and Anti-Colonial Education: The Intellectual Praxis

I would insist that our time, our energy, and our emotional and intellectual labour is far too precious of a resource to be spent engaging with scholars who do not share the desire to transform society. In broaching social justice, I have a political and intellectual desire to create spaces that make solidarity work possible. As a racialized, colonized, and Indigenous African body I am constantly and astutely aware of the power of critical questioning: For example, asking what are our entanglements with difference? How do we account for the dispossessions and dislocations of knowledge and a theory linking colonialism, ongoing colonizations, imperial practices, and the coloniality of power? The way talk [as speech] is shaped (i.e., the process of knowledging) is as much as important as the content of what is said. Difference is always threatening. Difference can be found oppressive when it seeks to challenge and deconstruct our universalized assumptions. Difference and knowledge construction in what I would call the "politics of knowledging" require us to work with cultural and historical specificities of knowing, to recognize the cultural logics of a given knowledge system, and to evaluate such knowledge on the basis of their own cultural logics and cultural dynamics (see Mudimbe, 1988). This is more the case when we look at how our interrogations of Indigenous knowledges are often informed through a Eurocentric lens.

I have often been enthused that criticisms of Indigenous knowledges have more to do with people's discomfort with Indigenous knowledge and its threatening nature to Western science knowledge (see also Battiste & Henderson, 2001). It is not because Indigenous knowledges lack theoretical sophistication nor the basic principles of an acceptable knowledge system. Knowledge is constructed and understood within the contexts of positionality, politics, social and ethical considerations, as well as relations and strategies of power. Knowledge makes sense in a given context. Knowledge is evaluated in terms of its inherent logics and the valid claims such knowledge asserts. Knowledge is demarcated by social differences and relations of power. In the "Politics of Representation", Larbalestier (1990) opined that "difference is a conceptual, cultural and material problem". I would add that acknowledging difference also has spiritual and emotional implications. Larbalestier's contention that "difference is embedded in politics of identity which are, in turn, embedded in relations of power" (1990, p. 155) brings to my mind the question of who is deemed worthy of knowing.

To do social justice work is to build anti-colonial solidarities. By "anti-colonial" I mean solidarities that are opposed to any form of colonization whether race, gender, class, sexual, [dis] ability or foreign imposed. The literature on anti-colonialism has been informed by Black/African, Indigenous and other racialized peoples' experiences with European colonization. In fact, as I have argued elsewhere, the struggle for Independence in Africa was an important avenue for producing much of the beginnings of anti-colonial literature (Dei, 2010). Anti-colonial theorizing is highly relevant today given these complex ways colonialisms continue to morph into new forms of imposition and domination of bodies, ideas, experiences and knowledges. These developments themselves have also served to offer new political, cultural and intellectual possibilities for using Indigenous-resistant knowledges to challenge the colonial order. To be effective, strategies of colonial resistance must be based on solidarities among colonized and oppressed peoples everywhere.

But, as many have noted, solidarity cannot be accomplished without a rethinking and reframing of our analytical and conceptual frameworks for political praxis. While we may tell the same story it does not necessarily mean the story is singular. Thus, we must be able to theorize difference critically within our frameworks in ways that challenge Eurocentric colonial differencing and its "parameters of dichotomous thinking" (Larbalestier, 1990, p. 154). The problem though is that, for us as racialized, colonized and Indigenous scholars, when we take up, challenge, and resist the impacts of Eurocentric binary thinking, we are often accused of inventing such dichotomies in the first place. This has been the problem for those who speak pointedly of the saliency and continuing significance of race. Instead of being viewed as intellectuals addressing a systemic issue, we are seen as inventing a problem!

My objective in the pursuit of social justice is to insist on particular anti-colonial representations of knowledge, ideas, bodies and politics. The struggle for representation implicates everyone, the dominant and the oppressed. The bidding of representation for those who are oppressed is disentangling how we have been represented; for the dominant, it is about cultural appropriation. Anti-colonial theorists enthused that identity and belonging have been sites colonizers pursued their practices of domination and oppression. It stands to reason, therefore, that for those whose identities have been oppressed with our sense of belonging always being questioned (and even threatened), we would view identity and belonging as sites to [re]claim, resist and transform. Such critical reading moves us away from the intellectual foot dancing around the plurality of oppressions – "we are all oppressed" and "we are simultaneously oppressors". No doubt, there are multiple and variegated sites, sources, and intersections of oppressions as well as relative complicities. How we evoke power to address our needs and concerns puts us in compromising situations ensuring multiple and varied complicities *and* responsibilities. But this reality is a far cry from the outright denial of the power of a colonial dominant. Their power is never in question. We cannot liberalize nor mute the oppressive position of the colonial dominant even as we insist power is diffused and relational.

Arguably, the body as a site of knowing and knowledge is continually contested but more so if the body happens to be non-dominant. I embrace and welcome such contestation. For me, it is an opportunity to raise new questions to ponder over in doing social justice work. There are definitely going to be gaps in discussions of social justice work. We must acknowledge these gaps and even appreciate them in terms of the limitations of our own knowing. This chapter, for example, is not going to be the end of the conversation. It is actually the continuation of a long story/journey that I/we want to tell by reflecting on some questions: How do we dislodge the dominant, racist, sexist, colonialist and patriarchal discourse and daily social practice in our institutions and within our local communities? How do we disrupt what has become the hegemonic stance and the taken-for-granted assumptions we each hold? What teachings inform the way we come to know about ourselves and our worlds? In particular, what and how are the teachings of the Land, place and resistance informing the politics of social justice work? How do we begin to produce, complicate and add complexity to existing readings, meanings and understandings of our practices and social categories? How do we ensure that the debate is not already framed in ways that preclude possibilities of other readings? Even asking and struggling with these questions is an important start to social justice work.

In revealing the complexity of social categories, we show a yearning to define and operationalize terms in ways that bring new, oppositional and subversive readings. This is not simply an exercise for conceptual clarity. It is an exercise to open up space for a myriad of voices to come to the table for discussion. We do not identify problems for the sake of the problem itself. We raise an issue because we want actions that move us toward achieving solutions. We do not raise a problem merely because we want clearly defined boundaries for our conversations. The way neoliberalism seeks to measure everything is clearly problematic. We may ask: how do we measure equality and inequalities? Should we get bogged down for lack of clarity? Should we even try to measure equality and inequality? To be on Indigenous peoples' Land makes this calling for social justice work extremely urgent. Such work is going to be hard, tough, painful and very emotionally charged and legitimately so. Such work is going to cause anger and frustration. However, we know that settler colonialism causes violence, dispossession and genocide. So what do we have to lose? We must frame the ways we teach social justice on settler lands through the paradigm of violence, genocide and colonialism. We must center the question of settler subjectivity and sense of entitlements in order to make sense of our positionalities and work together toward solutions.

For Indigenous and racialized bodies, there is the everyday "acts of refusal" that challenge placing our lives in a box or restricting what we write and say about our lives, experiences and histories (see also Simpson, 2014). For many colonized, Indigenous, and racialized bodies, our acts of refusal should include refusing the invitation into Whiteness, not to be seduced by Whiteness, nor to be caught in the trappings of it. We have differential routes and consequences of getting entangled in Whiteness. Invitations into Whiteness are about limited definitions of excellence, merit, scholarship, and intellectualism. What is rewarded in the academy is what Whiteness deems "knowledge" and the markers are objectified. These markers are not bestowed on just any subject. The subjects that perform Whiteness are the ones who are rewarded for such performativity. It is part of the project of policing and regulating "Whiteness as property" of a group. After all, such Whiteness, as Harris (1995) insists is founded on White supremacy, not social difference (p. 98).

Conventional Social Justice

Social justice continues to be a highly contested term in the 21st Century. Our contributions to the debate will be assessed in terms of the coherence of our arguments, attempts at denaturalizing social categories, and the ways we implicate the social contexts of how, why, and what we come to know and the politics we pursue. There is no singular model of social justice (see Slee, 2001, 2011; Ainscow, Booth, & Dyson, 2006; Ainscow & Sandill, 2010; Ainscow & Miles, 2008). As others have argued, promoting a hegemonic understanding of social justice is counter-productive. In the literature, much of the critical discussions of social justice focus on three urgencies:

First, is the *economic distributive justice* argument that calls for sustained measures to address *exploitation* (i.e., the ongoing exploitation of the efforts, contributions, and benefits of people in the larger citizenry by either the state or powerful social forces); *deprivation* (i.e., the systemic denial of adequate standards of living for everyone in society); and *economic marginalization* (i.e., the continuing lack of access to education, employment, housing, health to all citizens, etc.).

Second, is the pursuit of cultural justice as a consequence of *cultural domination* where the cultural rights, political sovereignty, and human dignity of certain groups are devalued, dismissed or negated. This approach calls for respect, recognition, and acknowledgement of different racial, ethnic, linguistic, religious, and other cultural groups.

Third is *associational justice*, which addresses the representation and participation of all, and especially marginalized groups in the task of nation-building and/or national development (see Fraser, 1997; Gewirtz & Cribb, 2002; and Keddie, 2012; see also Deenmamode, 2016). Taking these approaches some questions are key:

(a) How does every living subject have access to the valued goods and services of society as a fundamental right and a responsibility?
(b) How do we define rights to include access to health, education, employment, and housing?
(c) How do we define rights as respect for fundamental individual freedoms and rights, acknowledgment of collective and group rights and matching social and collective responsibilities of the citizenry to community and nation-building?

These questions in particular demonstrate how citizenship and justice are intertwined. The regimes of citizenship we contend with today produce the categories of "subjects" and "citizens". While some can claim rights to citizenship, for many their claims to citizenship are continually denied and rendered suspect.

Scholars have observed that the process of citizenship is riddled with the notion of outsiders and insiders to the nation (Bannerji, 1997; Thobani, 2007). We have merely become "subjects to be governed", or as Foucault would say, "docile" subjects (Foucault, 2002). For us, our citizenship is always in question and our quest for access to the valued goods and services of society places us in compromising relations with the nation/colonial state. The colonial state makes it clear that some have the right to claim and benefit from citizenship and others do not. A corresponding failure to challenge or join Indigenous peoples' struggles for self-determination and land rights implicates us deeply in the ongoing colonial relations between the state and Indigenous peoples. Given that we continually find ourselves engaged in debates to extricate ourselves from the state-sanctioned violence on Indigenous communities, we must remember that part of the social justice political project is to recognize how the diffusion of power operates in variegated ways through bodies and systems.

Social justice is dealing with power and the asymmetrical power relations structured along the lines of race, gender, class, sexuality, [dis]ability, sexuality, religion, and language. How these identities are lived and/or experienced in our worlds today brings to the forefront questions of power, knowledge and definitions. Social justice work entails that we work out existing contestations and contentions around these sites of difference, acknowledging the differential relations of power and the inequities in the distribution of social services and valued goods of society. Social justice lies in sharing power, resources and knowledge so we can create healthy livable communities. Social justice is about meeting individual and collective responsibilities to ourselves, and to each other, and ensuring that every member of our communities is able to live out and actualize their dreams, hopes and aspirations to the fullest. We create communities by respecting, acknowledging and validating each other's presence, as well as our collective experiences and shared destinies. Social justice is also about holding people accountable for their actions and includes accounting for the state's responsibilities to a larger citizenry. Social justice is also about respecting the Land and the environments we share with others including other living beings and inanimate objects.

Within the context of occupying Indigenous Lands, social justice work entails acknowledging our relative responsibilities, and complicities in settler colonialism, and supporting Indigenous peoples and their struggles for self-determination and Indigenous resurgence. This is where, how, and why social justice work meets the requirements of decolonization. In effect, social justice work is about decolonization for both the colonizer/oppressor and the colonized/oppressed. Social justice work must acknowledge our relative, contingent and intertwined histories in ongoing colonization of Indigenous peoples. Social justice work is about decolonizing minds, bodies, souls, and practices. It is about social, psychic, cultural, spiritual and emotional transitioning. Decolonizing is an unsettling process and cannot be about seeking acceptance from mainstream dogma. When that happens our decolonization is compromised. Social justice as decolonization must be about new futurities and changing the current order of things. Social justice work as decolonization is understanding how globalization and imperial economic forces script human lives as well as understanding that the resistances requires both to challenge our colonial investments and also to posit new counter futures.

Social justice is also about addressing the political and economic questions that are on the effects of globalization and the effects on different segments of our communities (e.g., the poor, racial, ethnic, linguistic, sexual, and cultural minorities, and women). Social justice is promoting radical education as a core avenue for "global redistributive justice" (Mundy, 2008, p.2) and seeking new relations of futurity. The forces of globalization have exacerbated poverty, particularly, in the Global South in its myriad forms, such as its economic, material, social, psychological, and spiritual areas. Many local people lack access to basic health, employment, housing and education. The individualized notions of success and wealth (whether material or moral) has undermined a collective capacity to eradicate poverty and there are entrenched systems of power that perpetuate poverty within local communities and marginalized populations. Globalization has exported neoliberal economies of schooling with profound effects on questions of social equity. There is a definition of education, as a private investment requiring individuals to take on debt. (e.g., the ways rising tuition fees, student loans, and debt all create barriers to accessing education for marginalized communities effectively serving as gatekeepers). What is needed is social justice education from a decolonial and anticolonial perspective to re-visioning schooling and education.

The feminization and racialization of the labour force through Western capital have affected racialized and Indigenous populations in disproportionate numbers creating a burgeoning working-class poor in these communities. On the international scale, global capitalism and Western modernity have worked in tandem exploiting human labour creating servitude among local peoples through the use of child labour, forced labour, sweatshops, maquiladoras, and other such mass production spaces, debt bondage, or indentured servitude all in the service of capital and the Empire (Walia, 2013). Transnational corporations continue to maximize their profits by reducing costs through uncompensated labour, and low wages. These developments have raised critical social justice questions to occupy the attention of social scientists and academic researchers.

New Framings of Social Justice for Anti-Colonial Education

The particular understanding of social justice education I hope to advance is grounded in the conceptual framings of three (3) philosophical tenets:

First, is the idea of *"multicentricity"* (Dei, 1996), that is, creating spaces for multiple centres of knowledge to co-exist. It is working with an understanding of the multiple knowledge that offers differential readings of our world and social realities. There is no *one* hegemonic understanding of social justice. The idea of multicentric knowledge means that we encourage multiple understandings to be brought to the table in order to achieve social transformation. Multiple knowledge and social realities gesture to the possibilities of how multiple readings of the world can allow us to think through and reflect on our social realities and posit a new future. This stance allows the different knowledge to contest each other in order to arrive at a more comprehensive understanding of our world.

An important reading of social justice affirms the saliency and centrality of race and by extension the pursuit of anti-racism. Race makes racism real. The two (race and racism) are in an uncomfortable tango. We cannot have one without the other. This assertion does not mean all social justice work is about race and racism. But we must be bold to name race and racism in our social justice work because of the discomfort and/or unspeakability of race. Any social justice work that fails to specifically name race, or intersections with race and other forms of difference (class, gender, sexuality, [dis]ability, language and religion), is a limitation. Race is everywhere and we cannot hide away from it. The way Euro-American society was founded all but guarantees that race will always be at the centre of identity no matter how one defines it. In such reading, I acknowledge the power of Whiteness and White identity and the consequences of dominant conceptions of Black and Blackness (see Dei 2017a).

Just as I articulate multiple models of anti-racism, I also would highlight anti-Black racism as an important dimension of anti-racism. Though distinct, the two share some common threads. Anti-Black racism is a particular negative reading, [re]action, and concrete response to Blackness. Such reading, practice and response are framed by a racist thought. Simply, it is racism directed at Black/African peoples for our alleged sub-humanity and our supposed roots to a dark, uncivilized, deviant, and criminal world (see also Benjamin, 2003). Anti-Black racism points to the permanence of skin colour as a marker for differentiation. It also alludes to an important truth about Blackness, that it is consequential (e.g., punishable and is seen as transgressive). The prevalence of a "Black-White prism/paradigm" as in the way a closer proximity to Whiteness is rewarded in society, also highlights the significance of anti-Black racism, and the unique status of anti-Black racism in anti-racist struggles.

The second philosophical tenet is the relevance of the "epistemic saliency" of the oppressed voice (see Dei, 1999). There is the power of subjective knowing of the oppressed to understand their own oppression. This knowing subverts traditional, worn-out critiques of "authenticity" which is often read as a search for purity, non-contamination, and single truths. Epistemic saliency of the oppressed voice, colonized, and racialized body, however, gestures to the fact that for far too long the dominant claims to know and understand the oppressed better than the oppressed subject themselves. When dominant voices declare they have this knowledge, their voice operates with privilege, furthering discursive authority in the native discourses of social oppression. If we are to understand oppression, epistemic saliency then highlights the importance of the oppressed voice (not as the only truth). We cannot claim to fight social oppression and injustice when the voice of the oppressed and colonized are missing. There is a recognition of the connection between knowledge and identity. The body is a site of knowing. For example, inhibiting a Black body in a white supremacist context is not just a claim of knowledge. It is also about the urgency of using the "epistemic saliency" of that body to refute dominant claims to know about my/our [racialized/colonized/Indigenous] lived experiences. This is not a claim to privilege the knowledge of the Black/colonized/racialized/Indigenous body. Through the epistemic saliency of the colonized/oppressed voice, the minoritized come to voice. As noted earlier, the body as a site of knowing and knowledge is continually contested. I highlight again the importance of embracing such contestation to raise new questions for us to ponder over in doing social justice work. There are many gaps in social justice discussions and as it was earlier stated we must acknowledge these gaps and even appreciate them in terms of the limitations of our own knowledge.

Third, is the urgency for a reframed "radical inclusion" (Dei, 2008). Radical inclusion centres power and sees social transformation as a bottom-up change. Radical inclusion is about rethinking inclusion as beginning anew, rather than simply adding to what already exists. How is it that many still hope to accomplish change by adding to what already exists, when what readily exists is the source of the problem in the first place? Radical inclusion challenges the depoliticization of difference since that difference is about power, change, and voice. We need to work with radical inclusion given that the liberal take on inclusion has merely been seductive, and multicultural in its outlook and has failed to place power, knowledge, identity, and representation at the center of discussions. Radical inclusion challenges sameness, homogeneity, and uniformity as problematic and aims to subvert the status quo. Radical inclusion does not seek inclusion on the terms of the dominant, but rather on the terms of those who have been excluded, marginalized, and devalued. It is in such marginal and marginalized voices, that the possibilities of counter-readings of the world emerge.

These three (3) conceptual frameworks are useful for critical anti-colonial praxis to achieve social justice ends. They help bring new questions to the forefront: for example, what is the role and place of Indigenous epistemology in the pursuit of socially transformative education; and, what are the possibilities of a new educational futurity when we engage Indigenous cultural knowledges? Indigenous philosophies help us to destabilize and subvert what is deemed conventional, normal, or everyday acceptable knowledge. Such knowledge is usually the knowledge of the dominant. These knowledges must be subverted for their inadequacies to offer a more complete account of our complex world. Indigenous philosophies can also be engaged as decolonial thinking with possibilities of decolonization for different bodies, histories, and experiences.

In situating Indigenous philosophies in social justice discourse, I affirm the relevance of spirituality, spiritual ontologies, and epistemologies (see Palmer, 1999; Miller, 1994). Equity flows from spirituality. Spiritual ontologies and epistemologies shape our thinking processes, implicate our embodiments and assist us in making social connections with each other. Indigenous spirituality makes claims about wholeness, relations, interdependence, love and compassion for humanity, as well as connections of the physical, spiritual and metaphysical realms of human existence (Cajete, 1994, 2000; Dilliard 2008). Spirituality makes us human. For oppressed bodies spirituality helps us to [re]claim our humanity that has been destroyed by colonialism and colonial dominance. Articulating Indigenous spirituality as anti-colonial knowing is creating epistemological and pedagogical spaces to interrupt conventional knowledge. Indigenous spirituality allows marginalized, colonized, and oppressed groups to center our worldviews in the understanding of social realities, and provide alternatives/counter perspectives to dominant knowledges, experiences, and colonial narratives as a way of decolonization (Postlethwaite, 2016; Shahjahan, 2009; Cajete, 1994). The educational site [like other institutional settings] can be a hostile, unfamiliar place – dismemberment, depersonalization, and the seduction to be "intellectual imposters", learners who are not true to their own authentic selves. Through our spiritualities, learners can develop a critical consciousness that allows us to center social justice, equity, power, and justice at the heart of our education (Shields, 2005; Postlethwaite, 2016; Wane 2002).

Africentric Schooling As Social Justice Education

Social justice education is ensuring that all learners are able to actualize their dreams. A major social justice question is regarding the differential educational outcomes for the diverse bodies in our school systems. Concerns around lack of curricular sophistication, differential [negative] treatment by race, gender, class, sexuality, dis/ability coupled with the absence of a diverse physical representation of faculty and staff have affected the ability of all learners to develop a sense of connectedness and identification to their schools. In what follows, I reiterate some of the long-standing arguments for re-visioning education for Black/African, racialized, and Indigenous youth. All youth are entitled to education as both a right and privilege. Such rights have corresponding responsibilities. Any education that fails to connect these dots is NOT social justice education.

I argue that insisting on schooling as a site of possibilities for a new future is to work with key principles of Afrocentric social thought as a form of decolonizing education. Proponents of Afrocentricity see it as a "grounding, orientation and perspective" (McDougal, 2011 cited in Pratt-Clarke, 2014, p. 220). Specifically, Molefi Asante describes Afrocentricty as a "mode of thought and action in which the centrality of African interests, values and perspectives predominate" (Pellebon, 2007, p. 171 cited in Pratt-Clarke, 2014, p. 220). Afrocentricity works with an "ideology rooted in African cultural values" including spiritual ontologies that highlight connections between the physical and metaphysical, the nexus of body, mind, soul, and spirit, as well as the interface of society, culture and Nature (see also Pratt-Clarke, 2014, p. 220). The Afrocentric perspective is about resistance to White supremacy or racial domination. Afrocentricity combines theory with practice for educational transformation. As an African-centred knowledge, it sees the education of Black/African youth as about drastically changing the colonial and re-colonial foundations of education and beginning to re-imagine schooling and education differently. It is about subverting current processes of validation evoked through the prism of Eurocentric standards of what constitutes scholarship and how such knowledge should be produced, interrogated, and disseminated internally and globally. African-centred education is also more than the search and use of African peoples' "interpretative virtues and analytical insights" to understand African experiences (Chabal, 1996; p. 50). Ultimately, it is about utilizing knowledge to rejuvenate our historical and spiritual selves.

Such education seeks to cultivate a sense of responsibility, community belonging, sharing and reciprocity, and mutual interdependence for young learners. In Canadian educational contexts, a main push for counter visions of schooling for racialized bodies emerges from the differential educational outcomes for youth and the dropout/push-out rates which are known to be disproportionately high for Black/African, Indigenous, and other marginalized communities. Identity, as already noted, is linked to schooling, education, and knowledge production. Education must help learners to develop a sense of identity which is crucial to self, group, and collective development. Education must empower learners in their histories and cultural knowledge in critical ways to learn from lessons of the past and use knowledge to reflect on the present and to project into the future. Learners should be equipped with the tools to fight for justice, fairness, and equity and to resist all forms of oppression. Teaching about race, gender, class, sexuality, dis/ability is part of a critical approach to anti-colonial and decolonial education.

In 2008, the Toronto District School Board (TDSB) board of trustees voted in favour of having an Afrocentric pilot school, the first of such state-funded (whether municipal, provincial, or state level) kind in Canada. The school opened in September, 2009 at the Sheppard Public School in Toronto to cater for junior Kindergarten to grade 6. In 2013, a second Africentric school was opened at Winston Churchill Secondary School in Scarborough. Unfortunately, since their establishment, these schools have been mired in controversies. These largely stem from stakeholder misunderstandings and systemic neglect. In the case of the 2009 school, the early years saw students performing well above the provincial average in academic EQAO test scores. In recent years the school's success has been impacted negatively by leadership challenges, frequent turnover of school principals, and tensions between the School Council and the school administration. It is no secret that the school has been under-resourced which lead to charges from the Black/African Canadian community that stated the school was deliberately set up to fail. At times the basic principles of Africentric education have been misunderstood or deliberately misrepresented serving to maintain the status quo of Eurocentric approaches to education. Africentric education is not the opposite of Eurocentric schooling. It is simply one of the many counter visions of education that aim to challenge the limited approaches of Eurocentric schooling which negatively impact educational transformation. Suffice it to say, the ideals informing the Africentric schools are what move us to confront questions of social justice in education as far as Black/African, Indigenous and racially minoritized communities are concerned.

In a few public speaking engagements and, perhaps, writings I have alluded to the words of Canadian legal expert, Sonia Lawrence (2009) who made some astute observations about the features of Africentric school. Her words are important and certainly worth repeating:

> First, it's [Africentric school] small scale: That is, it does not set up a broad model of segregation. Second, that it creates an optional model: that is, students are not required to attend the Afrocentric school as opposed to what I will label the "ordinary" curriculum. Third, entry to the school isn't based on race. In fact, the school is open to all students. The Afrocentric nature of the school is curricular. Arguably, restrictions based on race would be a legal problem, although it's not particularly easy to articulate, doctrinally, exactly what the problem would be. The fourth important feature of the Afrocentric school model is that it is intended as an "ameliorative" program: Under section 15(2), the Canadian charter explicitly preserves the ability of government to act in a way that attempts to further equality by recognizing difference. In other words, the Canadian charter explicitly ensures that affirmative action type programs won't be tarred with the brush of discrimination. There is clear statistical evidence about the way that ordinary schools fail Black students. Streaming,

completion rates, and test scores, all indicate that a significant proportion of Black students are not faring well in mainstream schools. Experimental methods for nurturing and appropriately educating these students are warranted under these circumstances. The Canadian charter explicitly recognizes that taking account of race is required if we are to address inequality.

Lawrence's observations above were overlooked by the media in favour of sensationalizing race politics. With the support of Lawrence and other intellectuals, the justification for the Africentric school is not a far-fetched idea. The initiation of the school is a response to the long history of demonstrated educational failure for certain segments of our community. Despite some educational successes, the fact remains that schools are failing a number of Black, racialized, and Indigenous youth. Those who even succeed, do so at a cost to their own identity, and the affirmation of their culture, history, heritage, and communal knowledges. The mainstream school system cannot provide all the answers. Educational inclusion is not, as stated earlier, simply "adding to what already exists" given that what already exists is the source of the problem in the first place. Integration by itself is not a guarantor of educational success. In the face of educational failures notwithstanding social integration in schools, some radical thoughts for counter-visioning schooling and education for our youth must be entertained. Integration may be good but we must ask at what cost? What do Black/African-Canadian parents have to show for their children's education despite all these years favouring social integration? What is deemed "democratic education" in the face of unequal access to the valuable goods and services of society? What are the prevailing discursive regimes of citizenship in Canadian contexts? In contexts where Black/African citizenship is always in question, what do we really mean when we speak of Canadian citizenship? What is our understanding of Canadian citizenship on stolen Indigenous peoples' Lands (see also Thobani, 2007)? And, what are our radical "politics of recognition" that may be pursued more as an anti-colonial recognition and a direct response to the structural, economic and psyche realms of our collective domination, oppression and resistance (see also Coulthard, 2014)?

The justification of Africentric schooling helps uncover these hidden aspects of our communities and calls on us to act for true education and social justice. Counter-visioning schooling and education through a social justice model recognizes the severity of issues and impacts for and on certain bodies. Such understanding is critical to achieving genuine educational transformation. This model of social justice insists there can be multiple approaches to educational justice, and that one approach can target groups historically disadvantaged by a system. If this approach is supported and successful, there will be lessons transferred into mainstream schools to serve the needs of all students. The thought that social justice is treating everybody the same, while it may sound ideal, can be limiting in the face of the already existing glaring inequities. These inequities point to the fact that not all learners operate from a level playing field.

There are lessons of the African-centered perspective relevant to the pursuit of African philosophies of education to assist the education of Black/African and other learners. This worldview as a system of thought is shaped by the lens of Africology that stresses the centrality of African culture, agency, history, identity, and experience. The African-centered paradigm offers an intellectual space for African peoples to interpret our experiences on our own terms, using culturally steeped worldviews and culturally contextualized understandings rather than being forced through a Eurocentric lens (see Asante, 1991; Karanja, 2014; Mazama, 2001; Ziegler, 1996; Van Dyk, 1996). A culturally grounded perspective that centers African/Indigenous peoples' worldviews helps resist the dominance of a Eurocentric perspective. Consequently, African-centered education stresses the notion of culture, grounding learners' histories, identities, and experiences, while focusing on the learner's agency to bring about change in personal and community lives. Culture is critical to knowledge production. In fact, cultural paradigms shape knowledge production. By working with the notion of "centeredness" of the learner, the student is best able to engage knowledge as meaningful to their experiences and histories. In promoting the agency of marginalized, colonized, and Indigenous peoples using local cultural knowledge systems the African Indigenous learners become subjects of their own histories, stories and experiences.

An Africentric school curriculum links bodies (learners) and the understanding of identity (as political) to help to promote pedagogical and instructional practices that are able to transform schools and the education system to ensure effective educational outcomes for all learners. Africentric schooling works with a broad definition of success as both academic and social. Success is not just students doing well on academic test scores, but also, how their success translates to the service of their communities. It is important that families, communities, and nations that have contributed to an individual's educational success also become beneficiaries of their education. Africentric teachings instill this sense of collective responsibility in young learners. Africentric schooling insists upon placing the education of learners, foremost, at the service of our communities. Thus, promoting community services is a big part of Africentric schooling and education.

Parents and local communities have a vital role in Africentric schooling which helps to provide leadership and a vision that ensures sustained community support for the official administration of the school. Parents are an important decision-making group of the school. They show their commitment by helping to provide some of the logistical and material support and requirements for the school. Parents have a role in major decision-making processes that affect the welfare of the school such as staff appointment, curriculum development and review, infrastructural development, as well as the development of the school's moral code of conduct. Parents' role is not simply advisory to the school leadership but is in fact *central* to the school's administration. In conventional schooling, when parental roles and responsibilities are addressed they are seen as largely advisory and in a few cases a select group of parents, usually the most wealthy and powerful, wield real power in schools. Africentric schools break down this barrier ensuring that fairness and justice concerns are paramount in letting local communities and parents have a seat in school governance. Providing such key roles for parents and community in the education of Black learners responds to the challenge of social justice education. Parents work with school leadership to re/articulate a clear, unambiguous vision for the school, cultivating decisive, visionary, and shared leadership for the school. This approach to Africentric schooling helps break down hierarchies in school administrative leadership structures creating a sense of collective ownership and shared destinies for the school. School leadership, as Africentric leadership, is based on Indigenous and African-centered principles of mutual interdependence, connections, relationality, and shared responsibilities. Parents and local community members are expected to collectively think through the varied opportunities and possibilities [not the challenge] of resourcing an Africentric school.

Bringing a radical race, anti-racist lens/perspective and a pro-Black/African philosophy to the Africentric school, in terms of curriculum, pedagogy, instruction, and the socio-organizational life of the school is significant. This is a social justice approach to Africentric schooling which gives the significance of race in the schooling of Black/African and Indigenous bodies. Africentric school places race and schooling at the table for discussion creating the space for students to acknowledge and discuss their identities (race, class, gender, sexuality [dis]ability and how they imbricate and impact schooling for contemporary youth. A critical anti-racist and pro-Black perspective means a decolonial/anti-colonial approach to the education of Black/African, as well as other racial minority and Indigenous youth. Students are taught to know who they are and to claim their Black/African identities as resistance, decolonization, and transformation. Such identities are political and knowing one's Africanness even in diasporic contexts can be empowering to Canadian youth of African descent. The Africentric school connects issues of race and Indigeneity, recognizing the Land as an important site of teaching and learning to appreciate the wealth of knowledge that Mother Earth offers. Such knowledge includes reverence and respect, sharing and reciprocity, love and appreciation, justice and fairness.

The Africentric school promotes a form of radical decoloniality by acknowledging race and other forms of learners' identities and how they connect to knowledge, stories and struggles of resistance. Such stories can be counter-narratives that challenge colonial metanarratives that affirm White dominance, unearned privileges and state-sanctioned violence against Indigenous and other colonized communities. Critical teachings about history and colonialism can help promote anti-colonial resistance to state-sanctioned violence. Africentric school is anti-colonial, decolonial, and anti-racist. It is education pursued as liberation.

Concluding Thoughts

I conclude this chapter with more questions: What does it mean to call social justice in education today? Why do we need such education? What is the language required for pursuing critical social justice work? As argued, schooling and education for social justice work is about presenting education that allows all learners to actualize their dreams, hopes, and aspirations. It is truly liberating education that does not disenfranchise the learner. It is education that allows students to handle tough questions of power, equity, and social difference. The search for a new educational futurity very responsive to the needs of contemporary society demands that we pursue education as nothing but anti-racist, anti-sexist, anti-classist, anti-homophobic, and anti-ableist. This is crucial today given the increasing diversity and difference within our communities and what this means in terms of power-sharing. We need such education for the main reason that education while serving as a tool for liberation, can also be a tool for domination and control. While education holds possibilities for social mobility for some, education has not advanced the welfare of all learners. Some learners and their cultures, knowledges, experiences, and histories have been marginalized in the school curriculum.

Similarly, the poetics of social justice education highlight some basic realities: First, the question of difference is nothing new. Social difference has always been part of the identity of our communities. Acknowledging and responding concretely to differences is a question of power. In social justice work, we must speak of difference not only as a fixation on Otherness or a "fixity to Otherness" (Keesing, 1989, p. 37). Differences must be spoken of in multiple, complex ways and understood and treated as a benefit to society. The colonial difference was and has always been about hierarchy, exoticization and inferiorization. Anti-colonial read of difference is about the strength and contributions of our diversity and multiple subjectivities of race, gender, class, sexual, [dis]abled identities. But, as we affirm such readings, we must also be mindful of the post-colonial and postmodern intellectual fancy footing about "irreducible multiplicity", and not leave unchallenged the arguments for "anti-essentialism" (see Howes 1996, pp. 156–157).

Second, is an ongoing quest for a just society where power is utilized to serve the needs of all. To ensure this social justice workers must be courageous to speak and fight injustice of all kinds. We must develop the language skills to name racism, sexism, homophobia, transphobia, classism, linguicism, and other oppressions. It also requires that we develop the language of interstices of differences whereby speaking race means speaking class, gender, sexuality, [dis]ability and vice versa. The language of intersections recognizes how oppressions are intertwined. Still, such language can have an entry point from which we address multiple oppressions. In my work, I have always advanced the saliency of race as an important entry point for social justice education. It is an important and deliberate tactic to highlight race because race is so unspeakable. Race easily becomes the disappearing act when we speak of intersections. We fail to name race and instead push it to the background.

Third, is the affirmation of the intellectual agency of racialized and Indigenous peoples to articulate their own lived realities, experiences, and concerns. We have our own understanding of the problems confronting our communities and what ought to be done about them. And, we cannot interpret them through Eurocentric conceptual frames of thought and Euro-colonial and racist conjectures of modernity. The claim to our intelligence is for us, as marginalized, colonized, racialized, and Indigenous bodies, to resist the persistent spurious claims to expertise and knowledge of our lives, histories and experiences by the dominant. We tell our own stories about social justice and not necessarily using narratives intelligible to the dominant. We must expand upon the languages, categories and technologies for understanding claims of social oppressions. We cannot be forced to narrate all experiences of social oppressions into the "parameters of acceptability" established by the so-called modernity and modern knowledge (see also Andreotti, Ahenakew and Cooper, 2011). For far too long, the racially oppressed have been asked to justify our claims of racism and oppression. If we cannot prove the claims and assertions we make, these are easily dismissed. Racism is not an objective science and the power of subjective knowing is equally important in working with the claims of the oppressed.

Fourth, the spiritual is a core axis of articulating an Indigenous theory/discursive framework for social justice. We do not often get to speak of the "spiritual" as part of our identities and what it means to pursue social justice work. But equity and social justice workflows from spirituality. It is work that engages the trialectic of the body, mind, soul, and spirit. This trialectic propels many of us to work for change (see Dei 2012). We cannot de-spiritualize our existence, our communities and our educational sites. The Eurocentric negation of the "spirit/spiritual" as a legitimate site of knowing is highly problematic. When we affirm the spiritual, what we do is acknowledge the power of "sacred knowledges" and the sanctity of what we do as social justice workers. The delegitimation of the spiritual through a process of denial, the commodification of life, and the disregard for the teachings of such knowledges of the metaphysical realms of social existence can only be deemed part of the ongoing colonizing practices of modernity.

Lastly, social justice work is not just about the process; it is also about expressions, symbols, and significations, as well as the pursuit of material and concrete activities and actions. Acknowledging the concrete materiality of social justice work does not mean social justice is a thing, an essence, or even a mere possession. It is about what we do to make us human [again]. This is where we relate social justice work to a new humanism that acknowledges what we share together as a people, community or a collective, what it takes to build new futures, and what it means to account for the differences that make us what we are as a people. In a forthcoming publication (Dei, 2017b), I have argued that what we term the human, is situated in a dominant Eurocentric notion, with its inherent limitations of Western humanism. We need contemporary schooling and education to engender a "community of learners" who pursue critical thinking, possess relevant knowledge to function in a global world, and is also able to "resist complacency, questions power, domination, oppression, injustice". A new educational futurity may help us answer with a resounding "NO" to the question anti-colonial theorist Aime Cesaire (1972) posed: why was colonization and imperial conquest deemed the only viable option by the colonizer? (p. 2). Racism and colonialism are the fundamental roots of social injustice and oppressions. These are problems Black/African, Indigenous and other racially minoritized groups did not create, to begin with. And yet we should be concerned because we have since become implicated and perhaps made complicit.

The current and future of the social justice landscape in respect to the next generation of social justice leaders, students and researchers, and I believe the next generation of scholars of Black studies will make what is complex more streamlined. For example, utilizing the universal language of Hip Hop culture as seen in Rhymes to Re-Education: A Hip-Hop Curriculum, (San Vicente, 2014) although rooted in the Black experience, it unifies people of struggle around the world. I also believe the future practitioners of social justice will be creating what KRS-ONE popularized through the song Edutainment (Parker, 1990) where education meets entertainment to reach and motivate their peers by creating edutainment in forms such as video blogs (vlogs), digital storytelling, film or other story-telling platforms via social media. As new media emerge, new questions and possibilities for social justice work will unfold.

To close, I would like to revisit a memory and share a story that gives me hope for the future of social justice work in the academy. I recall being a newly hired, tenure-track Black/African-Canadian male faculty in my department in July 1991 and students in the department were instrumental in securing my position. At the time, the department's governance structure included students in the faculty hiring process in such a way that their voices really counted. We worked together with students and other colleagues as an epistemic community, and we pushed anti-racist, social justice and equity scholarship despite institutional resistance. Some in-roads have been made and yet there is more work to be done. Our persistence and insistence offer useful lessons not to forget past work and sacrifices. There are lessons also for us to be mindful that there can be the "sensation of moving while standing still". An important challenge is to be able to sustain progressive efforts, learn from our limitations and failings, and work to continue the struggle. We cannot afford to be perpetual cynics and skeptics. That in itself is defeatist.

This is a time to write about social justice! A time when the sole global superpower is redefining its obligations to a world when its leader is filled with a ultra-right-wing racist ideology to pursue an isolationist agenda, cloaked in national security rhetoric. Racist populism disguised as heightened nationalism is intended, shamefully, to protect White privilege, power, and supremacy. For me, this is not a time for fancy intellectualism to debate the merits of social justice and whether or not social justice is even a meaningful term for us to work with. This is a time for speaking up, dissenting, and questioning hegemonic power structures that continue to animate through everyday acts of colonialism. One fact is clear; one model of social justice is not enough. We need to address social justice as a community with clear objectives that the goal is not to achieve an unrealistic ideal, but to work with existing realities and remake, reimagine, and re-envision the future.

References Cited:

Ainscow, M., & Miles, S. (2008). Making education for all inclusive: Where next? *Prospects*, 38, 15–34. doi: 10.1007/s11125-008-9055-0

Ainscow, M., & Sandill, A. (2010). Developing inclusive education systems: The role of organizational cultures and leadership. *International Journal of Inclusive Education*, 14(4), 401–416. doi: 10.1080/13603110802504903

Ainscow, M., Booth, T., & Dyson, A. (2006). *Improving schools, developing inclusion*. New York: Routledge.

Andreotti, V., Ahenakew, C., & Cooper, G. (2011). Epistemological pluralism: Ethical and pedagogical challenges in higher education. *AlterNative: An International Journal of Indigenous Peoples*, 7(1), 40 -50. https://doi.org/10.1177/117718011100700104.

Asante, M. (1991). "The Afrocentric idea in education". *Journal of Negro Education*, 60(2), 170–180.

Bannerji, H. (1997). "Geography lessons: On being and insider/outsider to the Canadian Nation." In L. Roman & L. Eyre (Eds.), *Dangerous territories: Struggles for difference and equality*. New York: Routledge, pp. 23–41.

Battiste, M., & James (Sa'ke'j) Youngblood Henderson. (2000). *Protecting Indigenous knowledge and heritage: A global challenge*. Saskatoon: Purich Publishing.

Cajete, G. (1994). *Look to the mountain: An ecology of Indigenous education*. Durango, CO: Kivaki Press.

Cajete, G. (2000). Indigenous knowledge: The Pueblo metaphor of Indigenous education. In M. Battiste (Ed.), *Reclaiming Indigenous voice and vision*. Vancouver, Toronto: UBC Press.

Cesaire, A. (1972). *Discourse on colonialism*. New York: Monthly Review Press.

Chabal, P. (1996). "The African crisis: Context and interpretation". In. R. Werbner & T. Ranger (Eds.), *Postcolonial identities in Africa*. London: Zed Books., pp. 29–54.

Coulthard, Glen Sean. (2014). *Red skin, white masks: Rejecting the colonial politics of recognition*.

Deenmamode, Lily-Claire Virginie. (2016). *Perceptions and practices of an inclusive education for social justice: The case of ZEP Schools of Mauritius*. Unpublished PhD dissertation, Australian Catholic University, North Sydney, New South Wales.

Dei, G, J. S. (1996). *Anti-racism education: Theory and practice*. Halifax, Nova Scotia: Fernwood Publishing.

Dei, G. J. S. (1999). "Knowledge and politics of social change: The implication of anti-Racism." *British Journal of Sociology of Education*, 20(3), 395–409.

Dei, G. J. S. (2002). Learning culture, spirituality and local knowledge: Implications for African schooling. *International Review of Education*, 48(5), 335–360.

Dei, G. J. S. (2008). *Racists beware: Uncovering racial politics in contemporary society*. Rotterdam: Sense Publishers.

Dei, G. J. S. (2010). "Fanon and anti-colonial theorizing". In G. J. S. Dei (Ed.), *Fanon and the counter-insurgency of education* (pp. 11–28). Rotterdam: Sense Publishers.

Dei, G. J. S. (2012). "Suahunu: The Trialectic space". *Journal of Black Studies*, 43(8), 823–846.

Dei, G. J. S. (2017a). *[Re]Theorising Blackness, anti-Blackness and Black Solidarities through anti-Colonial and decolonial prisms*. New York: Springer.

Dei, G. J. S. (2017b). "Reframing education through Indigenous, anti-Colonial and decolonial prisms". *The Radical Imagine-Nation*. Volume 2 [edited by In. Peter McLaren and Suzanne Soohoo].

Dilliard, C. (2008). "When the ground is black, the ground is fertile: Exploring endarkened feminist epistemology and healing methodologies of the spirit". In. N. Denzin, Y. Lincoln, & L. T. Smith (Eds.), *Handbook of critical and Indigenous methodologies* (pp. 277–292). Los Angeles: Sage Publications.

Foucault, M. (2002). "The subject and power." In *Essential works of Foucault power*. Ed. James D. Faubion. Trans. Robert Hurley et al., vol. 3. London: Penguin, pp. 326–348.

Fraser, N. (1997). *Justice interruptus: Critical reflections on the postsocialist condition*. New York: Routledge.

Fraser, N., & Honneth, A. (2003). *Redistribution or recognition? A political-philosophical exchange*. London: Verso, 2003.

Gewirtz, S., & Cribb, A. (2002). "Plural conceptions of social justice: Implications for policy sociology". *Journal of Educational Policy*, 17(5), 499–509. doi: 10.1080/02680930210158285

Griffith, R., Vidotto, D., (2019). New Approaches to Inclusivity: Race, Power, and Privilege in Ontario Schools, In R. Hughes & K. Cooper (Eds.), *Critical Issues In Education: Citizen Documentary in the Digital Age*. Life Rattle Press.

Howes, D. (1996). "Cultural appropriation and resistance in the American Southwest: Decommodifying Indianness". In D. Howes (Ed.), *Cross-Cultural consumption: Global markets local realities* (pp. 138–160). London and New York: Routledge.

Karanja Keita Carroll. (2014). An introduction to African-Centered Sociology: Worldview, epistemology, and social theory. *Critical Sociology*, 40(2), 257–270.

Keddie, A. (2012). *Educating for diversity and social justice*. New York: Routledge.

Keesing, R. M. (1989). "Creating the past: Custom and identity in the contemporary Pacific." *Contemporary Pacific*, 1(1/2), 19–42.

Larbalestier, Jan. (1990). "The politics of representation: Australian aboriginal women and feminism." *Anthropological Forum*, 6, 143–157.

Lawrence, S. (2009). "Afrocentric Schools and the legal framework of educational equality" remarks on the Panel: *Rethinking "Separate But Equal": A Discussion of Equality and Afrocentric Schools.*" Faculty of Law, University of Toronto, Faculty of Law, March 10.

Harris, C. (1995). "Whiteness as property". In Crenshaw, Gotanda, Peller, & Thomas (Eds.), *Critical race theory: The key writings that formed the movement* (pp. 276–291). New York: The New Press.

Mazama, A. (2001). "The Afrocentric paradigm: Contours and definitions." *Journal of Black Studies*, 31(4), 387–405.

McDougal, S. III. (2011). "The future of research methods in Africana Studies Graduate Curriculum". *Journal of African American Studies*, 72(5), 725–749.

Miller, J. P. (1994). Contemplative practice in higher education: An experiment in teacher development. *Journal of Humanistic Psychology*, 34(4), 53–69.

Mudimbe, V. Y. (1988). *The invention of Africa: Gnosis, philosophy, and the order of knowledge.* Bloomington: Indiana University Press.

Mundy, K. (2008). "Global politics and local realities in the realization of the universal right to education". In. S. Moor & R. Mitchell (Eds.), *Power, pedagogy and praxis: Social justice in the globalized classroom*. Routledge Adult and Professional Education Series. Routledge.

Nussbaum, M. C. (2007). Cultivating humanity and world citizenship. *Forum Futures*, 2007, 37–40.

Palmer, P. (1999). The grace of great things: Reclaiming the sacred in knowing, teaching, and learning. In S. Glazer (Ed.), *The heart of learning: Spirituality in education*. New York, NY: Jeremy P. Tarcher/Putnam.

Parker, C. (1990). Edutainment [Recorded by C. Parker]. New York City, United States of America.

Postlethwaite, M. (2016). "*Wairua* spirituality and motivation: The connection between *Wairua* and motivation for Maori Academics with Doctorates", Unpublished PhD, Dissertation, School of Indigenous Graduate Studies, Te Whare Wānanga ō Awanuiārangi. New Zealand.

Prah, K. (1997). "Accusing the victims – In my Father's House" A review of Kwame Anthony Appiah,s 'In My Father's House'. *CODESRIA Bulletin*, 1, 14–22.

Pratt-Clarke, Menah. (2014) "Building a Foundation for Africana Sociology: Black sociology, Afrocentricity, and transdisciplinary applied social justice". *Critical Sociology*, 40(2), 217–227.

Pellerbon, D. (2007). "An analysis of Afrocentricity as theory for social work practice". *Advances in Social Work*, 8(1), 169–183.

San Vicente, R. (2014). *Rhymes to Re-Education: A Hip-Hop curriculum: Resource guide for educators with social justice activities.* Toronto: A Different Publisher.

Semali, L. M., & Kincheloe, J. (1999). (Eds.). "Introduction: What is Indigenous knowledge and why should we study it? In *What is Indigenous knowledge? Voices from the Academy.* New York: Falmer Press, pp. 3–57.

Shahjahan, R. (2009). The role of spirituality in the anti-oppressive higher- education classroom. *Teaching in Higher Education, 14*(2), 121–131.

Shields, C. M. (2005). Liberating discourses: Spirituality and educational leadership. *Journal of School Leadership, 15,* 608–623.

Simpson, A. (2014). *Mohawk interruptus: Political life across the borders of settler states.* Durham: Duke University Press.

Slee, R. (2001). Social justice and the changing directions in educational research: The case of inclusive education. *International Journal of Inclusive Education, 5*(2–3), 167–177. doi: 10.1080/13603110010035832

Slee, R. (2011). *The irregular school: Exclusion, schooling and inclusive education.* New York: Routledge.

Thobani, S. (2007). *Exalted subjects: Studies in the making of race and nation in Canada.* Toronto: University of Toronto Press.

Van Dyk, S. (1996). "Toward an Afrocentric perspective: The significance of Afrocentricity." In D. Ziegler (Ed.), *Molefi Kete Asante and Afrocentricity* (pp. 1–10). Nasville, TN: James Winston.

Walia, H. (2013). *Undoing border imperialism.* Oakland: AK Press.

Wane, N. (2002). African women and spirituality: Connections between thought and action. In E. O'Sullivan, A. Morrell, & M. A. O'Connor (Eds.), *Expanding the boundaries of transformative learning: Essays on theory and praxis* (pp. 135–150).

Ziegler, D. (Ed.). (1996). *Molefi Kete Asante and Afrocentricity.* Nasville, TN: James Winston.

· 7 ·

TEACHING AFRICAN HISTORY TO FIGHT ANTI-BLACK RACISM

In coming to write this chapter I was deeply influenced by the way we have come to talk, valorize, and even defend history. We bring different perspectives to understanding history, depending on our positions of power. It is very interesting that as a society we seem to have difficulty speaking about reparations for the wrongs of history. And yet, many of us have no qualms about defending public statues and monuments of slave owners. The recent tensions over the removal of Confederate statues in the US are a case in point. I have often wondered about the visual landscape of our society (see Dei & Lara-Villanueva, 2022). We celebrate the powerful but not the powerless. In schools, we have portraits of dead, White, male leaders as making contributions worthy of remembrance. In these portraits very seldom do we see women and also Black, Indigenous, and racialized bodies. I have often wondered about the service workers, the janitors, and the cleaners, who always worked to make the school what it is. Did not these workers also make contributions to ensure the school/institution is what it is? Today, we call them essential workers. I also reflect on how African and Indigenous peoples' artifacts have arrived in our colonial museums in the West, and possibly, what it will take to return them to their rightful owners. And, by the way, if we are debating about naming streets for our heroes and heroines, and erecting statues/monuments in their honour, have we first asked the Indigenous peoples on whose Lands we sit?

Colonization and slavery are more than belief systems. They have been, and still constitute practices regulating human life and society. As I have argued in the preceding chapters, we cannot talk about colonization and slavery outside of anti-Black racism as institutionalized systemic violence on bodies and our histories. We need to be critical of the dominant historical narrative. One powerful story of African history is that there was a world before European colonialism. In other words, Euro-colonialism is only a part of world history to be told. We need critical conversations to reclaim our stories and ways of knowing outside the normalized Eurocentric lens. We must find and use African history to dismantle barriers to advancement for Black people and communities in education, employment, housing, rights, and income.

History must be thought of in the plural, histories. For Black and African peoples, history has created so many inequities that continue to impact our communities. The special organization of our communities have all been impacted by history. History is like a structure and a system that impacts us all deeply. Every question about contemporary society must be grounded in history. As the creator of the #BlackLivesMatter hashtag, Patrice Cullors' has opined, "if we sort of rewind time, what resources did they have in the neighbourhood? Do they have access to after-school programming? Do they have access to career development? I'm talking about really basic things that can lead to different life choices for Black people, that can lead to a different experience and a different interaction with law enforcement" (Touré, 2017).

I have been asking about what it means to be an African or Black body in history. To me, it is about resistance and resilience to the scripting of Black lives in wider society (Dei, 2017). Consequently, the narration of Africans has a structural understanding of what is implied and the consequences of having systems in place to exploit Black pain and suffering. It is also to understand history as resistance. The focus on structural forces also allows us to examine the way we have lived and continue to live our lives and how collective experiences have unfolded as part of human history.

In this chapter, I will position teaching history as a tool to fight anti-Black racism. As consistently laid on anti-Black racism is rooted in an ideology of racial hierarchies and a denial of African humanity (i.e.: Black life as devalued, wasted, disposable, dispensable). These ideas have been supported by African enslavement and colonization. We can hope to address this by making African history mandatory in the curriculum, even beyond K-12 education.

How we prepare teachers to teach and students to learn history is important. This may call for a critical review of history books and history lessons, placing emphasis on the analysis of historical content and critical thinking. Also, perhaps teaching historical events and developments beyond their political significance and relevance (e.g.: beyond the role of colonizers, and governments, to first-hand accounts and stories of the actual lived experiences of peoples) (see also Fancy, 2020). Teaching omissions and hidden histories that speak to social injustices, violence, and local resistance will be crucial. This will require teaching African colonization and enslavement critically to uncover White privilege, racism, violence, and African resistance.

The focus on the history of pre-colonial Africa and African Indigeneity, such as the history that validates African knowledge and philosophies, will be relevant. And so will be teaching such African history across all grades; beyond the Social Studies curriculum to all subjects; with African History Month integrated year-round in the curriculum, not just as "African History Month." The particular focus on pre-colonial (e.g.: African ancient kingdoms), colonial (e.g.: Berlin Conference, Middle Passage, Transatlantic Slave Trade); post-colonial (afterlife of slavery, Civil Rights Movement, African Renaissance, World War 2 and impacts on post-colonial/independent African nations); Contemporary Africa and Black Diasporic experiences, struggles, achievements and contributions (e.g.: Tulsa race massacre, Black Lives Matter, Black/African Indigeneities, etc.) will ensure students understand not just African challenges but African peoples' contributions to world civilizations, including resistance and struggles. This also places Africa as central in human history and the accounts of such collective history.

I see possibilities with educators encouraged to teach history by developing explicit lesson plans and curriculum units (including literature units on Black authors and engaging the work of artists, educators, politicians, and young and adult community activists). An Afrocentric narration of histories from an anti-colonial prism centring Black and African male, female, cisgender, queer, and non-binary voices and in their own stories will all serve to empower young learners. Similarly teaching African perspectives on anti-Black racism, Black struggles, and Black Lives Matter.

It has been observed that we are at an inflection point in our history. As a society, we have failed to reflect on our global schisms and the long history collectively and deeply behind our divides. Our colonial histories have been rife with pain and suffering for many of us. We erect monuments to honour, celebrate, venerate and remember the past for their contributions to society. I have never come across oppressed peoples' anywhere arguing for the erection of a statue or a monument for their oppressors. But the monuments and street names and other symbols we erect in society must reflect our true identity and what we want to be seen. We honour our freedom fighters and not those who sowed divisions and disunity. Is there something wrong with this picture?

History is not static. There is no end to history. As a society, we can rename our monuments to reflect the realities of our times. Why will we replace a $20 USD bill with an image of a slave-owning American President Andrew Jackson with that of a Black freedom fighter, Harriet Tubman, who worked to remove slaves from bondage? The recent raging debate about how we talk and remember our collective histories and shared memories of the past has a history to it. We do not support revisionist histories. We want accurate histories that are truly reflective of all accounts. But it is one thing to tell history and another to celebrate history. For so long we have failed to take a hard look at decolonizing our colonial architecture. The moment is past and it can be resurrected for now. We need histories and the remembrance of the past that heal rather than open wounds. Our public spaces must be welcoming, not excluding.

Certain questions are also worth asking as reflection points even if we do not have answers to all of them: Why do we want history to glorify oppression or oppressors? What does it say about us as a society when we celebrate the legacies of those who profited from slavery, which was a crime against humankind? What does it mean to look critically at our collective colonial histories, and to confront our past and its horrors of colonialism? What does it tell about a society that wants to celebrate/honour oppressors and colonizers in public spaces? Are there other ways we can tell history without glorifying the oppressor? Don't we have a new debate today as to who we want to mount a statute for? Who and what is erased in such moments and why? Where are the resistors and the vanquished in our remembrances? Are all the monuments in our public parks truly national treasures? How inclusive and democratic were decision-making processes at the point in history when decisions were made about having public monuments? How do we define heroes and heroines? To whom? When have we been in charge of our histories? And, more importantly, how were the Indigenous peoples on whose lands some monuments and street names situated part of the consultative processes in history?

Looking at the "problematic monuments and street names in Toronto – streets named for people who were slave-owners (like William Jarvis and Peter Russell), and statues that commemorate people with problematic histories, like Egerton Ryerson," (see Daubs, 2020) what message are we getting across? What does the monument of a slave owner in a public square symbolize? Does it signal to the world that we honour our heroes and heroines or do we honour a divisive past? The raging debate about monuments and colonial architecture speaks to the question of remembrance – Who, what, how and why of remembering (see Dei & Lara Villanueva, 2022). History and remembrance are often not the same things. There are some histories we may not want to remember. It does not mean it did not happen. Rather it has left deep scars on us we would rather forgive and forget. We often get this confused. History is about the totality of a people's lived experiences – about pain, suffering, satisfaction, glorification, victories and successes.

The way we discuss history today also brings our collective futurity into sharp focus. For example, where do we go from here as a society, when it comes to these symbols on our streets? It must be recognized that colonial architecture – moments etc. while representing the telling of particular histories, are stories of the victorious and conquerors. Similarly, the visuality of structures has become open reminders of pain, and suffering more so than a celebration of heroism. The way we teach history is to start with our schools and education. We must situate race and colonialism in the teaching of history. This means having an anti-racist, anti-colonial school curriculum that allows us to critically teach our histories raising questions about the absences, omissions, negations, denials, and devaluations. An anti-colonial/decolonial school curriculum can teach history that remembers oppressors differently rather than glorify them in public spaces. Critical anti-racist education must contribute to unveiling Eurocentric narratives in architectural education.

There is specificity to teaching African history to fight anti-Black racism and White colonial privilege and to help develop particular care for Black educational success. The way we teach history is to start with our schools and education. We must situate race and colonialism in the teaching of history. Classroom educators have an important responsibility to critically understand the teacher's identity. There is an African saying: "It is not what you are called that is important; it is what you respond to!". We must build "communities of learners" with the "community of schooling" and refuse to see our schools as "sites of refuge", but instead as "sites of liberation" (see Harney & Moten, 2013; Kelley, 2016).

African history must be understood broadly – a totality of a people's lived experience, inclusive of African Indigeneity, colonialism, enslavement, resistance, and the "afterlife". We need educational commitment to supporting

K-12, college and university teachers to strengthen their critical knowledge of Africa – to contribute to the possibilities of achieving the mission. Our educational strategies must include learning about Africa, African and Black epistemologies, and offering a fulsome and critical link for Africans and Black peoples in global diaspora and contemporary African culture and life.

Articulating the Educational Challenge

When we look at the education of Black, Indigenous, and racialized youth (particularly Generation Z and millennials) there is an under-resourcing of communities' education, supported with Eurocentric curricula and a lack of representation of, particularly, Black, and Indigenous teachers in the school system.

Whether federally (as in the US context), provincially, or at state levels, as well as local district, and school board levels, we see a standardization of curriculum. The linking of funding to educational performance continues to disproportionately under-resource and marginalize students of African and Latinx descent in the US. At the state level, school curricula continue to be Eurocentric (and while perhaps increasingly race-conscious), typically fail to address systemic issues (e.g.: anti-Black/African racism). At the local district/school board level, we have a predominantly middle-class White (female) workplace, meaning majority White teaching, leading to the inevitable dominance of White epistemic understandings and interpretations of the school curricula.

North American history has largely been a celebration of the dominant narratives. There is a need to understand the inaccuracies of "dominant history", and the cultural, racial and political-economic motivations underlying these inaccuracies. We need to uncover suppressed histories and knowledges in the school curriculum and everyday classrooms. We need to close the knowledge gap between the prevailing dominant prevailing historical narratives and the actual histories of the learners in school classrooms and communities. This begins with reconceptualizing Africa moving towards a decolonial [political and strategic] look at history that addresses colonialism, African Indigeneity and local resistance. History must be seen as the totality of a people's lived experiences, and connecting learners to their past, present and future. We must teach history beyond contestations to a decolonial and anti-colonial project of social and educational transformation. History must be presented as "a more accurate, complete and varied story of human history" (Kempf, 2020, p. 4), as "a dialogue (not monologue) … an interrogation (not a rhetorical polemic)" that materializes in a decolonial history curriculum and "not simply a critical historiography" (Kempf, 2020, p. 2; see also Kempf, 2006).

A decolonial and anti-colonial approach to critical historiography will move history beyond questions of appropriations, misrepresentations and discrediting of the history of ideas and events that have shaped and continue to shape human growth and development (see also Bernal, 1987, 1996, 2006; Olela, 1998; Asante, 2000). It will move history from suppressed histories to a resurrection of Indigenous knowledges into the school curriculum and classrooms, making African history (culture and knowledge) key aspects of the global historical record. Learners must be taught to know, understand and appreciate "African history" on its own terms – not on the basis of Eurocentric understandings and conceptions of "civilization", culture and development (see also Sardar, 1999).

Decolonizing African history also brings some important questions for interrogation. For example: Whose stories do dominant historical narratives tell, and how and why? Whose stories are absent from school curricula, how and why? Whose ancestors and ancestral knowledges are remembered, why and how? Who speaks for America as we remember "the national past"? How are the stories of genocide and conquest which have shaped the nation-building project told or not told to our children? Who and what is excluded in the (re)telling of history (e.g.: Classical civilization's exclusion of Afro-Asiatic contributions)? What does it mean to talk about curricular, pedagogic, and instructional changes within the broader context of demanding structural institutional change at our educational institutions? What often gets erased in our discussions about Africa and how do such exclusions, negations, and absences impact our own teaching and learning of African history? And, how do we openly address race and colonialism and not merely engage the language that dances around race in the historical text? (see also Kempf, 2020)

Implications and Practical Strategies for Teaching African History – Towards a Decolonial Curriculum, Pedagogy, and Instruction

Teaching African history is about a "philosophy of practice"- understanding why we do what we do as educators, "authenticity" – bringing true meaning to history that speaks about a people's lived experiences, including challenges and resistances, and "answerability"- educators becoming responsible to knowledge and their communities of learners. Among the specific educational strategies to address anti-Black racism and colonial oppressions, educators must situate race, Indigeneity, and colonialism in the teaching of history (i.e.: coming at African history from an anti-racist, anti-colonial school curriculum that allows us to critically teach our histories raising questions about the historical omissions and misrepresentations). It also requires interrogating and subverting racist historical narratives (e.g.: educators must name or call out what they notice or see for what it is). Educators should also interrogate power and knowledge in the making of histories (e.g.: what are the ideas, beliefs, stereotypes and prejudices as we produce particular historical narratives for consumption?). Educators must use critical texts to teach Africa(ness), race and Blackness (e.g.: historical texts that debunk Greek/Roman Whiteness assertions; the use of Walter Dean Myers *Monster* rather than the dominant's popular text, *To Kill a Mockingbird*). Part of anti-colonial teaching of African history is the teaching of African Indigenous languages in schools to assist learners' understanding of African people's cultures and identities.

Educators can strive to build community and caregiver relations, tapping into African cultural knowledge within local communities possessed by local Elders, to support the well-being and achievement of students. This can be approached by bringing Elders to tell stories and histories through cultural memories that allow students to see themselves reflected and also local communities, parents and Elders feel their voices are heard within school curricular programming. Educating youth by promoting the use of storytelling can assist students to express themselves in school and help in cultivating a greater sense of belonging for Black/African students and their families. Schools must pay attention to having a different library culture (i.e.: having resources such as historical novels that allow students to see themselves and their own representations). Given the power of dominant histories in constructing school knowledge, we need to pay attention to the inescapability of the "colonial library" (Mudimbe, 1988) that has been deeply influential in teaching, learning, and administration of education in our schools. Even assisting students to have difficult conversations about issues in the media, etc. such as George Floyd and the historical pattern of police brutality is significant.

For example, in North American schooling, children learn about European history and celebrations such as Easter, but relatively, very little about Black history or Indigenous peoples' histories prior to their contact with Europeans. During celebrations such as Eid, Muslim children must miss school because these are not considered to be school holidays such as Christmas. When children learn art, often we refer to European music or artists as classics such as Beethoven or Picasso. The musical canon in schools does not include African renowned artists such as Riad Al Subanti, or even contemporary Hip-hop artists (see Agawu, 2003; School children who will read Shakespeare but will not know Wole Soyinka, Chinua Achebe, Ama Atta Aidoo or Chimamanda Adichie. When Black students learn about contributions to society, such as mathematics or astronomy, books and schools sometimes erase the contributions of African, Asian and Mesoamerican civilizations to science and the things we know. This historical narrative gives the erroneous message to learners that Europeans invented *everything*! But, do our learners know that the oldest university to ever exist in the world was in Morocco? (see Edaich, 2019). Do they know that the development of geometrical thinking started in early African history? (see Joseph, 2000). Do learners know that ancient Egyptians considered a circle to have 360 degrees and estimated Π at 3.16? (See Coppe de Oliveira & Santos, 2020).

In his detailed exposition of the rich African history, we learn from Asante (2007) a lot about the contributions of African civilizations to global civilization with the achievements of ancient kingdoms and civilizations of Africa. There are some highlights in the teaching of African ancient civilizations and empires that all learners are informed of as a source of Black African pride and achievements in contrast to the continuing portrayal of African sub-humanity in some circles. First, there was the Kemetic (Egyptian) Civilization of 1550-590 BCE as the first major civilization of Africa. It was a civilization that invented a calendar and a form of writing hieroglyphics. It also developed papyrus, paper made from the papyrus plant, and built the magnificent pyramids (e.g.: Tombs of Kings) at Giza, notably the Great Sphinx (one of the seven wonders of the world). This civilization was unmatched at the pinnacle of its time given the notable achievements in arts, science and technology (e.g. mummifications), and mathematics (Asante, 2007).

The Nubian Civilization (3,100 – 1,000 BCE) is also noted for its two historical communities, Kush and Meroe. The Kushites, we are told, facilitated the vast economies of the iron ore industry and religious and spiritual achievements, noted in their flamboyant rituals and cultures. This civilization built important mining centres trading in minerals like gold and electrum. The African people also created an important centre for labour relations with local African peoples. We also know the people of Kush and Meroe developed a writing system, the second oldest in Africa, after the Egyptian hieroglyphics. There was also the great Zimbabwe Civilization of 1100 – 1,400 CE. It was a proud civilization named the Stone City of the South. It developed its own language, Shona, and had expansive trading networks, particularly, with the Kilwa and Swahili cultures in the coastal areas. These communities exhibited great culture, promoting wealth for the people. The stone city became a centre of economic activity for farming and the gold and ivory trade. The people also built an extensive network of monuments (notably, the Great Enclosure Wall) made out of granite stone (see Asante, 2007).

We should also not forget the Western Sudanese Empires and Kingdoms. For example, the Ghana Empire, was founded in the 2 or 3rd century CE. This Empire was notable for its trade in gold and ivory (from the South) and salt (from the North). It developed impressive markets and religious shrines with fortified royal forts and retreats that attracted foreign traders and merchants. The Mali Empire that arose after the fall of Ghana was similarly noted for its wealth and trade in gold, duplicating much of Ghana's achievements. The Kingdom's three famous rulers – Sundiata (1235–1260); Mansa Sakuru (1298–1308), and Mansa Musa were known to be great leaders ensuing significant developments in sciences, and arts education, economics, and health, including the famous Sankore University in Timbuktu. Also, the Songhai Empire came into prominence in the mid-C15th with its capital city Goa, exceeding the achievements of the earlier Empires of Ghana and Mali. With the fall of the ancient Empires arose the famous Western Sudanese Kingdoms: Mossi, Kanem Bornu, Hausa, Bambara, Wolof, Oyo, Yoruba, Benin, Dahomey, Asante, Bono and Akwamu.

To sum up the notable achievements and highlights of West African Kingdoms and Empires, one can point to the city of Timbuktu, Mali (with its famous Sankore University and the Madrasa) which became a hub for Islamic intellectualism in the 15th Century, attracting global scholars during the reign of Mansa Musa (Saad, 1983; Kane, 2016). We also know that Western fine art Masters (e.g. Pablo Picasso, Henri Matisee, and Jacques Lipchitz) were all heavily influenced by West African art (see Segy, 1962; Meldrum, 2006). For example, Picasso's groundbreaking Les Demoiselles d'Avignon (1907–09), which initiated Cubism in fine art, derives much of its inspiration from the ceremonial mask of the Dogon of Mali. The West African cities, Benin in Nigeria, and Kumbi Saleh all had great armies and were noted for their imposing architecture. The region became the source of the famous West African trade in gold and metals. This wealth and trade of the West African region also became the main source of inter-ethnic wars for Black African slaves sent to the New World, and the Arab enslavement of Africans prior to European colonization. Even in recanting the history of African enslavement, we must let learners also know the untold history of resistance of African Kings and Chiefs (e.g. Asantes) to European enslavement of African peoples. What is very clear is that European contact interrupted the path of West African civilization and subverted its political, economic, cultural and social systems.

The rich African history cannot exclusively be taught in school settings. Learners can be taught and emboldened to do their own research to understand the histories (beyond what they learn in school) and demand social justice in their schools and their wider communities. Black and Indigenous history taught year-round sends an important message of the significance of such education for all learners, not just Black and Indigenous learners.

African history transcends Africa to the global Diaspora. Many times the contributions of the African diaspora to Western societies are downplayed. For example, students can learn about Black Canadian history (use social media channels to advocate for change and research: for example, Africville, Black Nova Scotians, and Slavery in Canada). Several historical texts have documented the long history of African peoples in Canada going back to over 500 years ago (e.g.: Sadlier, 1994; Sadlier & Wang, 2003; Hill, 2010; Cooper, 2011; Mensah, 2002). What is clear is that in telling this rich history whether from the period of the "Early Descendants," the "Diaspora of post-Emancipation" (post-slavery) or the "Diaspora of Neo-Colonial Period" (see Nketia, 2009; Mensah, 2010, 2006, 2002), Africans and all peoples of African descent have made significant contributions to what is now Canada. Unfortunately, African peoples' contributions to Canada continue to be a much-untold story. This rich history includes the Harriet Tubman, and the Underground Railroad and African people yearning for freedom and our struggles of resistance and escape, as well as the sacrifices of ordinary men and women that laid the groundwork for race equity and social justice in our communities. For example, the role of the Negro Citizenship Association, fighting for the Bill of Rights and Freedoms that was to be a cornerstone for the Canadian Charter of Rights and Freedoms. There are the contributions made by enslaved Africans in building the frontier economy of Upper Canada, now Ontario. We also had the Brotherhood of Sleeping Car Porters who fight for a collective agreement, and fair wages for members become foundational for union rights in the country (Cooper, 2011; Foster, 2019; Mathieu, 2001, 2010; Winks, 2000).

History must be taught to learners as a study of politics and social movements. They can also learn about the history of protests and ask critical questions: Why are people still protesting in 2020? How is police brutality still a problem that does not go away? What other aspects of society need to change, and how and why? How can young people protest, and also, demand change? How can young people be global leaders and link their humanity to the humanity of others? Educators in teaching history can move beyond single issues and provide broader examples for multi-geo-spaces. We have gained many of the freedoms and rights that we have, because of protests. Students can be taught about these histories of protests and be encouraged to think about joining a protest with peers, family and parents or organizing for social justice causes in the schools informed by our rich history of protest movements.

The teaching of history must not centre Whiteness. African History must be taught in ways that do not displace Black and African peoples, our "intellectual thought and Black life itself." Furthermore, we need to problematize, and subvert, "the affiliation of Blackness, Africa(ness) with enslavement" and colonialism through an erasure of African Indigeneity (Harris, 2019; p. 216; Byrd, 2019). Black history is world history, and it is much more than trauma and resistance, it is also brilliance, art, beauty, joy, grandiosity, and excellence.

References Cited:

Agawu, K. (2003). *Representing African music: Postcolonial notes, queries, positions*. New York: Routledge.

Asante, M. K. (2000). *The Egyptian philosophers: Ancient African voices from Imhotep to Akhenaten*. Chicago: African American Images.

Asante, M. K. (2007). *The history of Africa: The quest of eternal harmony*. New York: Routledge.

Asante, M., & Berry, S. (2000). *African intellectual heritage: A book of sources*. Philadelphia: Temple University Press.

Bernal, M. (1987). *Black Athena: The Afroasiatic roots of classical civilization Vol. I*. London: Free Association Books.

Bernal, M. (1996). *Black Athena: The Afroasiatic roots of classical civilization Vol. II*. Piscataway: Rutgers University Press.

Bernal, M. (2006). *Black Athena: The Afroasiatic roots of classical civilization, Vol. III: The linguistic evidence*. Piscataway: Rutgers University Press.

Biondi, M. (2016, August 15). The radicalism of Black Lives Matter. In These Times. https://inthesetimes.com/features/black-lives-matter-history-police-brutality.html

Black Lives Matter. (n.d.). Herstory. Global actions – Black Lives Matter. Retrieved August 16, 2020, from https://blacklivesmatter.com/

Bristow, P. (1994). *We're rooted here and they can't pull us up: Essays in African Canadian women's history*. Toronto: University of Toronto Press

Byrd, J. A. (2019). Weather with you: Settler colonialism, antiblackness, and the grounded relationalities of resistance. *Journal of the Critical Ethnic Studies Association, 5*(1–2), 207.

Coppe de Oliveira, C., & Santos, A. P. (2020). African and Afro-Brazilian roots for mathematics teaching: Decolonize the curriculum. In *Ethnomathematics in action* (pp. 57–67). Springer International Publishing. https://doi.org/10.1007/978-3-030-49172-7_4

Cooper, A. (2011). *The hanging of Angelique*. New York: Harper Collins.

Daubs, K. (2020, June, 12). 'Toronto Star' reporter, email correspondence to request an interview on 'Monuments and History'.

Davis A. Y. (1989). *Women culture & politics (First)*. Random House.

Davis, E. (2017, November 7). Black Lives Matter Archives. Sydney Peace Foundation. https://sydneypeacefoundation.org.au/tag/black-lives-matter/

Dei, G. J. S. (2010). *Teaching Africa: Towards a transgressive pedagogy*. New York: Springer.

Dei, G. J. S. (2017). *Reframing blackness and black solidarities through anti-colonial and decolonial prisms*. Springer.

Dei, G. J. S., & Lara-Villanueva, M. (2022). Unveiling a design of erasure: In conversation with George Dei. In *The Routledge companion to architectural education in the Global South*. New York: Routledge.

Dei, G. J. S., & McDermott, M. (2019). *Centering African proverbs, Indigenous folktales and cultural stories in curriculum: Units and lesson plans for inclusive education*. Toronto: Canadian Scholars Press.

Edaich, S. (2019). The city of Fas and the University of al-Qarawiyyin: A common destiny. *Opolskie Studia Administracyjno-Prawne, 16*(4 (1)), 237–250. https://doi.org/10.25167/osap.1214

Fancy, N. (2020, July 31). If were going to tackle systemic racism, we need to rethink how we teach history. CBC News Opinion https://www.cbc.ca/news/opinion/opinion-high-shool-history-curriculum-racism-1.5658622?__vfz=medium%3Dsharebar.

Foster, C. (2019). *They call me George: The untold story of Black Train Porters and the Birth of Modern Canada*. Biblioasis

Harris, C. I. (2019). Of Blackness and Indigeneity: Comments on Jodi A. Byrd's "Weather with you: Settler colonialism, antiblackness, and the grounded relationalities of resistance". *Journal of the Critical Ethnic Studies Association, 5*(1–2), 215.

Hill, L. (2010). *The book of Negroes*. London: Black Swan.

Hillstrom, L. C. (2018). *Black lives matter: From a moment to a movement (Annotated-Illustrated ed.)*. Greenwood.

Holton, A. (2007). Decolonizing history: Arthur Schomburg's Afrodiasporic archive. *The Journal of African American History*, 92(2), 218–238. Retrieved from http://www.jstor.org/stable/20064181

James, G. G. (1990). *Stolen legacy*. Trenton: Africa World Press.

Joseph, E. (1987). Foundations of Eurocentrism in Mathematics. *Race and Class*, 3, 13–28.

Joseph, G. G. (2000). *The crest of the peacock : The non-European roots of mathematics* ([2nd ed.], reprinted with additional material). Princeton University Press.

Kane, O. (2016). *Beyond Timbuktu : An intellectual history of Muslim West Africa*. Harvard University Press

Kelley, R. D. G. (2016). Black study, Black struggle. *Boston Review* (March 7, 2016), https://bostonreview.net/forum/robin-d-g-kelley-black-study-black-struggle

Kempf, A. (2006). Anti-colonial historiography: Interrogating colonial education. In G. Dei & A. Kempf (Eds.), *Anti-colonialism and education: The politics of resistance*. Rotterdam: Sense.

Kempf, A. (2009). Contemporary anti-colonialism: A transhistorical perspective. In A. Kempf (Ed.), *Breaching the colonial contract: Anti-colonialism in the US and Canada* (pp. 13–34). New York: Springer.

Kempf, A. (2020). *North African knowledges and the western classroom: A brief situation of selected literature*. Unpublished paper. Ontario Institute for Studies in Education, University of Toronto.

Lefkowitz, R., & Rogers, G. M. (1996). (Eds.), *Black Athena revisited*. Chapel Hill: University of North Carolina Press.

McCaskie, T. C. (2015). *Asante, kingdom of gold : Essays in the history of an African culture*. Carolina Academic Press.

Mathieu, S.-J. (2010). *North of the Color Line. Migration and Black Resistance in Canada, 1870-1955*. University of North Carolina Press

Mathieu, S.-J. (2001). North of the Colour Line: Sleeping Car Porters and the battle against Jim Crow on Canadian Rails, 1880-1920. *Labour / Le Travail*, 47, 9–41.

Mbembe, A. (2015)."Decolonizing knowledge and the question of the archive." Africa is a Country. Retrieved from https://africaisacountry.atavist.com/decolonizing-knowledge-and-the-question-of-the-archive]

Meldrum, A. (2006, March 15). Stealing beauty. *The Guardian*. Retrieved from Stealing beauty | Art | The Guardian

Mensah, J. (2006). "West Africa: History and economic development". In *Encyclopaedia of the developing world*, pp. 1694.

Mensah, J. (2010). *Black Canadians: History, experiences, social conditions*. Black Point, N.S: Fernwood Publishing.

Mudimbe, V. Y. (1988). *The invention of Africa: Gnosis, philosophy, and the order of knowledge: Gnosis, philosophy, and the order of knowledge*. Indianapolis, IN: Indiana University Press.

Mukhtār, M. J.-D., & UNESCO. (1981). *Ancient civilizations Africa*. London: Heinemann Educational Books.

Nketiah, R. (2009). *KLM Babies: First-Generation Ghanaian-Canadian Womyn and Identity Formation*. University of Toronto. [unpublished MA thesis].

Nyoni, J. (2013). Decolonial multicultural education in post-apartheid South Africa. *International Journal for Innovation Education and Research*, 1(3), 83–92.

Nyoni, J. (2019). Decolonising the higher education curriculum: An analysis of African intellectual readiness to break the chains of a colonial caged mentality. *Transformation in Higher Education*, 4(0), doi.org/10.4102/the.v4i0.69

Olela, H. (1998). The African roots of Greek Philosophy. In E. Eze (Ed.), *African philosophy: An anthology* (pp. 43–49). London: Blackwell.

Parker, E. (2018, April 25). #BlackLivesMatter and the Power and Limits of Social Media. Medium. https://medium.com/@emilydparker/how-blacklivesmatter-resembles-activism-in-the-authoritarian-world-24d1200864f6

1ncognito_(2019, August 31). I noticed African Architecture isn't really showcased compared to Asian, European, Middle Eastern and Indian. So here is a thread of African Architectural styles. Starting with Nubian. (Twitter Post). Retrieved from https://twitter.com/Thevinchy_/status/1167748981188902914

Rodney, W. (1972). *How Europe underdeveloped Africa*. London: Tanzania Publishing House.

Saad, E. N. (1983). *Social history of Timbuktu : The role of Muslim scholars and notables, 1400-1900*. Cambridge University Press.

Sadlier, R. (1994). *Leading the way: Black women in Canada*. Toronto: Umbrella Press.

Sadlier, R., & Wang, Q. (2003). *The kids book of Black Canadian history*. Toronto: Kids Can Press.

Sardar, Z. (1999). Development and the location of Eurocentrism. In R. Munck & D. O'Hearn (Eds.), *Critical development theory: Contributions to the new paradigm* (pp. 44–61). London: Zed Books.

Segy, L. (1962). African sculpture and Cubism. *Criticism (Detroit)*, 4(4), 273–301.

Stewart, M. H. (1993). *Borgu and its kingdoms: A reconstruction of a Western Sudanese polity*. Lewiston, N.Y: E. Mellen Press.

Touré. (2017, December 7). A year inside the Black Lives Matter Movement. Rolling Stone. https://www.rollingstone.com/politics/politics-news/a-year-inside-the-black-lives-matter-movement-204982/

Winks, R. W. (2000). *The Blacks in Canada: A history* (2nd ed.). McGill-Queen's University Press.

Zinn, H. (1999). *A people's history of the United States: 1492-Present*. New York: Perennial Classic.

· 8 ·

THE INTERSECTIONS OF ANTI-COLONIAL SOLIDARITIES

Solidarity will also be a challenge for anti-colonial politics. Long ago, Alfred's and Corntassel's (2005) writing on Indigenous resurgences and colonialism referred us back to the work of anti-colonial theorist Franz Fanon. They point to his argument that,

> The most important strength of Indigenous resistance, unity, is also constantly under attack as colonial powers erase community histories and senses of place to replace them with doctrines of individualism and predatory capitalism: In the colonial context…the natives fight among themselves. They tend to use each other as a screen, and each hides from his neighbour, the national enemy (p. 603).

For Indigenous peoples, the authors cautioned that we cannot let divisions, "distract us from the bigger picture of decolonization and sap the crucial energy and solidarity that are essential to an effective confrontation of imperial power in whatever form it presents itself (Alfred & Corntassel, 2005, p. 603). What lessons can we draw here going forward in political work for justice?

How do we spatialize and theorize now from our different locations and politics for meaningful solidarity work? This question is made all the more difficult to answer. What may at times appear to be our competing struggles, when looked at carefully, calls for collective work to fight broader systemic and structural problems. Subjectivity and politics are always aligned. So, for example, how do we center Blackness and Indigeneity in our analysis while noting the "historical messiness of Black and Indigenous encounters" (Byrd, 2019, p. 207)? How do we "enact solidarities across disparate histories, [experiences] and geographies, embody resistances at the intersections of identities and imagine [new] futures outside the colonial registers of possession and dispossession" (Byrd, 2019, p. 207)? I agree that we need to move beyond the specificities of place, "toward a spatialization of simultaneous oppressions that define the conditions of possibility that make our contemporary now possible" (Byrd, 2019, p. 211). I'd like to think that our intellectual inclinations will help us respond to these questions in meaningful and actionable ways.

In the past (Dei, 2017), I examined Black solidarities working with our often contested, complicated, and heterogenous Blackness to foster Black unity and power across global spaces. Now, I will extend that discussion to not only promoting Black solidarities through the intersections of Blackness (class, gender, class, sexuality, language and religion) but more so, how we can pursue social movement politics broadly to address multi-faceted struggles of Black, Indigenous, racialized and colonized communities. The learning objective is to work with political friends, specifically "critical friends" who come together through the interstices of struggles employing the discursive political frame of anti-colonial solidarity for social change. In effect, I propose anti-colonial solidarity to expand the thesis of Black solidarities. Anti-colonial solidarity is working with our intersections of privileges and oppressions and across multiple geo-spaces to address all forms of colonialism ("foreign", "alien", "external", "internal", "imposed" and "dominating" relations).

This chapter looks at a simple question: How do we engage in anti-colonial solidarity in pursuing social movement politics broadly while keeping certain goals at the centre? We have our respective entry points to politics. Particularly for social movement struggles the idea or the notion of saliencies of oppressions and the recognition of the severity of issues for certain bodies (see Dei, 1996) in our communities must undergird our conception of anti-colonial solidarity. Intersectional anti-colonial politics is a worthy pursuit provided we do not lose sight of the intensities of oppression for different groups in anti-colonial solidarity. The question of power and privilege, knowing when to use voice and to listen to voices, and how we conceive leadership roles in solidarity work are all critical to discussions of anti-colonial, intersectional politics of solidarity including the intersectionality of racism, capitalism, patriarchy, gender, sexuality, and disability. Violence must be engaged in everyday politics for change as these oppressions intersect. They also compound the lived experiences of diverse communities in ways that not only stress the importance of linking struggles, but also, making such linkages in the right way not to reproduce the very things we are contesting (e.g.: power, privilege, entitlements, dominance, and void responsibilities, and complicities).

Fanon (1963) exhorted that as anti-colonial scholars we should not become a "conveyor belt" for Eurocentrism. This means we must also bring a critical eye to political practice. As a Black scholar, Fanon's words, "Oh my body, make me always a [hu]man who questions" (Fanon, 1963, p. 231) is a call for the anti-colonial scholar to be an interrupter, subversive, a distinctive Black voice, and to reveal an authentic self. As argued in previous sections, while the Black scholar identity is a racial, cultural, and political construct, it is also intersected with ethnicity, gender, class, and sexuality, as well as multiple geographies and locations. The rooting of Blackness in different places like Africa, the Caribbean, Latin America, North America, Europe, and Asia is attached to Indigenous expressions globally. We see intersections of anti-Blackness, anti-Indigeneity and anti-Indigenous racism, and settler colonialism as an epitome of violence (including acts of human devaluations, colonial theft and appropriations of Land, culture and resources), in different geographical spaces. These have implications for the interstices of anti-colonial solidarity work using Black social justice causes as an entry point.

In pursuing anti-colonial solidarity, we can examine, interrogate and, where required, reconstruct the meanings and understandings we bring to our social categories. Like race, we can see how gender, sexuality, class, dis/ability, religion, and language all constitute sites and sources of identity and knowledge, as well as relations of difference and power. These are social constructs that also reveal contested, fluid and, oftentimes, paradoxical meanings. These constructs are politically constitutive and are relationally informed. They are about conceptions of the body, skin, body images, and representations of who and what we are, ways of being, and feeling, as well as expectations, fears, anxieties, hopes, aspirations and dreams. Throughout human history, we have seen colonial and imperial projects of selective misreading or misrecording of gender, sexuality, faith, religion and spiritualities and the nature of their intersections. Colonial binaries continue to pit groups and identities against each other as dominant conceptions of these social categories predetermine life chances. Prevailing racist, sexist, ableist, and classist hierarchical structures and social relations are often viewed as "normal", "natural" and "inevitable." In anti-colonial solidarity, we can work together to disrupt, subvert and topple.

For example, heterosexuality as a privileged and acceptable social norm and practice, which unfortunately reinforces structures of White supremacy and colonial capitalism, including White settler colonialism (see Smith, 2006, among many others).

Contesting knowledge is always powerful for political work. The dominant conception of gender and sexuality has negated African and Indigenous/African understandings of sexuality, and Two-Spirit people (see de Rachewiltz, 1964; https://malidoma.com/main/; Maat, 2014; Some, 1994). Even when useful to work with, we need to question if these categories - gender, lesbian, gay, bisexual, trans*, cisgender, queer, inter-sexed – have universal explanatory power in Black, African, and Indigenous communities globally (see Asanti, 2010; Epprecht, 1998; Mkasi, 2016; Oyewumi, 1997; Parpart, 2010). Certain facts and developments are profound and in need of anti-colonial solidarity action. Racial, gender, sexual and class violence continues to be a primary tool of colonialism, White supremacy and social domination. Through the power of everyday hegemonic thinking, often served as ideological orthodoxies, we are often seduced to frame the violence oppressed peoples encounter in their daily lives as problems stemming from racial, cultural, sexual, classist, religious, and linguistic differences, and not, the result of oppressive systems and structures.

To understand anti-colonial solidarity, we must appreciate what it means to be implicated differently in political struggle. Just as we collectively work to bring racism to the fore in the public consciousness, we should recognize the intersectional privileges we may enjoy given our layered identities. This is why, as we fight racism, we cannot forget about classism, sexism, genderism, heterosexism, hetero-patriarchy, ableism, and linguistic violence. Our different and myriad identities also mean we have collective and differing responsibilities and roles. We must be welcoming of all forms of identities that are part of our community that have long been silenced. Our community is broad because it is inclusive of all. No one must be pushed to the margins by virtue of their sexuality, class, gender, dis/ability, linguistic, or cultural identities. This must start by acknowledging the hate and violence endured by our 2SLGBTQI+ communities and by first confronting the colonial legacies that deny space for our multiple identities. We must lift up and support all members of our community by acknowledging our different lived experiences in a collective effort to fight transphobia, homophobia, gender violence, and all forms of human oppression and how these relate to anti-Black racism resistance.

Before proceeding any further let me give examples of how I am reading intersectional geographies, space, knowledge, and politics as essential to the pursuit of anti-colonial solidarity. I point to the case of Latin America, Blackness and Indigeneity. As we seek to learn about, hear, and see Latinx communities, our representations of global Black communities and their struggles must challenge the imposed singular dominant narratives that erase Black/ Afro-Latinxs, Indigenous Peoples, and Black/ Afro-Indigenous peoples. We must unveil the nuances and complexities of LatinX identities to see how schooling impacts various groupings within the Latinx community similarly and differently. In the Latinx communities' context, centring Black/ Afro-Latinxs, Indigenous Peoples, and Black/Afro-Indigenous peoples' experiences and voices in schooling and beyond can bring liberation for all Latinx peoples. It includes learning from shared histories and resistance of global Black/ African continental and diasporic bodies as well as global Indigenous peoples, and global Black/ Afro-Indigenous peoples outside of Latin America and its diaspora context. We must also uncover how global White supremacy implicates Latin America. Hence, acknowledging how White supremacy within Latinx communities has perpetuated anti-Blackness, anti-Indigeneity, transphobia, homophobia and so forth.

Also, there can be a shared anti-colonial framework for understanding the construction of Islam as a threat and the impact it has on Muslims. It is about the question of power and who actually benefits from the "Othering" of Muslims. The nation-state in the West has a racist caricature of Islam and the Muslim identity. Anti-colonial solidarity struggles against global anti-racism and must examine policies aimed at targeting Muslims (e.g.: the Muslim ban in the U.S., the Hijab ban in France, etc.) and the ways people's bodies, as well as particular religions and dress attire (e.g., hijab, niqab, burka, etc.), are all racialized by the dominant group regardless of the body's skin marker as salient and consequential. We must understand how intersectionality impacts people's lives, individual and collective stories, experiences and everyday practice (e.g., the intersectionality of Black/ Muslims among other intersectionalities and identity markers – gender, ethnicity, sexuality, dis/ability, dress attire). The social construction of what constitutes a person who is Black, who is a Muslim is embedded in the dominant's imaginings. This imagination affects how one is read and whether one is included or excluded as Black, Muslim, Black Muslim, etc. and the materialized impact and consequences they endure. Furthermore, the identity of Muslims is connected to "inferior" and racialized geographical locations and yet everyone can be a Muslim (see Dei & Mohamed, 2021).

We are complicit in each other's oppression. Kitossa (2021) shows how Black sexuality continues to be a subject of intense discussions in academia and public discourse in part given the dominant's eroticization of the Black male body. Such eroticization serves to reduce Black male sexuality to the physical "thingness," an object of the Black body and the desire of the dominant gaze, often within a consumptive capitalist culture. There is the mythology of the Black man (and female) matched with distorted representations of gender, sexuality and class identities. Particularly, in school and educational settings, we see a reification of "problematic masculinity" locating a particular "brand" of Blackness as residing in the Black male heterosexual body. While not located in all Black youth, this is a concrete reality that is congealed and experienced in the very physicality of Black male bodies (e.g.: the racist readings of Black physical formidability as hostile, threatening, violent and to be feared). Our youth are often seen as exercising a form of hyper-masculinity that is threatening to the established order as very misogynistic, violent, anti-school, etc. I want us to dislodge the racist knowledge-making in a way that allows us to solve problems, and also, does not claim somehow Black bodies have a monopoly on social ills. These tropes are too often congealed as biologically determined aspects of Blackness itself. How do we interrupt this through anti-colonial solidarity that involves educators, community workers, young learners, and communities from diverse classes, genders, sexualities, dis/abilities and Indigenous backgrounds? How do we work together to deconstruct colonial representations of Black masculinity? How can we take up a decolonized Black masculinity as an interruption of race, class, gender, and sexuality? How do we take up our different complicities in White male patriarchy in a collective politics for healthy environments in educational spaces? And how do our collective politics disrupt the idea and practice of "Black men as emblematically appealing and appalling sexualized beings" (see Kitossa, 2021)?

Our global economic system has created deep schisms and inequities in health, education, employment, justice and law, and the transportation system. The current global pandemic, Covid-19 has, unfortunately, read this system very well. Covid-19 has taken advantage of the deep structural disparities among groups to cause unimaginable deaths, particularly in the most vulnerable segments of society. The disproportionate numbers of Black, Indigenous, and racialized in the health and social service sector have not been spared as revealed in the death statistics at the time of writing this chapter. Dei and Lewis (2020) point to the Johns Hopkins University Corona Resource Center data of more than 846,877 deaths worldwide. The U.S.A. has the highest mortality rate at 183,068 deaths and Brazil at 120,828 (see Johns Hopkins University, 2020). One in 1,125 Black Americans has died (or 88.4 deaths per 100,000 people), 1 in 1,375 Indigenous Americans have died (or 73.2 deaths per 100,000), and 1 in 2,450 White Americans have died (or 40.4 deaths per 100,000) (see APM Research Lab, 2020).

The intersections of race and class are very clear. We are living in a moment of racial and economic anxieties stoked by political fears which have actually intensified White racial resentments against Blacks, Indigenous and racialized communities. As Howard (2020) notes, globalization, technological changes and mobility of finance capital have had a disastrous impact on the incomes and livelihood of many workers. We have uneven economic opportunities for social groups leading to an ever-increasing economic equality gap between the working and middle classes. Clearly, Black and Indigenous communities are also communities disproportionately employed in low-paying jobs, constituting a working class that has historically been disenfranchised by the economic system. Their woes were compounded by structural and system racism which has necessitated a rallying call for all groups to mobilize, protest and demand fundamental structural change in society. The jury is still out on how these voices will be heard by political leaders and decision-makers. The issues cut across communities and nation-states. Many countries, particularly the working poor in the Global South, continue to face austerity in economic measures creating untold hardships due to policies engineered by an international financial market system that favors the rich and powerful and the Global North. Economic privatization measures and primacy and liberalization of markets (under the cloak of globalization as universal opportunity) have worked to create economic benefits for the wealthy while ensuring an even wider economic gap between the rich and poor. People have to come together to fight for economic justice and more. This includes fighting for justice in basic health, jobs, education, media, transportation, housing, environment, law, as well as race and policing. There is the intersectionality of these struggles for justice revealing relational aspects of social difference – race, class, gender, sexuality, dis/ability, religion, language, etc., and responding to the urgency of what is required to have a fairer social system in place through collective political mobilization.

The foregoing examples all have implications for anti-colonial solidarity work. In Dei (1996), I used the term "integrative anti-racism" (see also Dei, Calliste, & Belkhir, 1995) in contending that race, while intersected with other forms of social difference, must still be held up as the entry point to gender, class, sexuality, ability, dis/ability oppressions in anti-racist work. Like many others, I will continue to be unapologetic about the centricity of race, the necessity of lodging a fierce struggle against anti-Black racism, and anti-Black violence, and to continually insist on the idea that Black humanity "matters too". I have been criticized as the "race man" who reads the world in simplistic "Black/White" binary terms. But this intellectual practice of the centricity of race was a strategic positioning in my earlier anti-racist work. If one cannot centre race in anti-racist analysis, where else can one call on race as a centre? And, while race was more than skin colour, race has everything to do with skin colour as a salient marker of human differentiation. We cannot deny this fact. We cannot downplay that we live in our world, our anxieties, fears, pain, and suffering in colour-coded terms. Skin colour racism and skin colour privilege are real and consequential.

Still, we must leave room for others to have a different entry point (e.g.: gender, sexuality, dis/ability, class, etc.) in social movement politics or solidarity work. The most important fact is that whatever politics we choose strategically, we seek an intersectional analysis that connects social oppressions. We just have to keep the gaze of our practice so that we do not leave others' oppressions behind as we do this work. This does not mean we will give equal treatment. We must recognize the limits and partiality of our own knowledge and be intellectually honest about what we are doing. I do not believe that arguing that oppression while intersecting, may not necessarily have the same consequences irresponsive of geography and location is being anti-intellectual. Similarly, just as there is the relative saliency of different oppressions and identities so must we recognize that there are going to be situational and contextual variations in the intensities of oppressions (see Dei, 1996).

Racism is cancer, a deadly virus, in our global society that fails to go away. We ought to put the same energies into finding cures for viruses that affect our health, and anti-Black racism is a huge virus. But we cannot fight even anti-Black racism without linking it with other racism, sexism, patriarchy, homophobia, ableism, religious bigotry, and linguistic discrimination. Similarly, as the global struggles for Black lives have shown, we must connect racism with patriarchy, gender, sexuality, class, dis/ability and violence, as well as issues of capitalism, the climate crisis, global health, housing disparities, and education. Fighting for Black lives means standing up against housing discrimination, housing segregation, and low-income housing in all our cities and particularly, in North American suburbs.

My focus is to take up "intersectional theory" broadly as a lens for anti-colonial political action to interrogate and challenge solidarity work beyond the question of allyship. There is the seduction of liberal social oppression work, and consequently, a need to reframe radical, anti-colonial politics of solidarity. The continuing blatant forms of racial, classist, and gendered violence and hate (e.g.: the rise in White nationalism and anti-Black hate and violence) speak to the severity of issues for certain bodies but also, how oppressed bodies can become complicit and implicated in oppressive relations.

The growing intellectual interest (and sometimes fascination) in "Indigeneity", "decolonization" and "internationalization" cannot leave out racialization and global anti-Blackness. To do so will constitute what may be termed "the poverty of intersections" as a framework for solidarity. Allyship has been corrupted as part of this "poverty of intersections". Intersectional theory is supposed to help us link oppressions and work in solidarities. Yet allyship as shared oppressions and intersecting privileges necessitating the creation of "communities in solidarities" has been spiritually and emotionally wounding for Black, Indigenous and racialized communities. Allies are not really critical friends. For Black and African people, this abuse of allyship is a big problem for moving forward. Sometimes a liberal read of allyship has been a hindrance to moving forward. We have seen it in White benevolence caught in the paradigms of dominant framings, the mindset of "do good," the "imperial saviour"; Kipling's tutelage of the "Whiteman's burden," and the continuing patting ourselves on the back for doing good. Allyship has become an escape route, a moral distancing, and a sense that we all share in oppressive acts and their impacts. And, we have seen it with the pursuit of social justice without ethics, transparency, and accountability. Allyship has never allowed the dominant to trouble their prevailing "logics of possession" (Moreton-Robinson, 2004, p. 192; see also Wolfe, 2006), a definitional power of the dominant to reproduce their privilege.

I am often asked: How does a "critical friend" differ from someone in actual allyship? Allies are simply those who see themselves in coalitions and shared struggles with a determination to work together. However, this is a definition of politics not what allies do. This is because allies do not centre their complicities, implications, and their relative power and histories of privileged positions, and how these inform their political practice. Allies are not willing to seriously give up power and privilege. They largely see their part in the struggles as helping someone else but not themselves. There is usually a moral distancing from the "bad ones." Critical friends in solidarity work are prepared to accept critiques of their practice and their complicity in oppression, even as they fight in the struggle. Critical friends see themselves as the problem. Critical friends see themselves as having a greater responsibility to raise the issues and work for social change and justice. They do not leave it to the oppressed/ minoritized. Critical friends start the work by dismantling their privileges. The idea of critical friends is a new mindset that challenges the imperial saviour complex. It moves from the "I am going to help them syndrome" to a practice that says, "we have to start this." There is no defensiveness. Critical friends will acknowledge their participation in colonial violence and the power of self-determination (see Dei, 2020).

I have found it relevant to connect an interrogation of allyship with those sympathetic to the term, "implicit bias." The phrase has been appealing in that it has become a mainstream mantra used to delegitimize critical thought and commentary. As I have argued elsewhere, the term is an attempt to implicate everyone, liberalize our critiques, and dodge the saliency of anti-Black racism (see Dei, 2020). It is a way of shifting the gaze away from interrogations of structures and systemic racism toward individual prejudices, bias, and discrimination. An understanding of bias does require an acknowledgement of race, systemic racism, or oppression. It is an apolitical term that can be applied to everyone. The de facto understanding of "bias" is that we all have it within us. And if we all are implicitly biased, there is no need to even speak of systems, structures, and institutions. Bias is rendered an individualized problem of attitude, preference, and prejudice. Well folks, if the fight for social justice was simply a case of individual bias, the "Social Justice Warriors" of the world would have won by now. Joyce King's (1991) "dysconscious racism" (notwithstanding limitations) was not about implicit bias. King named race specifically in her analysis.

At this juncture let us briefly review some ideas of intersectional theorizing that can be useful for
conceptualizing anti-colonial solidarity with intersectional theorizing. To begin with, rethinking the concept of solidarity as a pedagogy and critical praxis (Gaztambide-Fernandez, 2012) in ways that set the parameters for a decolonizing strategy in education.

How do we bring intersectional theorizing into the foregoing analysis? In examining the discursive history and politics of intersectional theorizing, the focus was on the law and the legal system and the inadequacy in accounting for Black lesbian/ female experiences. The continuing neglect of Black, Indigenous, and racialized women's experiences in accounting for theory has always been clear pushing for Black, Indigenous, and racialized scholars always to search for the possibilities of translating theory into political action. Not only have we often seen issues affecting the very people but the intersectional theory was created in mind left behind. There is a failure to subvert or even complement our conventional thinking for our diverse lived experiences that ground the saliency of issues for Black, Indigenous, and racialized women. There is the polarization of theories (e.g.: intersectional theory about social reproduction theories) which end up as class/ economic reductionism, thereby subsuming race below class.

The domestication of intersectionality theory leads one to ask whether dominant bodies can be in solidarity as partners in the struggles against anti-Black racism and Black Lives Matter. There is no one model of solidarity politics. We must be able to read the possibility of progressive discourses and politics on all bodies. The goal of solidarity politics is not just "sharing power" but understanding our complicities in power and privilege such that we may think simply by being in solidarity we have done the work required. Solidarity statements of Black Lives Matter can simply be expressions of sentiments not backed by action. We have seen this in the aftermath of the George Floyd murder in Minneapolis. There was a rush to issue such statements of solidarity from progressive groups. This became a play in itself, a privileging and hierarchy of knowledge, progressivism, and radicalism. It was like, "let us see who's statement is more critical and punchy than the other." Critical words are not enough.

There is a need for Black, Indigenous, and racialized scholars to mobilize the collective culture as revolutionary practice. We need to think through collaboration from our shared political struggles, to create solidarities among people, "suffering through a particular set of circumstances/struggles", and an understanding that, "we are all struggling with life and death questions" (Black Ink Info, 2020, p. 6). There must be a realization to collectively work through liberation together and not simply because we agree on everything. We must want change to the current social order, something different, and the possibilities that come with something different.

To spell out the principles of intersectional, anti-colonial solidarity, we must confront additional questions: How do we speak/ engage/ dialogue on the intersectionality of struggles and rootedness of oppressions (particularly today) in White supremacist capitalist structures and logic, while at the same time hanging on the saliencies of issues for Black/ African and Indigenous bodies? For the oppressed and communities in struggle, how do we convey such understandings without reproducing the colonial divides of pitting ourselves against each other? Do we continue to injure Black/ African and Indigenous bodies when we read/ interpret moves to centre saliencies of particular oppressions as claims of oppression Olympics? When such claims of oppression Olympics emerge, how do Black and Indigenous bodies see and feel the violence repeating itself again in decolonial spaces? Should the concepts of "saliencies" and "intersections" be read as binaries (either/ or), rather than reading as complementary (and/ with)? How do we explain and account for the dominant appropriation of intersectionality and intersectional theory and politics? We may not have answers to all these questions. However, it is about the questions raised about our thinking on anti-colonial solidarity and what/ how it will look like.

Framing the Principles of Intersectional, Anti-Colonial Solidarity

In thinking through solidarity, I am informed by Sexton's (2015) words in search for, "a solidarity that seems to persist, in principle and in practice, despite problems of asymmetry or even antagonism; a solidarity that does not join the struggle, but exceeds it from within" (cited in Garba & Sorentino, 2020, p. 778).

A discursive and political practice of intersectional solidarity in addressing power and privilege, and also, owning up to our respective complicities and responsibilities. The global everydayness of intersectional oppressions and privileges requires collectively interrogating the spaces we occupy, and the work required to come together to address power, privilege, and oppression. Since we cannot be effective in using oppressive institutions or spaces to teach and learn about our oppressions. We must begin with the power of ideas that will challenge oppressive spaces. Teaching and learning are more effective in decolonized spaces. Such spaces are created and are continually in a process if we let our guard down. But we can respond to the paradox of using institutions that are themselves oppressive in teaching and learning about and fighting against racism, and other social oppressions, by making our education count. We can ask critical, anti-colonial questions about power, privilege, history and identities in the "community of learners" or the "epistemic community." In the current climate of global anti-Black racism, the power of politicizing social location and acknowledging the saliency of Blackness and its different geographies is significant. As noted earlier, "critical friends" ask us to interrogate solidarity work informed about intersections, and remind us that at the heart of this politics should be relations between and among people, different Lands, and geographies. Critical friendship is to bring to the table the politics of ensuring unheard voices lead discussions.

White supremacy needs gender, race, and class intersections to function. Whiteness continues to be a colonial fabrication and is very enticing and seductive. We must be critical of our politics. We cannot fall into the trap of colonial knowledge that reinforces the same things we are contesting. We cannot engage in the hyper-sexualization of Black bodies, even as we claim to do solidarity work. We cannot reduce racism, gender, sexuality, class, dis/ability, or religious violence (including anti-Semitism, Islamophobia and anti-Muslim racism) to psychology which often leaves institutions and systems off the hook. We must not allow our irrational fears to lead to hate and systemic violence. We cannot adhere to dominant conceptions of identity that flatten and cheapen us out of complexities, heterogeneities and, in fact, our humanity. We can still hold on to a reading of "Muslim" as a racial identity or as a significant racial category that constructs, determines, and defines people's lives, while people continue to resist White supremacy. We must hold to the idea of geographic and locational specificities to our identities. There is a queering of Blackness and a colonial reading of Blackness as simply all races can be colonizing and oppressive to other Black bodies. Blackness with Africa, Africanness, and African Indigeneity absented is equally oppressive. Blackness did not start with Euro-colonization.

We must begin to think of collective lives and a politics of futurity with mutual responsibilities and reciprocity in mind. This means building anti-colonial solidarities that connect struggles, Lands, and relations of different geographies. Our anti-colonial politics can be strengthened with a gaze on Indigenous peoples in settler-colonial North American contexts and similar struggles in different geographies of African, Caribbean, Asia, Europe, and Latin American contexts and Land spaces. Educators can also promote pedagogical practices that challenge colonialism, settler colonialism, anti-Black racism, heteropatriarchal racial capitalism, and the coloniality of power as part of global anti-colonial educational struggles. There is much to be learned in global social movement politics from the examination of settler-colonial contexts in Brazil and Latin America in formulating anti-colonial theory and practice and developing opposition to neoliberal global capitalism. We must pursue dialogues that are complementary to each other while recognizing the differences, specificities, as well as potential challenges in "epistemologies in dialogue." We can speak, engage, and dialogue on the intersections of struggles with their rootedness in White supremacist logic and oppressive capitalist structures, and at the same time hang on to the saliency and severity of issues for particular bodies. For "communities in struggles" we must convey understanding of particular saliencies without reproducing the colonial divides or implying a hierarchy of oppressions.

In moving toward new conceptualizations of anti-colonial solidarity with an intersectional frame, it is important to detail the why, what, when, and how we do solidarity work. This means examining the particular understandings of White logic(s) that govern claims of solidarity and the ways we can weave the dominant logic out of our daily individual and collective practices. We should also be interrogating the spaces we each occupy and the politicization of these locations. To reiterate, the idea of critical friends is a relation among peoples, Lands and geographies, and is built with an assumption that decolonization and anti-colonial politics is centred on building new relationships (see Dei, 2020). In understanding the nature of co-relational status among ourselves in solidarities, we could work hard to ensure marginalized voices are made epistemic salient in the study of oppression. This does not mean only oppressed voices can speak in solidarity work, but rather, that we make sure hitherto, unheard, discounted, and devalued voices lead our discussions. Beyond understanding the structure and mechanics of oppression we should also examine how we each become complicit, implicated, and have responsibilities in each other's oppression. At the end of it all, understanding intersectionality in anti-colonial solidarity work is also about resistance and rewarding resistance to dominant practices that have continually maintained and sustained the status quo.

I highlight the following 10 ideas for pursuing anti-colonial solidarity practice:

First, an engagement with anti-colonial politics of solidarity through a search for the "Trialectic Space" (Dei, 2012) and a "sacred learning landscape" (Garcia & Shirley, 2012, p. 77) with body, mind, soul, and spirit connections.

For many of us, race equity and social justice workflow from spirituality. We bring a shared understanding of the universe as interdependent, interrelated, and interconnected sharing the Land and Mother Earth with living and non-living, animals and humans as one. We also understand our ontological existence as "fundamentally spirit and spiritual with material manifestations" (Carroll, 2014, p. 259), and that our values system prioritizes interpersonal relations, and collective, communal and community gain. Such a philosophical worldview crystalizes the interface and nexus of body, mind, soul and spirit as coming to know, understand and act within the physical and metaphysical realms of existence. Solidarity work is informed by both the "sanctity of life" and "sanctity of activity."

Second, decolonial solidarity works with the notion of "saliency" in understanding the confluence of multiple oppressions. While oppressions intersect and political work proceeds on all oppressions, we must recognize the saliency of oppression depending on situations and contextual variations in the intensities of oppressions. Saliency is not a privilege of one struggle or oppression over the other. It is more about a recognition of primacy, prominence, and pre-eminence that allows all workers in solidarity to define their respective entry points to political struggles. Dei (1996) speaks of the "saliency of race" suggesting the politics of anti-racism calls for placing race on the axis of oppression. Solidarity work is political, and the project and practice of fighting myriad oppressions allow for race, class, gender, sexuality, and dis/ability as entry points for people as strategic choices to make. Working with the notion of saliency in solidarity work is also political in the sense of a recognition of the salience of the White body and White racial identity in a supremacist society. The notion of saliency as an entry point in our theorizing and practice of anti-colonial solidarity means beginning with and implicating the self.

Third, related to this understanding of saliency, is the significance of the epistemic saliency of the oppressed voice and the "epistemologies of the colonized" in coming to know about social oppression. As enthused in the proceeding chapter, the oppressed voice must be recognized as salient in oppression work because of lived experiences, understanding of one's experiences, and the ability to theory the experience while connecting the particularity of experience to the broader socio-political system. The idea of epistemic saliency in anti-colonial solidities is also intended to address and distinguish the metaphor and reality surrounding discourses about the fluidity or flux nature of identities as continually shifting which tends to leave racialized peoples with nowhere to stand. It also brings a critical awareness to the limitations of White bodies doing critical race and anti-Black racism work, like the needed scrutiny of those who are privileged by a system working against it. The dominant must understand their Whiteness and cannot profit from doing work from which they have historically benefitted.

Fourth, the diverse bodies in anti-colonial solidarity (from different races, classes, genders, sexualities, religious backgrounds etc.) constitute we are in "relations of power." This is the way our socio-political system is structured. Political work in such solidarity movements must ensure that these relations actually work to transform society and not necessarily lead to "states of domination." This is the difficult work of social movements. There is always the risk of people in such political spaces reproducing their relations of power in ways that maintain their respective privileges and entitlements, rather than transforming relations of domination. If we are not careful, solidarity runs a risk of reproducing privilege and power. We need to maintain a gaze that at all times, our work must be geared toward subverting domination for it to be anti-colonial. We cannot enter into solidarity and hope that our privileges and power remain intact coming within the movement and even coming out of this relationship.

Fifth, we must not expect anti-colonial spaces to be safe spaces. The oppressed have never known a space that allows them to work against their oppression. So, this knowledge of the difficulty of not knowing a "decolonial space" or that there are no safe spaces to do social movement politics does not mean we should not try to create one. It is a critical knowledge base that this is a given and to begin to work from there. It also allows us to raise questions about what constitutes a safe space, a space for whom, and how, and what, are the ground rules to begin to create such a safe space in anti-colonial solidarity work. There are risks and consequences in the politics of solidarity that play out differently for the bodies doing such work. Recognizing such differential risks, consequences, and perhaps responsibilities is an important part of this work.

The success of our politics of anti-colonial solidarity would depend on an informed understanding of the philosophical grounding of what we are seeking to do and the resolve to accomplish the task irrespective of safety, risks, as well as losing power and privilege. What is required in anti-colonial solidarity is to welcome safety concerns and to strategize collective survival under a climate of fear, intimidation and violence (see also Leonardo & Porter, 2010).

Sixth, anti-colonial solidarity is about creating community and communities. These communities are created (not given), meaning we work hard to have them in place. In other words, we do not pluck communities from the sky but demand hard groundwork and a willingness to sacrifice. These communities are "sameness" and "difference." They are about shared histories and the connections between histories and struggles. These communities also eschew relations of identities and subjectivities. The most important point of this all is that we seek to create communities not necessarily for the oppressed, but for our collective. We need communities for our collective welfare and we create these communities working to address injustice, privilege, false entitlements and the discretionary use of power to dominate and subjugate. Communities will always be a work in progress, remaking, and redirecting our focus and energies. It is these synergies and dialectics of change that make communities worth pursuing in solidarity work. No community is static. And it is also important to always remember that as we seek to build communities, there will be resistance to such moves.

Seventh, history is very important to anti-colonial solidarity. To do anti-colonial solidarity work we must be prepared to divest ourselves from our colonial inheritance and colonial investments as made possible by our diverse and yet contingent and intertwined histories. Many times, our privileges are unearned and have come to us through our place in history. Similarly, it places before us certain burdens and challenges. Anti-colonial solidarity is embracing history and our place in these histories. We must understand such history and responsibilities in history. History calls on us differently to act. But history also places differential responsibilities when it comes to working for change. This is why understanding our place in history is particularly important in being part of collective working for change. Solidarity work requires an understanding of the politics of geography and space. Why and how we come into spaces and do the work is required, and the obligations we have to ensure these spaces are free of injustice and violence. Anti-colonial solidarity work must be more complex than merely coming together. It must involve navigating difficult questions, and histories, and developing a philosophical understanding of how and why we seek such coalitions in the first place. Through history, we connect our struggles in different Lands and spaces. The politics of geographies and space places onerous responsibilities to understand the history that brings us into a community and work with the knowledge to create even better spaces that we came to meet through a new politics of territoriality.

The Eighth is to recognize that our political work does not absolve us of complicities and responsibilities. We may feel that because we are in solidarities with oppressed communities, we have played our bit in terms of both understanding our complicities and performing our obligations and responsibilities. In fact, there is seduction and complacency that solidarity work may bestow covering up our continued roles and complicities in oppression and violence. Solidarity work requires a constant exploration of self and politics to the extent that we view the self as both parts of the problem and the solution. We never leave our role as being part of the problem of oppression simply because we are in solidarity or collective political struggles. This realization must keep us on our toes, be vigilant, and strive for a better future. In fact, solidarity work and the struggle for justice never end. It is a continual process, working for change to create a better world, a new future, one in which there is no moral distancing away from our roles and responsibilities in oppressive behaviours. This realization should push us further. We are to never be complacent that the work is never done. It also means acknowledging the progress we have made while working harder, rather than being comfortable in our skin.

Ninth, a major difficulty in carrying out anti-colonial solidarity, is a failure to understand how our intersectional privileges, intersectional oppressions, and intersectional struggles play out in mutually reinforcing ways in the context of White colonial and supremacist logics. It is also such dialectics that justify why we need to come together to resist collectively. There is a place for the radicalization of thought for anti-colonial objectives. Notwithstanding, the relations we each have to the varying geographies of home, place, and Land, we come to solidarity with the purpose to create better worlds or new futures. Our task is not simply to theorize or frame the end of the world but to work towards the beginning of new futures. As noted earlier, colonialism has been an interrupter of history for many Black, Indigenous, and oppressed peoples. We will never know what might have happened. In thinking through new futures, we must ask ourselves, what do we want to happen? Is it the end of capitalism? To be human again? To self-define one's sense of collective existence? To get rid of the falsity of Western democracy – freedoms, liberty, rights? Contesting these questions as we engage in solidarities gets closer to addressing a key question: How do we shape the change we want?

Tenth, there is a shared belief in anti-colonial solidarity for participants that life must be worth living and that we must struggle collectively to design new futures however contested this will be. Part of the struggle for new futures is contending with the competing views and ideas of members in such communities. The contestation is both over ideas and practice. There is an understanding that ideas must propose change, but that change is the eventual outcome of competing ideas about the futures we want. Out of that navigation and struggles will arrive new futures that we can conveniently own and claim to be part of bringing to fruition. We must watch out for the "logic of possession" (Moreton-Robinson, 2004, p. 192; see also Wolfe, 2006) that interstices of privileges uphold, as well as the temptation of colonial binaries and divides that easily pit us against each other- as if we are one camp (privilege) or the other (oppression). We can simultaneously hold privilege and oppression while at the same time be oppressed at another level of our identity. So, we need to work with both sides of privilege and oppression, given the relationality that needs to be drawn for more effective anti-colonial solidarity. This is why we need to decolonize and unchain our minds (see also Womack, 2013, p. 44).

References Cited:

Alfred, T., & Corntassel, J. (2005). Being Indigenous: Resurgences against contemporary colonialism. *Government and Opposition*, 40(4), 597–614.

APM Research Lab. (2020, August 18). The color of Coronavirus: COVID-19 deaths by race and ethnicity. Retrieved from https://www.apmresearchlab.org/covid/deaths-by-race

Asanti, I. T. (2010). "Living with dual spirits: Spirituality, sexuality and healing in the African Diaspora." *Journal of Bisexuality*, 10(1–2), 22–30.

Black Ink Info. (2020). "Solidarity Is Not a Market Exchange": An interview with Robin D. G. Kelley by Black Ink. https://Black-Ink.Info/Author/Blcknk/

Byrd, J. A. (2019). Weather with you: Settler colonialism, Anti- Blackness, and the grounded relationalities of resistance. *Journal of the Critical Ethnic Studies Association*, 5(1–2), 207.

Crenshaw, K. W. (1991). Mapping the margins: Intersectionality, identity politics, and violence against women of color. Stanford Law Review, 43(6), 1241–1299.

Dei, G. J. S. (1996). *Anti-racism education in theory and practice*. Halifax: Fernwood Publishing.

Dei, G. J. S. (2012). "Suahunu: The Trialectic Space". *Journal of Black Studies*, 43(8), 823–846.

Dei, J. S. S. (2017). *Reframing Blackness and Black Solidarities through anti-colonial and decolonial prisms*. New York: Springer Publishing.

Dei, G. J. S. (2020). Black theorising: Indigeneity and resistance in Academia. In S. Styres & A. Kempf (Eds.), *Troubling the trickster* [in press].

Dei, G. J. S., & Lewis, K. (2020). "COVID-19, Systemic racism, racialization and the lives of Black People". Position paper, Working Group on Racism for the Royal Society of Canada [RSC] Task Force.

Dei, G. J. S., Calliste, A., & Belkhir, J. (1995). Canadian perspectives on anti-racism and race, gender and class. *Race, Gender and Class*, 2(3), 5–10.

Dei, G. J. S., & Mohamed, R. (2021). "Mapping the contours: African perspectives on anti-Blackness and anti-Black racism". In *African perspectives on Anti-Blackness and Anti-Black racism*. New York: Dio Press Inc. [forthcoming].

de Rachewiltz, Boris. (1964). *Black Eros: Sexual customs of Africa from prehistoric times to present*. Lyle Stuart Publishers.

Epprecht, M. (1998). The 'Unsaying' of Indigenous homosexualities in Zimbabwe: Mapping a blindspot in an African masculinity. *Journal of Southern African Studies*, 24(4), 631–651.

Fanon, F. (1963). *The wretched of the Earth*. New York: Grove Press.

Garba, T., & Sorentino, S. M. (2020). Slavery is a metaphor: A critical commentary on Eve Tuck and K. Wayne Yang's "Decolonization is Not a Metaphor." *Antipode*, 52(3), 764–782. doi:10.1111/anti.12615

Garcia, J., & Shirley, V. (2012). Performing decolonization: Lessons learned from Indigenous youth, teachers and leaders' engagement with critical Indigenous pedagogy. *Journal of Curriculum Theorizing*, 28(2), 76–91.

Gaztambide-Fernández, R. A. (2012). Decolonization and the pedagogy of solidarity. *Decolonization: Indigeneity, Education & Society*, 1(1), 41–67.

Harwood, J. (2020). "Trump's race-baiting might come at a cost to his economy". https://www.cnn.com/2020/09/20/politics/election-2020-trump-race-economy/index.html

Johns Hopkins University. (2020). COVID-19 Dashboard by the Center for Systems Science and Engineering (CSSE) at Johns Hopkins University. Retrieved from: https://coronavirus.jhu.edu/map.html

Kelley, R. D. G. (2000). *A poetics of anticolonialism*. New York: Monthly Review Press.

Kitossa, T. (2021). *Appealing because he is Appalling: Black masculinities, colonialism and erotic racism: Essays honouring Baldwin and Fanon*. The University of Alberta Press.

King, J. (1991). Dysconscious racism: Ideology, identity, and the miseducation of teachers. *The Journal of Negro Education*, 60(2), 133–146.

Leonardo, Z., & Porter, R. K. (2010). Pedagogy of fear: Toward a Fanonian theory of 'safety' in race dialogue. *Race Ethnicity and Education*, 13(2), 139–157. doi:10.1080/13613324.2010.482898

Maat, Sekhmet Ra Em Kht. (2014). Towards an African-centered sociological approach to Africana lesbian, gay, bisexual, transgender, queer, and intersexed identities and performances: The Kemetic Model of the Cosmological Interactive Self. *Critical Sociology*, 40(2), 239–256.

Mkasi, L. P. (2016). African same-sexualities and Indigenous knowledge: Creating a space for dialogue within patriarchy- original research. *Verbum Et Ecclesia*, 37(2), 1–6.

Moreton-Robinson, A. (2004b). Whiteness matters: Australian studies and Indigenous studies. In D. Carter, K. Darien-Smith, & G. Worby (Eds.), *Thinking Australian studies: Teaching across cultures*. St Lucia: University of Queensland Press, pp. 136–146.

Oyewumi, Oyeronke. (1997). *The invention of women: The making of African sense of western gender*. Minneapolis: University of Minnesota Press.

Parpart, J. L. (2010). African Womanhood in Colonial Kenya 1900–50, by Tabitha Kanogo. *African Affairs*, 109(435), 346–348.

Sexton, J. (2015). Roundtable on anti-Blackness and Black-Palestinian solidarity. Noura Erakat   http://www.nouraerakat.com/blogi/roundtable-on-anti-blackness-and-black-palestinian-solidarity
Some, Malidoma Patrice. (1994). *Of water and spirit: Ritual, magic and initiation in the life of an African Shaman*. New York: Penguin Books Ltd.
Wolfe, P. (2006). Settler colonialism and the elimination of the native. *Journal of Genocide Research*, 8(4).
Womack, Y. (2013). *Afrofuturism: The world of Black Sci-Fi and fantasy culture*. Chicago, IL: Lawrence Hill Books Press.

· 9 ·

THE BLACK SCHOLAR AND ACADEMIC MENTORSHIP

We are at an inflection point in the African learners experience in the academy. Those with the privilege of being familiar with history have a responsibility to mentor and be mentored by our young colleagues and promote capacity building through the power of knowledge. I have said earlier that our history is about reclaiming the past, reflecting on the present and projecting toward the future. In this section, I reflect on academic mentorship from nearly four decades of my experiences teaching and researching in the academy. I have had the honour of mentoring, through teaching and engaging in research with, over a thousand graduate students, including supervising nearly 60 completed Ph.D. candidates who are now scholars in various places in the academy. I draw on these myriads of experiences to reflect on the possibilities and limitations of academic mentorship.

Similar to the previous sections, I seek to advance a decolonial and anti-colonial perspective on what it means to speak of a particular location of the *African Scholar* in an institution of higher learning (see Dei, 2014). I see the *decolonial* as a process with the end goal of an anti-colonial stance. As I note in Dei (2014), the African Scholar must not contend with charges of betraying our communities by either failing to champion the causes and issues that are of utmost concern to community survival or coming to know about our communities' historic struggles "from a distance" (Harding, 1974; Kelley, 2016; Dei, 2014, 2019; King, Council, Fournillier, Richardson, & Akua, 2019). The scholar is also responsible for developing genuine reciprocal relations, a co-relational status with ourselves, students and communities, and to co-produce knowledge in mutually beneficial ways.

My goal is to share concrete practices, challenges, and opportunities related to academic mentorship from my interactions with students and colleagues in various contexts because I see mentorship as a pillar of Black scholarship. This discussion will weave together an exploration of African Indigenous spatial conceptions and narratives of mentorship. The version of mentorship discussed will push against colonial schooling hierarchies and create communities of learners within a context of "schooling as a community". The intended political project is to assist African scholars in pursuing Indigenous mentorship strategies and intellectual possibilities to advance new African educational futures. The phrase "schooling as a community" fits into mentorship, specifically within the African Indigenous context of community building within schools and schooling. The phrase is about reciprocity, sharing of knowledge, the mutual interdependence of all learners, and knowledge production as a collective undertaking. "Schooling as community" broadly implies shared responsibilities to ensure knowledge serves a collective interest. Mentorship can facilitate this process in that those privileged by history have the responsibility to assist young learners.

Mentees can assist mentors in developing a shared sense of community. In promoting "schooling as community", the mentor is usually an individual who desires to create communities by assisting others in pursuit of knowledge. For such knowledge to be considered relevant, it must be placed at the disposal of a broader community to compel action. Therefore, it is the responsibility and obligation of academic and educational institutions to assist one another in the pursuit of learning. Academic mentorship must assist learners in realizing their dreams and goals as active participants in academic culture.

Academic mentorship is a crucial aspect of institutional capacity building, particularly in student training and mentorship. I see academic mentorship primarily as knowledge building and dissemination by equipping learners with critical thinking skills to challenge the taken-for-granted assumptions and emphasize that knowledge should compel change. This academic mentorship is about learners and mentors, specifically, what each person does to actualize change and transformation. In the discussion, I ground "student mentoring" concerning personal experiences, pointing to the benefits and challenges, best practices, and pathways to expand knowledge and capacity building in enhancing educational capacity. Moreover, I will be reflecting on my work, *African Scholar in the Western Academy* (2014).

Theorizing Mentorship

We must connect mentorship and capacity building in cultivating a pool of academic scholars and young learners capable of presenting knowledge for social change in our institutions and communities. Capacity building refers to having human power in place to sustain teaching, learning, and the administration of education. Capacity building is not just recruitment and training. It is also about retaining and promoting the relevant human bodies and developing the skills and aptitude to ensure educational change. It is generally agreed that African schooling and education need to develop the human capacity to deliver education to learners. Some questions to ponder despite appearing too elemental are: Who are the educators? Who are the learners? How do we prepare these educators to deliver critical knowledge? How do we prepare learners to work with such knowledge to ensure change? What human power is available within our institutions to deliver education to young learners? Educators must be well-trained to assume their responsibilities. Training is about knowledge, creation, and dissemination. It is about developing the human capacity to teach, learn, and administer education. Effective education delivery depends on the existence of well-trained educators. Therefore, we would expect academic mentorship to contribute to human capacity development in our educational settings.

Academic mentorship must be tailored to a particular learning objective, which is to enhance educational delivery and learning outcomes. The most common theorization surrounding mentorship is that it strengthens the learning between mentee and mentor. However, the core of mentorship theory is the presumption that one person must learn from the other. This assumption that one must be positioned as a teacher and the other as a learner is hierarchical and requires an anti-colonial analysis. Learning in mentorship relations must occur through knowledge sharing, shifts in perspectives, and a deepened awareness of the lived experiences of both the mentee and mentor (Arnesson & Albinsson, 2017). An issue often overlooked in mentorship theory is the potential for effective change in students and mentors. Academic mentorship can assist scholars in exploring Indigenous, anti-colonial strategies of mentorship; however, this involves knowledge surrounding what academic mentorship looks like within an African Indigenous context.

The understandings of academic mentorship points toward the possibility of new educational futurities intended to build on the learner's strengths. Such strengths should be developed through reciprocal, dialectic, and collective engagement that promotes respect, relevance, reciprocity, and responsibility (Kirkness & Barnhardt, 1991). Western, hierarchical understandings of mentorship have positioned students as solely absorbing knowledge from their mentors without actively engaging in a dialectical process or exchange. Mentees are not just passive receptors of knowledge, they are more than that, and such realization can contribute to a rich relationship of trust, respect, and knowledge potential. All invested in academic mentorship and capacity building within educational institutions must actively work to disrupt Western canons of education that fail to interrogate what student success and mentorship look like.

Oftentimes, academic mentorship programs fail to inspire change when operating with a "neutral space" lens. In educational institutions where educators do not feel supported, the ability to sustain teaching is limited. It cannot be denied that formal mentorship programs continue to grip white supremacist ideals and hierarchical structures in education that reproduce racism. Many mentorship programs rely on ideologies that institutionalize white supremacy hidden between the lines of individualism, multiculturalism, and colourblind logic (Vargas, Saetermore, & Chavira, 2020). Therefore, mentorship requires radical and transformational thought rooted in anti-colonial resistance. This resistance must incorporate futurities while imagining new spaces that affirm Black thought, Indigeneity, and put simply, other ways of existing, thinking, and making meaning of the world. Indigenous strategies of mentorship are mainly instrumental in supporting Black, African, Indigenous, and racialized students. Black scholars require space and positionality that recognizes excellence rather than questioning and invalidating abilities and experiences.

To further understand the contestations surrounding mentorship theory, it is essential to discuss a mentor's role in mentorship relationships. A mentor is someone familiar with the educational institution and its practices. The learning experience of the student/mentee is therefore dependent on how the mentor sees themselves as either connected to or disconnected from the privileges of higher education. Moreover, the failure to understand learners as change-makers has led to a dilemma within mentorship, presenting challenges for research and mentorship. Therefore, instructors, educators and researchers with lived experience of practices desirable to improve success, and experiences of institutional barriers and how to challenge them, can and should spearhead mentorship opportunities. Throughout my own experiences, my academic journey has benefitted from my mentee relations with the learner. Reflexive practices such as journal writing, creative group inquiry, and mentorship have allowed for genuine discussions and learning and provide contextual evidence of how and why specific issues occur.

Indigenous conceptualizations of mentorship have always centred mentorship on being collective, reciprocal, dialectic, and mutually responsive. Such knowledge does not emerge from the Western academy, which positions mentorship on a hierarchical basis; instead, mentorship should be centred on an Indigenous worldview, which includes an inherent shared responsibility of learning and the belief that learning is relational. Participants in all roles should see mentorship as a pedagogical tool to combine theory and practice geared toward learning and growth in higher education. Western mentorship fails to situate race and racial hierarchies as shaping higher education. There is an urgent need to include alternatives to traditional research and mentorship and situate mentorship within racist hierarchies. Anti-colonial theory can be used to theorize mentorship and understand the failures of mentorship in its institutions. Anti-colonial theory highlights that mentorship relationships are situated within racist structures that present challenges to students and push out Black and racialized students from higher education settings (Vargas, Saetermoe, & Chavira, 2020). Situating mentorship relationships within racist hierarchical structures provides insight into the ways "intrapsychic and interpersonal actions and discourses unfold" (Vargas, Saetermore, & Chavira, 2020, p. 1043). Such arguments emphasize the need for alternatives to traditional research and mentorship by highlighting the failure of higher education to take accountability for the hierarchies that continue to disproportionately impact racialized students within higher education. Black, Indigenous, and racialized students are often not presented with the same opportunities as White students, which can manifest in discouraging racialized students from producing innovative ideas. Students are deterred from pursuing goals and producing remarkable scholarship by silencing Black, Indigenous, and racialized students in higher education. Therefore, racism is reproduced through higher education without race-conscious mentor training, consequently failing to understand how mentorship can lead racialized students to disconnect from the academy altogether.

The "Personal" as "Intellectual and Political"

My initial work on "African and International Critical Development Studies", was followed later with a focus on race, schooling and Black and minority education, culminating in the current examinations of the intersections of Indigenous Philosophies, decolonization and anti-colonialism. This search of knowledge has taught some significant intellectual politics that I have always sought to impact students with through academic mentorship: First, to assist students to understand that our epistemological frameworks and academic engagements must recognize the body of the knowledge producer, politics, desires, as well as place, contexts in which knowledge is produced. As McKittrick (2021) points out, who we cite is important because it frames our argument, methodologically and theoretically – in other words, "if we begin with Michael Foucault as our primary methodological and theoretical frame...we will most certainly draw Foucauldian conclusions..." (p. 23). This means the theories and frameworks that we work with are fundamental to enhancing our intellectual capacity and we must make conscientious choices.

Second, is an understanding that the anti-colonial is intimately connected to decolonization, and by extension, decolonization cannot happen solely through Western scholarship. This entails learners advancing new knowledge to unravel and subvert the particularities of knowledge masquerading as universals, for example, dominant Western analysis frames and the imposition of colonial systems of knowing African communities (Oloruntoba-Oju, 2021). Subsequently, decolonizing African education "is not just de-Westernizing, but rather a total re-assertion of Africa at the center of knowledge discovery, interrogation, validation and dissemination" (see Asante, 2013, p. 12).

Third, there is a particular place of Indigenous epistemologies from multiple Lands, geographies and spaces to challenge, threaten, replace, and re-imagine alternatives to colonial thinking and practices of conventional schooling and education (see also Styres, 2019; Smith, Tuck, & Yang, 2012; Tuck & Yang, 2019). This is significant for reclaiming African knowledges and challenging the colonial appellation of African Indigenous, which is always in question as if colonialism destroyed the entire knowledge systems of African peoples. Moreover, the complex problems and challenges facing the world today defy universalist solutions but can be remedied by multi-centric ways of knowing/doing/being. We need different and multiple forms of knowledge that work with synergies of body, mind, soul, and spirit, and as such, the

African learner ought to continually search for a "Trialectic Space" [Suahunu] when we do our work to survive (Dei, 2012; see also Garcia & Shirley, 2012).

Practical Strategies

One cannot engage in academic mentorship through research collaboration with students and not confront the challenges rooted in the political economy of the academy, as well as the coloniality of the academic space, with its attendant colonial mimicry and questions of Black/African authenticity. The marketplace of ideas in academia is such that knowledge can be commodified and privatized to gain privilege and dominance without necessarily being subversive knowledge. It has to be intentional on the part of the African scholar to produce knowledge that subverts dominance and the status quo. Black, African, Indigenous and racialized students in the Western academy are often seduced to seek validation, acceptance and legitimation in White colonial spaces (see also Fanon, 1961, 1967). This reveals deep traces of epistemological and academic imperialism and tends to have emotional, spiritual, mental, and psychological consequences on learners. It requires an academic strategy of building confidence in the power of self-knowing as bodily knowing. Part of transformative academic mentorship is instructing students to respond to this problem of academic hierarchies of knowledge and challenging the coloniality-modernity dialectic (see Mignolo, 2007, 2010; Quijano, 2007). As Smith (2012) notes, "imperialism frames the Indigenous experience. It is part of our story, our version of Modernity. Writing about our experience under imperialism and its more specific expression of colonialism has become a significant project of the Indigenous world" (p. 57). Likewise, imperialism and colonialism have shaped and informed Black writing in multiple nuanced ways.

Academic mentorship emboldens students to question dominant Modernity articulations and, for example, separate or disentangle Indigenous articulations of "Indigeneity" from the dominant articulations or conceptions of Aboriginal/Indigenous or White nationalism from anti-colonialism nationalism. African and Indigenous learners must be able to reclaim "Indigenous Modernity", insisting that the "Indigenous world does not conceive history as linear, (but that) the past-future is contained in the present" [and therefore a project of] "Indigenous modernity can emerge from the present in a spiral whose movement is a continuous feedback from the past to the future, (offering) a principle of hope or anticipatory consciousness that both discerns and realizes decolonization at the same time" (Cusicanqui, 2012, p. 97). In the present and past lessons, this is a grammar of Black futurity, striving and living for the future (see Campt, 2017).

This is also about the power of "Writing Back" (see Dei, 1998). The "Global" assumes Western Europe [and its Euro-colonial Modernity] transcends human history and intellectuality. Colonial, colonizing and imperial relations and practices (including racist, sexist, ablest, homophobic and other oppressive systems) follow this thinking process. Such thinking and practice must continually be resisted and subverted. Therefore, African, Indigenous, racialized and anti-colonial scholars cannot afford not to "write back" to the imperial narrative. This is a necessary exercise in our decolonization. The problem and clarity sought are what does "Writing Back" really mean? Writing back entails the necessary situating of our critiques and interventions foremost in a critique of Europe and Euro-colonial Modernity and beyond. The conundrum is anti-colonial scholars always risk being accused of engaging in a reactionary discourse to Europe! However, can we talk about Africa without Europe while still recognizing that Europe is not the advent of human history? So, what is beyond and going this is our complicities and responsibilities (e.g., not speaking truth to power, being seduced by silence, Whiteness, privilege and a false sense of entitlement without responsibilities)?

Specific strategies to achieve this objective learning are cultivating the power of knowing, coming to know differently and affirming their cultural knowledges. There is also a need to work with students to develop a comfort zone speaking from their own experiences, histories, knowledge base and ancestral memories. I encourage the students themselves to build learning communities through the mentorship of peers. Part of the strategy is to develop the student's sense of ownership of the academic space and to know that the university is worth fighting for and that their work must break down colonial structures in schooling and education. I have come to realize that a pedagogy of subversion framed from an anti-colonial lens strengthens, builds and empowers all learners rather than disenfranchises, marginalizes and devalues certain bodies. The spatiality of Blackness reveals that racism transcends particular geographies, borders, Lands and spaces. So, we must encourage and mentor our learners to work with their [self and collectively generated onto-epistemological] understandings of Blackness, anti-Blackness and Africanness to pursue a radical politics of new Black global educational futurity.

Another strategy of academic mentorship is to understand that knowledge and action create futures, that futures are being contested, and that the academy itself is a contested space. There are contestations over knowledge, representation, power, and identities. Life can be messy, and students must develop the courage to speak out and defend their stances while showing a willingness to learn beyond where they are. Given the coloniality of Western science knowledge that has devalued African knowings, we need African learners to be part of this academic contestation over knowledge in search of new futurity as a collective, a community of differences. Community is a search for anti-colonial solidarities. So, for example, to assist students as part of the learning process to see the question of Black liberation and connect with Indigenous struggles for sovereignty. This is the idea of developing Black and Indigenous radical relationalities.

Long ago, Ghanaian philosophers had a charge for African/Black scholars to pioneer "new analytical systems for understanding our communities steeped in our home-grown cultural perspectives" (Yankah, 2004, p. 25). Strategies to assist students to meet this call include working with them on the possibilities of counter-visioning schooling and education. In 2019, I began to engage with several graduate students on a research project on African Elders' cultural knowledge to counter-visioning schooling and education (Dei, 2023 forthcoming?). The study relies on Indigenous knowledge rediscovery and recovery to counteract and challenge epistemological imperialism and bring such knowledges to reframe schooling and education. This research works with Earthly teachings on relationalities, reciprocity, sharing, equity and justice, community building, Land and Environments, and responsibility enshrined in local proverbs, songs, fables, folktales, myths, and mythologies. This solid knowledge base challenges knowledge hierarchies by bringing African Elders into schooling and education. Elders' teachings have instructional, pedagogic, and communicative values that we can consider as learning communities to educate ourselves. These teachings also constitute local cultural resource knowledge as influential sites of multiple knowings, a different way of explaining our realities and thinking through solutions to our problems.

Students must be mentored in their learning to arrive at a critical understanding that local cultural resource knowledge of African Elders has been the least analyzed for their contributions to schooling, education and development. Schooling must promote social values of local cultural knowledges, and challenge the neo-liberal economic values of competitive individualism, consumerism, efficiency, and productivity. Creating a community of learners transforms schools into supporting and welcoming spaces, a spiritual healing space, and a community of learners.

Another strategy of academic mentorship is to help students frame their learning in terms of possibilities and limitations. This is crucial if we are to confront the liberal narrative that posits liberation in education. The Covid-19 pandemic has presented critical questions about education globally. We as educators must ask ourselves, "What is education really for?" The urgency of this conversation unfolds as education globally has been paralyzed, perhaps like never before in our times. We also need to think about the institutional negligence around the experiences of Black learners, including anti-Black racism. Academic mentorship is to assist students to repurpose Black political agendas and Black thought in educational institutions. It is to betray and push our institutions to re-imagine Black futurities. Academia has long manipulated Black and African excellence. We are used as calling cards when convenient. Our institutions always find a "path to redemption", or as Mandela Gray (2021) puts it, to do "penance" that gets in the way of true liberation. Envisioning African educational futurity needs to encompass all peoples of African descent for true liberation, not just African-Americans or Black Canadians. We cannot be complicit with the imperial project that does not allow us to see our commonalities. For example, it is true liberation to betray our institutions when they approach anti-Black racism as a way to do "penance and have their conscience cleansed" (Gray, 2021).

Another strategy I have employed in my academic mentorship is forming a study group of students who work with me at the University of Toronto. The group is likely my supervisees, and we meet once a month to discuss students' school work, share ideas, and bring in local community members to ensure the academic space connects with real-life community issues.

The group has published four books, each spearheaded by a group of students as editors. This has been a space for students to present their work and receive collective feedback. It has also given space for students to work on "think tank" theoretical pieces and conceptual notes.

As a strategy of academic mentorship, I have developed a student buddy-buddy system that pairs senior and young students at different stages of their academic careers to support each other on their academic journey. This has been especially useful in mitigating hierarchical mentoring relationships and increasing participation among students. A communal mentoring approach emphasizes that learning takes place in all directions and consists of interconnected layers.

Another strategy I have employed through academic mentorship is to ensure a co-edited book publication from student papers in my courses at the University of Toronto. This has served to build the confidence of graduate students as future academic writers.

One strategy that has proven effective in creating spaces for graduate and postdoctoral studies students is to outline personal short and long-term goals and find practical ways to achieve those goals with alumni and others in the field. This process includes practical goal setting, constant self-reassessments, and aligning students' goals with their department.

Finally, a critical approach I have taken to promote confidence in students has been providing a space where students witness transparency when dealing with institutionalized barriers such as financial resources, biases, and outdated policies. As many others have articulated, transparency and trust are difficult to establish through mentorship relations (Saha, 2019; Fries-Britt & Snider, 2015). Nonetheless, with the exposed vulnerability of the mentor, mentees realize that they are not alone in experiencing barriers and challenges within educational institutions. This creates openness and mutuality between mentors and students necessary to establish in academic settings, especially when considering the growth of relationships and partnerships (Fries-Britt & Kelly, 2015).

Academic Mentorship for Publication

I now address an important area of academic mentorship – developing learners' capacity to publish academically. My own "publishing career" has spanned continents, as well as areas of scholarship and different text forms [e.g., school newspapers, newspaper Opinion editorials, other media texts, Journal articles, books, co-authorships, sole-edited and co-edited works]. It began as a student at Ghana National College in Cape Coast, Ghana, when I published a short piece on why Black shoes attract sunlight. It continued into Ontario universities as a graduate student, a Social Science and Humanities Council (SSHRC) postdoctoral fellow, and later, tenured faculty. Along the way, I have mentored graduate students and faculty members, including having joint publications. I find this whole process reciprocal as my students have been my best teachers. I am, thus, speaking from my personal experiences with the belief that publishing for academics is a vital component for knowledge production, construction, and dissemination. Young Black scholars, who are desirous of academic mentorship must confront this question: How do we assist learners in developing their academic publications capacities? My personal accounting below, written as friendly advice, highlights substantive content and process issues throughout the publication journey.

Lessons Learned from Personal History and Contexts

Start this journey early. Establishing your writing career takes time and commitment.

Have something to say that makes a difference, but do not fall into the academic trap of publishing to publish or to increase your publications. Frequently, academic writing risks being simply theoretical and self-gratifying. Be passionate about your subject matter and the purpose for which you write. In doing so, your work and your writing will mean something more significant to both you and the audience for whom you wish to write.

Do your homework: Look for Journal articles, this could be peer-reviewed Journals, public record texts or refereed articles. Consider current debates or points of contention alongside their focus and audience. As you read, reflect on the editorship, the intellectual frame of reference present in the writing and the market for readership. A critical aspect of publishing is to seek advice from established publishers. If you cannot find someone established to publish with, be willing and ready to start from the bottom. Ask mentors and other established academics for their experiences with specific publishers and tailor your approach to their publication needs. For students, in particular, finding a publisher who wants to work with an "up-and-coming academic" is always challenging—as such, finding an academic who is willing to nurture your career and co-publish with you is an immense advantage.

Working with Oppositional Scholarship

It is essential to recognize that if you wish to engage in writing deemed to be oppositional to dominant narratives, your work will be perceived in a specific manner. This is particularly true if you are a member of a racially and historically oppressed group. As such, the publishers you wish to collaborate with must have an anti-colonial/anti-racist/anti-oppressive agenda. You must not sacrifice your politics for publications. It may mean that fewer publishers will want to work with you. However, you will ultimately find yourself in a niche market.

Openness to Knowledge

Two African proverbs highlight the journey we engage in as we collect, examine and filter the knowledge and experiences we acquire throughout our daily lives:

1. Like the turtle, every man must stick out his neck if he wants to go forward.
2. Wisdom is like a baobab tree; no one individual can embrace it.

Do not be afraid to cross theoretical and methodological boundaries in your work. In order to avoid circular reasoning, one must be open to seeking out and acquiring feedback from a linear thinker. This is one of the best ways to approach established theory through a fresh lens.

Reciprocity and collaboration are fundamental principles in the knowledge production and dissemination process. Be prepared to learn as much from others as they learn from you. Collaborative work has its advantages in that colleagues are the best measure of your theoretical focus and success. If your arguments or approaches do not make sense to them, they will likely be problematic for other readers as well. Always have your work checked and critiqued by colleagues that you trust.

Searching for Support Networks

Support networks are individuals in your life who help you to achieve your personal and professional goals. Within the publishing realm, support networks must engage those with the power and privilege to help you get published and partners in the project within student communities. For example, study groups that include other students in your publication projects enhance knowledge collection, sharing and critical reflection. Ultimately within these communities, if one individual succeeds, everyone succeeds – all other parties become allies within the collective journey.

Dealing with Rejections

Almost all writers suffer setbacks and rejections. This is part of the growth and development process. You will likely receive rejections, so make sure you are prepared for them. Rejections must encourage you to work harder and explore alternative approaches to refine your writing. It is essential to always be prepared to rework your desired publication and resubmit.

Collaboration

I have found collaborative work to be more satisfying as an opportunity to learn alongside individuals and engage in dialogue toward change. The challenging part is finding colleagues and partners who will aggressively support your writing projects. Be wary of individuals who do not share similar interests or goals. In such partnerships, you have to expect that collaborators will be differently engaged and thus differently responsible for completing the work. Accept this and move on.

Seek collaborative opportunities with individuals who are already established in the field in which you wish to engage. Do not be afraid to bring ideas and take on extra work to get the project done. Those who are already established will likely have other responsibilities. You must ensure you are motivated to see the project to its end.

Additional Significant Tips

1. Identify peer-reviewed journals in the field of study for which the research is appropriate. Avoid open access Journals if possible because some of them require payment. In addition to peer-reviewed academic journals, it is good to publish in non-academic places such as magazines, blogs, and social media. This allows you to make your writing available to either the general public or a target audience.
2. Do a regular check for "Call for Papers" in the field of study. Sometimes publishers and journals will call a "special issue" with topics that may be of interest.
3. Create opportunities for joint publications. This can be done in multiple ways. Consider writing op-ed pieces for media publications so that your work can be amplified outside of academia. Learning to write short

pieces in an accessible way makes you a better writer. Furthermore, being a part of an academic/writing community supports collaboration and engaging in critical conversations that will ultimately enhance your writing.
4. Promote your publications. Consider creating a website or platform to promote all of your publications.
5. Find ways to work through writing blocks. Creative work is a process that takes time. When you experience writing blocks, read poetry, listen to music or do something that inspires you. Take breaks when you need to – be kind to yourself.

Refereed Journal Publications

Choosing the right Journal requires critical reflection and careful assessment. Here are some points for consideration:

1. Analyze the "aims and scope" of the journal to determine whether your writing is an excellent fit for the publication. One should probably do this in the early stages of the writing so that one is not doing many last-minute revisions to make a fit.
2. Carefully assess the founding context of the journal: when was the journal established? Who created it and why?
3. Research the Journal's mission statement and guiding principles. Authors should be sure that the assumptions and principles guiding their scholarship align with whether journal editors and reviewers will be disposed to offer critical and fair judgment of your submission.
4. Identify whether the Journal a) clearly states the role of editor(s) and b) offers clear guidelines to reviewers for ethical and collegial reviews such as that provided by the Committee on Ethical Publication Ethics.
5. Is the Journal ranked for "impact factor"? There are essentially ideological, methodological and normative questions to be asked about such metrics.
6. Determine whether the journal's disciplinary focus/foci match with the disciplinary approach of your research.
7. Does the journal engage in predatory publishing: meaning, do you have to pay to get published?
8. Is the journal Open Access or restricted access? You will need to decide whether the knowledge you produce is for the intellectual commons

or if you only speak to a highly restricted and economically endowed audience that treats knowledge as private property.

As a general rule, submit your research publications to Journals that publish the scholarship you appreciate and value. Once a Journal is selected, the second journey of engagement must be centred around the writing process. Here are some points for consideration:

1. Determine a few articles in the journal that speak to your topic of interest. Examine whether and how you might bring your writing into conversation with these published articles. Keep in mind that these writers may very well be the scholars who will be called on to review your submission.
2. Practice writing as early as possible with their citation format in mind. If you can, purchase a citation program, as working on in-text citations and bibliography after the fact is highly time-consuming.
3. Before submitting your scholarship, have colleagues and people who have successfully published critically assess your writing.
4. Ensure that it is carefully copy-edited (follow journal submission guidelines) before submission. It sets negative precedence if reviewers feel you have not taken the care to review your work carefully or if you have otherwise made their job more complicated than necessary.
5. Submit anyone who works for publication review to onejournal at a time.
6. Be patient with reviewers once comments come back. Feedback should always be taken as an opportunity to improve your writing. If you feel you have been misunderstood, take responsibility for your lack of clarity and reflect on how you can ensure the intention and purpose of your writing is readily accessible and understood by your audience. Ultimately, if the journal has been well chosen, you should be speaking among scholars with similar commitments.

Book Publications [including sole/joint authored monograph or sole/joint edited collection]

Determining the publishing house that aligns with your direction of scholarship requires an in-depth review of presses and careful analysis of the publication series. Here are some points for consideration:

1. Carefully review prospectus design and submission guidelines
2. Decide whether you want to work with a university versus a trade press.

3. Put together a solid proposal. During this process, you must be willing to revise your proposals based on the requirements of each publisher. This entails ensuring you are writing on a topic of relevance, not only in subject matter but also in approach.
4. If you are working towards an edited reader, do not be afraid to contact established allies in the field. These individuals likely remember their experiences as young academics and may provide you with some guidance.
5. Concerning subject matter, this applies to dissertation work; choose a topic that will build on existing knowledge and be dynamic to a readership. After all, if you do not have something original and exciting to say, who will want to read your work, let alone publish it?
6. Be clear about the focus of your book. Ask yourself what it contributes to the literature in a given area of scholarship and how it is positioned relative to at least ten other books that have addressed a duplicate or related topic within the past 5-10 years.

If your book will be an edited collection and the press approves it, ensure the following:

1. Circulate a call for papers on appropriate email lists and journals catering to the area of scholarship to be found in your book.
2. Be clear about the division of labour regarding who the primary and subsequent editors will be, or if it is a collective effort rather than individually named authors.
3. Have clear and transparent guidelines for judging the quality of submissions and the conditions that may disqualify them, even if their abstracts and subsequent papers are accepted. The latter may include quality of research and argument, correct citation format, quality of writing, timely submission and responsiveness to editor commentary.
4. Be reasonable about due dates, as it takes much longer than you may think.
5. Invite colleagues you trust to review and offer critical friendly commentary on your prospectus confidentially.
6. Submit your prospectus to only one editor at a time.

What Makes for an Excellent, Cutting Edge Publication?

Many features can enhance your publication. Ask yourself the following questions:

1. Have you conveyed discursive authority or intellectual confidence in your writing?
2. Have you identified the key points you wish to convey?
3. How clear are your arguments to diverse audiences?
4. What have you done to ensure you are grounded in existing literature?
5. How have you gone beyond the literature to ask new questions? This includes bringing a new theoretical/discursive gaze to the scholarship.
6. Expanding the scope of arguments into new terrain.
7. Have you used examples/illustrations (where applicable) to support, enhance, or provide clarity to your key ideas?
8. Have you ended your writing with the direction the study is going or hopes to go and future questions for investigation? This includes presenting unanswered questions/challenges to further your contributions to the scholarship.

Conclusion: Sustaining a Publishing Career

Sustaining publishing requires three things: (i) work, (ii) work and (iii) more work.

You must be willing to do more than is asked of you and aggressively seek publication avenues. This means setting goals such as developing a plan to publish at least one book or two articles a year and actively exploring ways to ensure that goals become a reality. Above all else, publishing means genuinely loving the work and area of scholarship that is of interest. Research and writing must go hand in hand, and you must believe that publishing can indeed make a difference in one's academic career.

Institutional Responsibility

My own academic and professional growth in African Studies and Indigenous Knowledge Systems interacting and working with African scholars and students on the continent has been enriched. In addition, I have had the privilege of mentoring countless students in Canada, shaping my own perception of mentorship tremendously. My academic journey has benefitted from my mentee relations with learners, as the perspectives shared have been profoundly influential in my practice as an educator. The measurable outcomes of the academic engagements and mentorship reveal themselves on the impact of students' academic progress such as completion rates, publications, conferences attended and papers presented, success in competitive grants, honours and awards, academic grounding in theory and method of social inquiry.

Universities face various challenges in creating the capacity for students to expand educational boundaries, in that many struggle with excellence being defined in terms of expectations created within the Global North (Dei, 2014). The issue of legitimacy is experienced worldwide, and it is the responsibility of mentors to recognize pedagogical concerns, socio-political issues, and power imbalances in mentor/mentee relations (Saha, 2019). Here it is essential to understand that collaboration in mentoring exposes the flaws of environments which is why the approaches to mentorship must consistently be re-evaluated and assessed from the perspective of students and mentors. Most importantly, mentors must recognize the values of mutuality (Saha, 2019). As this is an essential part of these relationships.

Concluding Thoughts

Academic mentorship does not only require communication and commitment; it requires resources to sustain teaching and retain educators who are dedicated to educational change and transformation. Human capacity development in educational settings must strengthen our critiques of the failure of mentorship to keep students engaged in long-term projects while retaining mentors. We also must interrogate the ways mentorship opportunities operate through an understanding of institutional hierarchies. To mitigate this issue, educational institutions must emphasize the importance of turning toward African and Indigenous knowledges and approaches to mentorship that center dialectical learning. Moreover, engaging with schooling as a community in mentorship relations allows for mutually beneficial relationships built from reciprocity, collectiveness, and transformational growth.

Success cannot be attributed to individual actions but rather from things produced within the dialectic of interpersonal relations. As outlined within this paper, the multitude of experiences I have with mentorship in all capacities has provided me with knowledge surrounding processes that require attention to sustain and provide successful opportunities for academic mentorship. I continue to support students in envisioning and creating new methodological and practical approaches to transform institutions. This aspect of academic mentorship enhances my understanding of education and consistently positions me as a learner in the process. There are responsibilities that mentors must address in efforts to move beyond individualistic aspects of mentorship towards a mentorship that acknowledges the complexity of different practices, beliefs, and thoughts in education. It is critical to ask ourselves, how can academic mentorship truly move beyond individualism toward collectivity that emphasizes new African futurities?

Moreover, how do we subvert colonial legacies of mentorship that have historically pushed African, Black, Indigenous and racialized students away from academic success and research opportunities? When carefully executed, mentorship can create endless possibilities for students to transform their visions into tangible practices that expand knowledge and emphasize collective success.

References Cited:

Arnesson, K., & Albinsson, G. (2017). Mentorship – A pedagogical method for integration of theory and practice in higher education. *Nordic Journal of Studies in Educational Policy*, 3(3), 202–217. https://doi.org/10.1080/20020317.2017.1379346

Campt, T. (2017). *Listening to images*. Duke University Press.

Cusicanqui, S. R. (2012). Ch'ixinakax utxiwa: A reflection on the practices and discourses of decolonization. *South Atlantic Quarterly*, 111(1), 95–109. doi: 10.1215/00382876-1472612

Dei, G. J. S. (1998). "Why Write Back?": The role of Afrocentric discourse in social change. *Canadian Journal of Education*, 23(2), 200–208. https://doi.org/10.2307/1585981

Dei, G. J. S. (2012). "Suahunu: The Trialectic Space". *Journal of Black Studies*, 43(8), 823–846.

Dei, G. J. S. (2014). "The African Scholar in the Western Academy". *Journal of Black Studies*, 45(3), 167–179.

Dei, G. J. S. (2022). *The Black Scholar Travelogue*. New York: Routledge [proposed].

Fanon, F. (2004) [1961]. The wretched of the earth. New York: Grove Press.

Fanon, F. (1967). Black Skin, white Masks. New York: Grove Press.

Garcia, J., & Shirley, V. (2012). Performing decolonization: Lessons learned from Indigenous youth, teachers and leaders' engagement with critical Indigenous pedagogy. *Journal of Curriculum Theorizing*, 28(2), 76–91.

Gray, B. S. (2021). [Tweet]. *@BikoMandelaGray*.

Harding, V. (1974). The vocation of the Black scholar and the struggles of the Black community. In Institute of the Black World (Eds.), *Education and Black struggle: Notes from the colonized world*. Harvard Educational Review (Monograph no. 2), 3–29.

Kelley, R. D. (2016). "Black study, Black struggle". Boston Review, March 7. http://bostonreview.net/forum/robin-d-g-kelley-black-study-black-struggle

King, J., Council, T. M., Fournillier, J. B., Richardson, V., & Akua, C. (2019). "Pedagogy for partisanship: Research training for Black graduate students in the Black intellectual tradition." *International Journal of Qualitative Studies in Education*, 32(2), 188–209. doi:10.1080/09518398.2018.1548040

Kirkness, V., & Barnhardt, R. (1991). First nations and higher education: The four R's—Respect, relevance, reciprocity and responsibility. *Journal of American Indian Education*, 30, 1–15.

McKittrick, K. (2021). *Dear science and other stories*. Duke University Press. https://doi.org/10.1515/9781478012573

Oloruntoba-Oju, T. (2021). Email correspondence. July, 2021.

Quijano, A. (2007). Coloniality and Modernity/Rationality. *Cultural Studies*, 21 (2–3), 168–178. DOI: 10.1080/09502380601164353

Saha, M. (2019). Contextual Mentoring: Theory and Practice Alignment. *Canadian Journal for New Scholars in Education*, 10(2)

Smith, L. T. (2012). *Decolonizing methodologies: Research and indigenous peoples*. Zed books.

Smith, L. T., Tuck, E., & Yang, K. W. (2019). "Introduction". In. L. T. Smith, E. Tuck, & K. W. Yang (Eds.), *Indigenous and decolonizing studies in education: Mapping the long view*. New York: Routledge.

Styres, S. (2019). Literacies of land: Decolonizing narratives, storying, and literature. In L. T. Smith, E. Tuck, & K. W. Yang (Eds.), Indigenous and decolonizing studies in education: *Mapping the long view* (pp. 159 -174). New York: Routledge.

Tuck, E., & Yang, K. W. (2012). "Decolonization is not a metaphor". *Decolonization: Indigeneity, Education & Society*, 1(1), 1–40.

Vargas, J. H., Saetermoe, C. L., & Chavira, G. (2020). Using critical race theory to reframe mentor training: Theoretical considerations regarding the ecological systems of mentorship. *Higher Education*, 81(5), 1043–1062. https://doi.org/10.1007/s10734-020-00598-z

Yankah, K. (2004). *Globalization and the African scholar*. Faculty of Arts University of Ghana Monograph.

· 1 0 ·

THE UGLY FACE OF A NEW "DIVERSITY PLAY"

In Concluding this book, I could not help but reference a recent "Opinion piece" in a British newspaper. Kehinde Andrews (2022) makes the point that "Britain is as close as it has ever been to being run by a prime minister who is not White....but rather than being a signal that we are at a watershed moment in British politics, this whole episode is the perfect example that diversity is often the enemy of anti-racism". This is so true, plain and simple. In truth, diversity politics, or might we say the "true identity politics" has been co-opted by Ultra Right conservative to champion their self-assured intentions and causes. Long ago, Dei, Karumanchery, and Karumanchery-Luik (2004) wrote a book we purposely titled "Playing the Race Card: Exposing White Power and Privilege". We never liked the term, but we were arguing then that it is White bodies who actually "play the race card", if ever there is anything as such. Unfortunately, the term is affixed to Black, Brown and Indigenous body politics when we use race to seek justice the same way White has used race to amass White privilege. When the Ultra Conservatives champion their skewed understanding of diversity, it is not for the love of diversity and representation in the workforce or any facet of wider society. They decry it. Yet they love to see a Black, Brown or Indigenous face who is anti-diversity leading all their charges of "wokeism" and the vehement against racial justice charges. Unfortunately, for the layperson it gives the false impression society has made headway in, for example, selecting a Black, Brown or Indigenous leader in a White-dominated context. But in truth, this minoritized body is merely doing its bidding. The Black, Brown or Indigenous face Whites love to see as signs of representation in the top echelons of power is simply enabled to say things Whites cannot say and get away with. Why? All because she or he is Black, Brown or Indigenous thereby lending credence and credibility to the assertion that "they cannot be racist".

Of late, in the case of Britain, Andrews (2022) opines that "despite all this diversity, the government has pursued the most openly racist policy agenda in living memory'. Andrews (2020) continues "it is no coincidence that the most racist policy has come from a non-White spokesperson". A non-White leader's anti-stance on diversity allows them "to get away with words and deeds someone of a different hue could not". He or she lends credibility to White who decries there is racism or that race is irrelevant. To her, a racialized body mouth of such views carries weight and is used against the broader causes to which we fight as Black, Indigenous and racialized bodies. Andrews (2022) points out the case of a "Nigerian immigrant who became the queen of the anti-woke brigade with her attacks on critical race theory, Black Lives Matter and her defence of the British Empire". Andrews (2022) further enthuses that "the idea that Black and Brown faces leading the party is progressive is as insulting as it is absurd. This is the real identity politics, the idea that just because of their colour people like Patel, Badenoch and Sunak must have the best interests of Black and Brown communities at heart……In truth, there have always been those who chose to align with the forces of racial oppression in order to enrich and enable themselves. The British Empire simply could not have run without countless Black and brown middle managers. The fact that one may now be elevated into the most important role is no kind of victory". This is an astute observation and it shows how Black, Indigenous and racialized groups are not just a monolithic group, but that sometimes many of us fail to see the forest beyond the trees. Bodies matter but so also is the politics of the body.

Andrews (2022) concludes his piece with this observation. A "Sunak victory would put British race relations back even further than the Johnson government did. There is nothing more damaging than the illusion of progress because it masks the real problems that continue to exist"……..If Sunak wins, he will be leading an openly racist government, hell-bent on continuing its devastating agenda. But because a non-White prime minister has been such a long time coming, many of us will delude ourselves into believing a change has come". Right on. As I write we don't know the result of the British election. But it does not matter. Many White who supports Sunak may share his policy stances and economic views. But many are also fine and happy that a racialized body carrying the mantle of a harsh agenda against Black, Indigenous and racialized peoples' social justice causes is just fine with them. The irony is not lost on them.

My main point in bringing up Andrews (2022) exhortation is simple: Given its misuses, the rhetoric of diversity is no substitute for genuine decolonial and anti-colonial shifts within our systems and institutional settings. As noted repeatedly in this book, schools are carceral places with violence marked on particular and different bodies. In truth, schools can also be fulfilling places if good critical anti-colonial learning and teaching are allowed to flourish. Race is, and continues to be a salient lens through which educational inequalities and disparities take shape. "Decolonization" itself has become a way to uphold Whiteness in academia [e.g., how has our university become an arm of the settler state (Hill, 2022)]. As noted, a critical understanding of the ways Equity, Diversity and Inclusion (EDI has been a distraction through race evasiveness, colour-blind ideology and the inability to name and act on race, racism, particularly, anti-Black racism and White Supremacy is significant. There continues to be settler crimes against Black and Indigenous humanity (Grande, 2018, p. 48, Dei, 2017). From open denials of Black and Indigenous suffering to quick scapegoating and the lack of power-sharing. Settler crimes are diverse and complex. By resisting a monolithic construction of White settlerhood and the settled Land, we are best positioned to engage in critical anti-colonial theorizing as social agents inhabiting our multiple ways of Being and being seen and heard on multiple fronts (Dei & Lordan, 2013).

I would venture to opine that what really threatens liberal democracies today is the continuing problem of coloniality devaluing and valuing different lives and aspirations. This, associated with expectations of Whiteness, in terms of conformity, policing, surveillance and punishment is scripting Black and Indigenous lives and crippling social justice overall. Clearly, the project of dismantling White supremacy calls for building new futures, not just living in the present. We build for the future with the lessons of the past and the present much in our gaze. I am attracted to the idea of "fleeing from without leaving" (see Harney & Moten, 2013). It is about our complicities and shared responsibilities as members of a community. This reading is important as we seek multiple and complex strategies with an "and/with" rather than an "either /or" mindset. In other words, to develop strategies that allow us to flee ourselves from carceral logics without leaving the possibilities within such carceral spaces nonetheless, places in which we live, work and study. As many have noted, our schools, colleges and universities are gatekeepers of knowledge, research and methodologies. How we all question these bodies of knowledge is very critical. As contested spaces, schools, colleges and universities can also be turned into spaces for radical and speculative imaginaries.

This is why working together and in different yet connected lanes is always significant for ensuring collective success. Although education is one of the main sources of contemporary and past troubled relations between Indigenous and non-Indigenous people, education also has the potential to remedy some of the harm inflicted by schools (see also Vowel, Tucker, & HighWater Press, 2020). Social justice, anti-racist, decolonial and anti-colonial work is for all of us, not something reserved for a few – Black, Indigenous and racialized bodies. With power and privilege comes great responsibility, and we must always commit to something bigger than ourselves. In our anti-racist, decolonial and anti-colonial work, showing humility and respect for history is equally important. We should never arrive late and yet proceed to claim all the credit. Let us recognizes the sacrifices and hard work that has been done by those before us and resolve to build upon these struggles.

The current reckoning of race, anti-Blackness and decolonial challenges can lead to a path of meaningful and productive change, if we completely denounce ongoing developments. For example, the blatant disregard for lives that happen to be non-White. We cannot be oblivious to how Black, Indigenous and racialized tragedy is normalized in the global media imagination. The world is outraged seeing White pain. It cannot fathom White death. And yet, Black death is normalized, we have all become desensitized to it. The continuing devaluation and negation of Black/African, Indigenous, racialized peoples' social theorizing and knowledge, whereby the White, Western liberal subject/knower is universalized as an archetype of humanity, and the "all knower" (see also Furo, 2018; Abidogun & Toyin, 2020; Santos, 2002). Black, Indigenous and racialized experiences always reveal a rich trope of knowledge to learn from and act upon.

This is why we cannot remain silent when bodies of knowledge that challenge the status quo are being dismissed. Our cries matter. It is worth repeating things that have been reiterated in earlier sections of the book to put a cap on matters. Today, we have to contend with the "calculated to distract" and often misguided cries of "wokeism" and how "misinformation, conspiracy theories, lies, culture wars, and barely concealed racism now dominate public discourse and politics", particularly in the US context (Collinson, 2022). We can at least speak out against the muzzling of anti-racist speech and this dominant desire for a return to a "colour-blind" world. We must also address the prevailing race-coloniality tandem, that is, the silence, denial and hypocrisy on particular identities, connections to knowledge production and the impacts on racialized bodies. The twin problems of settler colonial retrenchment and Conservative backlash through legislation is a serious concern. In the US, the vicious and calculated backlash to anti-racist education as posing a threat to the American way of life; exacerbates and influences divisions rather than creating an inter-ethnic bridge is just fiction with real consequences (Asmelash, 2021). There is the deliberately manufactured "problem" of Critical Race Theory (CRT) when it is not even taught in American public schools! To call for a Parents' Bill of Rights that a select group of privileged White parents are allowed to dictate what all learners must learn in our schools is deeply offensive. These antics not only deny teachers creativity to teach on important subjects of history and social justicebut also, demonstrate the seeping of thought speech police in the school system. The classrooms can never be a place for critical learning under such conditions. The hypocrisy of those who cry "cancel culture" being at the helm of regulating what can be taught in our schools, what books can be taught etc. is deeply worrisome. The idea that teaching "Black History" makes White kids feel bad and therefore we must silence such teachings does not bode well for the future of schooling and education in any true democracy.

White grievances and victimhood as bearing the onus of racism, such as the "angry White male" are laughable. But it is a serious mantra that demands we call out White supremacist logics and how it engenders settler consciousness. The shameful US Supreme Court confirmation process of Judge Ketanji Brown Jackson laid bare White Conservative hypocrisy, specious, vile and outrageous attacks, and disrespect of the historic confirmation of the first Black woman Supreme Court Judge. It is an important case in point to the length that some may go to deny history or when history is being made. Rather than addressing power and privilege culture wars and conspiracy theories are now seen as avenues to political power with histrionics and viral media moments becoming "vicious political play for base politics" (Collinson, 2022). Guess who is showing up at White supremacist rallies these days? We must ask: where are our souls?

Going Forward and Making Discursive Links of Blackness and Indigeneity in Reconciliation, Decolonization and Restitution

Systemic anti-Black racism has been continually denied within institutional settings. Yet, in Toronto, a recent review of race-based data examining more than 86,500 interactions Toronto Police had with members of the public in 2020 confirmed that non-White residents are more likely to face disproportionate levels of violence at the hands of police (see Toronto Police report, June 15, 2022). Indeed, the findings were disturbing but not surprising:

- Blacks were 230% more likely to have a Police Officer point a firearm at them than White people.
- Blacks are 1.6 more likely to have police force used on them.
- When force was used, Blacks were overrepresented in higher types of force used.
- Compared to Whites, Blacks were 150% more likely to have a police firearm pointed at them during the enforcement action.
- Whites were 40 percent more likely to have less-than-lethal force [e.g., physical contact, a bean-bag shotgun, baton or Taser] used against them by police, even when they were thought to be in possession of weapons.
- Latinos were overrepresented in use-of-force incidents by a factor of 1.5 while Middle Eastern and Southeast Asian people were overrepresented by a factor of 1.2. Indigenous people were overrepresented in enforcement actions by a factor of 1.5.

We need anti-colonial education to examine the precarity and containment of Black, Indigenous and racialized lives. The fact that Canada has been a site of Black and Indigenous displacements, dispossessions, and has served as "controls of Black [and Indigenous] mobility" (Maynard, 2019, p. 134; and see also, McKittrick's, 2011). We need to teach young learners about how and why Black and Indigenous peoples have been "targets of social and spatial controls (deriving from our) anomalous position in relation to (Canadian settler state) citizenship" (Maynard, 2019, p. 129). This particularly implies teaching and learning Blackness and Indigeneity in "radical relationality" in terms of our shared Land dislocations, displacements and dispossessions, as well as the intersectionality of bodies and labour on different Lands and geospaces (see also Harris, 2019; Byrd, 2019).

Our classroom pedagogies must name the "settler" pedagogically in terms of what it means and politically, in terms of what action called for. This will lead us to the possibilities of developing strategies of co-resistances and anticolonial solidarity discussed earlier. We need a "Radical Black and Indigenous Pedagogy" (RBIP) to raise questions about the absences, omissions, negations and denials; engage critical educational texts that debunk Greek/Roman Whiteness assertions; and ensure the production and promotion of knowledge and resources that allow our diverse communities to see themselves and their own representations. RBIP must advocate and support the development of self along with collective-healing processes/outlets within Black, Indigenous and racialized communities (e.g., for communities to embark on personal and collective (un)learning and healing journeys). Also, RBIP must address the perception of the White subject as the "producer of knowledge" and Black/African, Indigenous or racialized subject as the "objective of the dominant gaze" (see also Davis & Walsh, 2020, p. 12). RBIP must be a critical praxis of "re-storying" Black life and the "carceral projects" of Black social and spatial exclusions in schools and spaces. For example, the geographies and logics of over-policing; criminalization and panoptic surveillance of Black bodies through a culture of "weaponized and prisoned Black hyper masculinities" (see Crichlow, 2014, pp. 113–120). In teaching Blackness, there must be a corresponding focus on "Trauma free Blackness" (see Blake, 2021) Pedagogically this means paying attention to aspects of Black life as joy and happiness (not just pain and suffering); a change from the relentless and persistence of Black grief and anguish.

Calls for reparations have been silenced for Black and African bodies. But reparations must be understood as restitution for colonial wrongs to Black and African bodies. Black and Indigenous peoples are on the same bridge. We cannot be more vociferous on the power of Black and Indigenous solidarities. The White settler colonial nation-state in Canada has co-opted reconciliation into a goal that to "be attained with empty promises and mandates that ultimately serve to maintain colonial power and colonial futurity" (Dhaliwal, 2022). The settler/colonial nation-state uses the reconciliatory rhetoric to cloak the repositioning of settler violence and to reify colonial power (Gaudry & Lorenz, 2018; Daigle, 2019, p. 710). Additionally, Daigle (2019, p. 704) argues that in practice, "the process of truth and reconciliation has "naturalized and fetishized Indigenous suffering and trauma" through "colonial spectacles" in which White settler Canadians stage empty performances of recognition and remorse (cited in Dhaliwal, 2022). A decentering of settler responsibilities to Indigenous people has offloaded the burden of reconciliation onto Indigenous peoples. In Canada, we see this move in the Truth and Reconciliation Council's "Call for Action". We must ask: what are the institutional responses to the TRC's Call to Action, and what are they accomplishing? What are the lessons for a decolonial and anti-colonial future? Reconciliation cannot be attained with empty promises and mandates that ultimately serve to maintain colonial power and colonial futurity by using reconciliatory rhetoric to cloak this repositioning of settler violence. The Reconciliation bandwagon has evolved into an academic currency, prompting Canadian universities to adopt Indigenous course requirements. As noted such hollow institutional tendency has added to the expansive nature of colonial violence found at educational sites (Daigle, 2019, p. 706).

In discussing Reconciliation and Restitution, it needs emphasizing that there are many paths to decolonization and to ground our decolonial and anti-colonial projects in Black and Indigenous ontologies and epistemologies. Decolonization cannot be hidden as a secret activity nor an "undercover scholarship". Moten and Harney (2004) exhortation to be in, but not of the university is so powerful. In effect, we must see the university as a site of action. And, to reiterate we must seriously take decolonial and anti-colonial spaces to include those "fugitive spaces" where we combine work, study and activism to meaningful effect. As already alluded to in this book, it is important to recognize decolonization as a pathway toward an anti-colonial end. Decolonization is messy and confrontational. Decolonization is not about mainstreaming practice (i.e., a decolonial project cannot seek legitimation and validation from the dominant!). We need to continually be vigilant of how a "decolonization" can be domesticated/liberalized to uphold Whiteness. For instance, see how our institutions easily become "arms of the colonial settler state" (see Grande, 2018; Hill, 2022). Decolonial education stresses the importance of History, that is teaching our students, particularly our White students to acknowledge their Euro-ancestry of privilege and to use such knowledge to work for educational change & human liberation.

There is the urgency of decolonizing school curriculum and its crimes against Black and Indigenous bodies (Grande, 2018, p. 48), its colonial hierarchies and the ideology of sameness (e.g., "one size must fit all" thinking and the "standardization recipes" Lewin, 2008). As hooks (1992) long noted such "imposition of sameness is a provocation that terrorizes" (pp. 22–23).

A more radical/subversive take on decolonial "inclusion" as about breaking down structures and subverting instructional processes at play. A decolonial curriculum works with the idea of a curriculum as a path to follow, a course of action to take, further acknowledging that curriculum is everything about the educational system – what long ago we called the "Deep Curriculum " (Dei, Mazzuca, McIsaac, & Zine, 1997). That is, culture, climate, environment and the social organizational lives of schools; besides texts, instruction and pedagogy. Curriculum is power-saturated and contested, and more profoundly is requiring us to work with generative knowledges and radical, speculative imaginaries for new futures.

Indigeneity, Land and Earthly teachings offer a counter Indigenous Black/African education evoking physical, spiritual, social & cultural conceptions of Land, inclusive of sky, water & seas] as powerful literacies, ontologies & epistemologies (Simpson, 2014, 2017; see also Tuck & Yang, 2012; Styres, 2019; Dei, Wambui, & Erger, 2022). Land and Earthly teachings (literacies) of relationality, sharing, reciprocity, connections, mutual interdependence, building relationships, social responsibility and accountability to enrich conversations that promote "communities of learners" and "schooling as community" (see Dei, 2008). We must be able to problematize the racialization of the (Black) "Human" and the bifurcation of "Human" & "non-Human" in affirming African/Black humanity, that sees the "human" broadly as inclusive of animate/inanimate objects, plants, animals, water, rocks, etc. as having Life and offering something to teach us; and further, to break colonial binaries (see also, Whitehouse, 2016; Andreotti, Stein, Ahenakew, & Hunt, 2015).

To reframe decolonial and radical inclusion from the standpoint of school curriculum, educators must evaluate the appropriateness of curriculum materials/resources (e.g., who, what, how, and when questions regarding the "making of texts"). We must also examine procedures for centring, infusing/integrating/synthesizing relevant anti-racist/anti-colonial materials that speak to questions of coloniality, [Euro]modernity and power. There must be a critical analysis of texts and materials for omissions, bias, exclusions of experiences and the violence of practices around race, gender, sexuality, disability, class, religion and, we must also respond to issues of availability, access and adequacy of anti-racist, anti-colonial, Indigenous instructional materials and resources for students, educators, parents and community workers, and to combine school (academic/official), off-school, community and local cultural resource knowledges (see Dei, James, James-Wilson, Karumanchery, & Zine, 2000; Dei, James-Wilson, & Zine, 2002).

Anti-colonial education requires a total commitment from us as Black, Indigenous and racialized learners and educators. For some, it may just require just striving to make a contribution. History places responsibilities on all of us. History is all our burden but it is also differently shared. We build communities one day at a time working in collectivities.

There is the power of thinking and acting anew on anti-racism and de/anti-colonial possibilities. We are called upon to become "prophets of what could be" (Coghlan, 2022, p. 13). That is to create an "Otherwise" and "Other World". As noted we are both "living a new present" (Simpson, 2017) and building a new future. It is not an "either/or" reading. We can work with the past but also not allow the past to imprison us. This means we shed the past atrocities that constitute to have lasting legacies and impacts on human lives. We must reframe the "politics of refusal" as disruption, divestment, resistance, strategic, building our politics around, within and outside institutions and communities, generative and creating something anew, radical imaginaries. We must also affirm schools as contested spaces for us "to be in, but not of" (Moten & Harney, 2004, p. 26). It requires us to engage in combat and become "academic warriors" (Dei, 2014) with shared responsibilities and accountability. We cannot afford to become "products" of our institutions like "intellectual imposters" (Nyamnjoh, 2012). Rather, we must be "products" of our own decolonization and resistance in those fugitive spaces. Our anti-colonial educational moves must be towards a "Spatiology of Reparations". Going beyond the conventional posture of "not expecting anything from our institutions" to "making demands", embracing education as the "sanctity/sacredness of activity" that is learning and seeking knowledge to compel action. The conversation began a long time ago, it continues today and will in the future with a spiral back and forth. The only thing I ask is our conversations must show the fruits of our actions, because a lot has happened but not a lot has changed. Yet we must not be discouraged.

References Cited:

Abidogun, J., & Toyin, F. (Eds.), (2020). *Palgrave handbook of African education and Indigenous knowledge*. New York: Palgrave MacMillan.

Andreotti, V., Stein, S., Ahenakew, C., & Hunt, D. (2015). "Mapping interpretations of decolonization in the context of higher education. *Decolonization: Indigeneity, Education & Society*, 4(1), 21–40.

Andrews, Kehinde. (2022). "Opinion: Britain is closer than ever to a non-White prime minister. Don't think it's racial progress". https://www.cnn.com/2022/08/08/opinions/uk-leaders hip-race-prime-minister-rishi-sunak-andrews/index.html

Asmelash, L. (2021). Idaho moves to ban Critical Race Theory Instruction in all Public Schools, including Universities. https://www.cnn.com/2021/04/27/us/critical-race-theory-idaho-bill-trnd/index.html

Blake, J. (2021). "The Author of 'White Fragility' takes on 'Nice Racism'". https://www.cnn.com/2021/06/26/health/robin-diangelo-nice-racism-blake/index.html

Byrd, J. A. (2019). Weather with you: Settler colonialism, antiblackness, and the grounded relationalities of resistance. *Journal of the Critical Ethnic Studies Association*, 5(1–2), 207.

Coghlan, Catherine. (2022). Secret spaces of freedom: Re-humanization through Marronage. Unpublished paper, SJE 1921: Principles of Anti-Racism Education, OISE, University of Toronto.

Collinson, S. (2022, April 6). Obama and Romney are back, and show how American politics have changed for the worse. *CNN Politics*. Retrieved on September 1, 2022.

Coulthard, G. (2007). Subjects of empire: Indigenous peoples and the 'Politics of Recognition' in Canada. *Contemporary Political Theory*, 6, 437–460.

Coulthard, G. (2010). "Place against empire: Understanding Indigenous anti-colonialism". *Affinities: A Journal of Radical Theory, Culture, and Action*, 4(2), 79–83.

Coulthard, G. (2014). *Red Skin White Masks: Rejecting the colonial politics of recognition*. Minneapolis: University of Minnesota Press.

Crichlow, W. (2014). "Weaponization and prisonization of Toronto's Black Male Youth". *International Journal for Crime, Justice and Social Democracy*, 3(3). doi: 10.5204/ijcjsd.v3i3.120

Daigle, M. (2019). The spectacle of reconciliation: On (the) unsettling responsibilities to Indigenous peoples in the Academy. *Environment and Planning D: Society and Space*, 37(4), 703–721. https://doi.org/10.1177/026377581882434

Dei, G. J. S. (2008). 'Schooling as Community': Race, schooling, and the education of African youth. *Journal of Black Studies*, 38(3), 346–366.

Dei, G. J. S. (2014). "The African Scholar in the Western Academy". *Journal of Black Studies* 45(3), 167–179.

Dei, G. J. S. (2017). *Reframing Blackness and Black Solidarities through anti-colonial and decolonial prisms*. New York: Springer.

Dei, G. J. S., Mazzuca, J., McIsaac, E., & Zine, J. (1997). *Reconstructing 'Dropout': A critical ethnography of the dynamics of Black Students' disengagement from schools*. Toronto: University of Toronto Press.

Dei, G. J. S., James, I. M., James-Wilson, S., Karumanchery, L., & Zine J. (2000). *Removing the margins: The challenges and possibilities of inclusive schooling*. Toronto: Canadian Scholars' Press.

Dei, G. J. S., James-Wilson, S., & Zine, J. (2002). *Inclusive schooling: A teacher's companion to removing the margins*. Toronto: Canadian Scholars' Press.

Dei, G. J. S., Karumanchery, Leeno, & Karumanchery-Luik, Nisha. (2004). *Playing the race card: Exposing White power and privilege*. New York: Peter Lang.

Dei, G. J. S., & Lordan, M. (2013). (Eds.). *Contemporary issues in the Sociology of race and ethnicity: A critical reader*. New York: Peter Lang.

Dhaliwal, K. (2022). Continued settler violence & educational sites: (re) conciliation? lessons for decolonial futurity. Unpublished paper. OISE, UT. Course 3914H.

Furo, A. (2018). *Decolonizing the classroom curriculum: Indigenous knowledges, colonizing logics, and ethical spaces*. Ottawa: Doctoral dissertation, Université d'Ottawa/University of Ottawa).

Gaudry, A., & Lorenz, D. (2018). Indigenization as inclusion, reconciliation, and decolonization: Navigating the different visions for Indigenizing the Canadian Academy. *AlterNative: An International Journal of Indigenous Peoples, 14*(3), 218–227.

Gaudry, A., & Lorenz, D. E. (2019). Decolonization for the masses? Grappling with Indigenous content requirements in the changing Canadian Post-Secondary Environment. In L. T. Smith, E. Tuck, & K. W. Yang (Eds.), *Indigenous and decolonizing studies in education: Mapping the long view* (pp. 159–174). New York: Routledge.

Grande, S. (2018). Refusing the University. *Toward What Justice?*, 47–65.

Harney, S., & Moten, F. (2013). *The undercommons: Fugitive planning and black study*. Minor Compositions.

Harris, C. I. (2019). Of Blackness and indigeneity: Comments on Jodi A. Byrd's "Weather with you: Settler colonialism, antiblackness, and the grounded relationalities of resistance". *Journal of the Critical Ethnic Studies Association, 5*(1–2), 215.

Hill, J. (2022). Pedagogies and politics of hope and refusal in higher education and beyond. Unpublished course paper, SJE 1921Y.

Lewin, K. M. (2008). Strategies for sustainable financing of secondary education in Sub-Saharan Africa. Human development series World Bank Working Paper No. 1 3 6. Washington, D.C. World Bank].

Maynard, R. (2019). Black life and death across the U.S.- Canada Border: Border violence, Black Fugitive Belonging, and a Turtle Island View of Black Liberation. *Journal of the Critical Ethnic Studies Association, 5*(1–2), 124–140.

McKittrick, K. (2011). "On plantations, prisons, and a Black Sense of Place". *Social and Cultural Geography, 12*(8), 947–963.

Nyamnjoh, F. (2012). "Potted plants in greenhouses': A critical reflection on the resilience of colonial education in Africa". *Journal of Asian and African Studies*. 1–26 [On line version: http://jas.sagepub.com/content/early/2012/02/14/0021909611417240

Santos, B. (2002). "Toward a multicultural conception of human rights". In. B. Hernandez-Truyol (ed.). *Moral imperialism: A Critical Anthology*. New York: New York University Press.

Simpson, A. (2014). *Mohawk interruptus: Political life across the borders of settler states*. Durham, NC: Duke University Press.

Simpson, L. (2017). *As we have always done: Indigenous freedom through radical resistance*. University of Minnesota Press.

Smith, L. T., Tuck, E., & Yang, K. W. (Ed.). (2019b). *Indigenous and decolonizing studies in education: Mapping the long view*. New York: Routledge.

Styres, S. (2019). Literacies of land: Decolonizing narratives, storying, and literature. In. L. T. Smith, E. Tuck, & K. W. Yang (Eds.), *Indigenous and decolonizing studies in education: Mapping the long view* (pp. 24–37). New York: Routledge. Retrieved from https://ebookcentral-proquest-com.myaccess.library.utoronto.ca

Tuck, E., & Yang, K. W. (2012). Decolonization is not a metaphor. *Decolonization: Indigeneity, Education & Society, 1*(1), 1–40.

Vowel, C., Tucker, B., & HighWater Press. (2020). Monster: The Residential School legacy (pp. 171–180). *Indigenous writes: A guide to first nations, Métis, and Inuit Issues in Canada.* HighWater Press.

Whitehouse, H., Lui, F. W., Sellwood, J., Barret, M., & Chigeza, P. (2016). *Sea Country: Navigating Indigenous and colonial Ontologies in Australian Environmental Education.* New York: Routledge, Taylor & Francis Group.

INDEX

A

Abdi, Abdirahman 88
academic freedom 31
academic mentorship 4, 187–8
   advice from established publishers 198
   African Indigenous spatial conceptions and narratives 188
   as assistance to students 192
   for dealing with setbacks and rejections 200
   decolonization 192
   Indigenous epistemologies 192–3
   oppositional scholarship 198–9
   outcomes 204–5
   practical strategies 193–7
   for publication 197–204
   reciprocity and collaboration 199–200
   support networks 199
   theorizing 189–91
academic scholarship 3
accountability 66, 92, 130, 191, 217
academic warriors 218
allyship 173
   of Black scholars 39
   state and political 2
Achebe, Chinua 157
Adichie, Chimamanda 157
Africa, portrayal of 15
African anti-colonialism 40
Africana thought 38
African-centred education 135–41
   anti-racist lens/perspective 140
   in Canadian educational contexts 136–7
   features 137–9, 141
   justification 138
   role of parents and local communities 140
   success 139
African Elders 48
African history, teaching 149–51, 213
   of African ancient civilizations and empires 157–8
   Afrocentric narration of histories 151

Arab and European enslavement of
  Africans 159
challenges 154–5
contemporary Africa and Black Diasporic
  experiences 151
contributions of African civilizations 157
decolonial and anti-colonial approach
  153, 155
to fight anti-Black racism and White
  colonial privilege 153
global diaspora 159–60
of Indigenous knowledges 149, 152, 155
monuments 152–3
politics and social movements 160
practical strategies for 156–60
of pre-colonial, colonial, and
  post-colonial 151
race and colonialism in 153
role of local communities, parents and
  Elders 156–7
teacher's identity 153
wealth and trade of West Africa 159
West African art 159
African Indigeneity 3, 56, 101,
  103–4, 116–17
African redemption 40
African traditionalism 40
Afrocentricity 135–6
Afrocentrism, Afrocentricity, and
  Africology 38
Aidoo, Ama Atta 157
allyship 173–4
Al Subanti, Riad 157
American Educational Research
  Association (AERA) 123
Andrews 210–11
Andrews, Kehinde 209
Ant-Black racism 84
Anti-Apartheid Network 15
anti-Blackness 14–16, 20, 28, 36–7, 43, 45–
  7, 53, 82–6, 93, 96–7
  oppressions 86–7
  specificity of 95–7
  as systemic disparities and barriers 96

anti-Black racism 1–2, 14–17, 19, 22, 90,
  92, 168, 172, 180, 196, 211, 214; see
  also Black Lives Matter (BLM)
capitalism and 20
in Civil rights struggles 5, 88
in the context of Blackcentricity 67–71
during Covid-19 pandemic 5–6, 18
culture of denialism 93
current events of 83–4
history 21
protests 19–20
saliency of 174, 177
specificity of 96
support of capitalism 20
teaching history as a tool to fight 150,
  153, 156
in terms of skin colour 133
White supremacy and 45
anti-colonial education 103, 122, 218
  Blackcentric agenda 69
  Indigenous knowledges 125–6
  as Land-based education 47
  theorizing 125–8
anti-colonialism 32, 38, 40, 53–5, 57,
  59–62, 101–2
  distinction between decolonization
    and 102
anti-colonial solidarities 5, 31, 96,
  117, 165–83
  allyship 173–4
  conceptualizations of 178–83
  creation of community and
    communities 180–1
  critical friends, role of 174
  importance of history 181
  leadership roles 166
  notion of saliency 179
  in political struggle 168–9, 175, 182
  poverty of intersections 173
  principles of intersectionality
    171, 173–83
  relations of power 180
  sanctity of life and sanctity of
    activity 179

in social movement politics 166, 172, 175
anti-colonial spaces 47, 113, 180, 216
anti-colonial struggles 58, 60, 62, 88, 96, 105–7, 112–14, 116–17, 126–7, 130–1, 141, 144, 151, 159, 166–9, 171–8, 181–3, 188, 195
anti-colonial studies/scholarship 14–16, 30, 53
Anti-Colonial Theory (ACT) 62–7, 126–7
  anti-colonial solidarities 126
  coloniality of knowledge 56, 65, 112
  coloniality of power 64
  colonial/re-colonial relations and its implications 62–3
  cultural criticism 64
  as "imposed" and "dominating" 63
  literacy of resistance 64
  power of Indigenous 65
  in terms of bodies, identities, places, and Lands 66–7
  territorial imperialism and state/ cultural control of resources 63
  White supremacy 66
anti-Indigeneity 22, 36, 167, 169
anti-Islam violence 22–3
anti-racism 17, 32–3, 38, 123, 132–3, 209; see also anti-Black racism
anti-Semitism 22
Arbery, Ahmaud 82, 88–9
Asante, Molefi 38, 67–8, 136
associational justice 129
authenticity 133

B

Bell, Derrick 38
Black Action Defence Committee (BADC) 14
Black/African identities 39, 141
Black/African nationalist sensibilities 25
Black and Indigenous body/subject 3, 29–32, 36–7, 46–7, 68, 74, 83, 124, 176
  environmental conditions 94
  hypervisibility of 84–5
  social and spiritual death of 84
Black Canadian history 159
Black centricity 67–77
  Black/African Indigeneities 68–9
  for Black intellectuality/ scholarship 70–7
  diaspora 76–7
  educational research agenda 69–70
  idea of unashamed Blackness 68
  for re-claiming of Blackness 76
Black criminality 36
Black Crit Theory 38
Black death and Black loss 1
Black existentialism 38
Black feminism 37–8, 58
Black healthcare workers 18
Black immigration scholarship 36
Black Intellectual Tradition 30, 37–8
  contested understandings 38–9
  definition 37
  major traditions 38
  origins 38–9
  possibilities and challenges 42
Black life 44, 87
Black Lives Matter (BLM) 2, 5–6, 19–20, 37, 69, 82, 95, 151, 210
  #Blacklivesmatter 87–8, 150
  as global movement 20
  idea and politics of 88
  symbolism of painting 20
Black Marxism 38, 41
Black Nationalism 38
Blackness 8–9, 21–2, 29–31, 36–7, 42–4, 76, 83, 85, 88, 90, 115, 133, 160, 167, 170
  commodification of 74
  paraontology of 84
  places and spaces 85
  predicament of 75
Blacknesses 117
Black postmodernism, poststructuralism, postcolonialism, and cultural and queer studies 38
Black pragmatism 38
Black radical politics 38, 41–2

Black religious thought 38
Black resistance movements 16
Black responsibility 89
Black scholar and Black scholarship 3, 17, 37–9, 45, 67, 69–73, 81, 86, 167
Black self 8
Black sexuality 170
Black Star Steamship Line 39
Black theorizing 28, 37–42
  in academia 42–9
  African humanity and humanness 48–9
  Black/ African identities 43
  contested understandings 38–9
  culture of anti-Blackness 46
  historicizing and contemporizing Black education 44
  issues of Indigeneity and resistance 43
  major traditions 38
  sociology of knowledge 37
  value of schooling and education 47–8
  as a weapon of change and social transformation 45–7
  White Eurocentric perspectives 44–5
Black values, forgetting and forgetfulness of 83
Black/White binary 17, 54
Black women's experiences 57–8
Blake, Jacob 19, 90
Bland, Sandra 88
Brathwaite, Keren 15
British Empire 210
Brooks, Rayshard 89
Brotherhood of Sleeping Car Porters 160
Brown, Michael 88
Buffalo massacre 82, 91
Butler, Judith 18

C

Campbell, D'Andre 19, 88
Canada 12–13, 47
  Africentric schooling in 17
  Black Canadian history 159–60
  racial issues 14
  TRC's Call to Action 216
Canadian Charter of Rights and Freedoms 160
Canadian Education Association (CEA) 121
capitalism 9, 53, 75, 97, 115–16
Carby, Jermain 88
Castile, Philando 88
Cesaire, Aime 38
Chauvin, Derek 90
citizenship 9, 115, 130, 214
  Black/African 138
  White national 116
climate change and global warming, impact on racialized communities 1
Collins, P. H. 57–8
Collins, Patricia Hill 38
Colonial education 16
Colonial genocide 29
Colonialism 1, 6, 9, 21, 23, 29, 32, 35, 53, 56–7, 103, 124, 182
  Black women's experiences 57–8
  colonial modernity 24
  epistemic challenges 56
  exploitation of Land, space, place, and resources 56, 60–2
  genocide and African enslavement without 59
  impact on women's lives and knowledge production 57
  living traces of 4
  practices of Otherness 58–9
  racist colonial practices 59
  understanding 35–6
Coloniality of Being 24
Coloniality of knowledge 56, 65, 112
"coming to know" 4
"coming to theory" 28, 35–7
Cooper, Amy 89–90
Cooper, Anna Julia 39, 71
Cooper, Christian 90
Covid-19 pandemic 5–6, 18, 21–2, 90, 93–4, 170

impact on Black and racialized
    communities 93–4
Crenshaw, Kimberle 38
Critical Anti-Racist Theory 38
Critical Race Theory (CRT) 1, 38, 81, 213
Cullors, Patrice 150
cult of individualism 5
cultural appropriation discourse 33
cultural domination 129
Cusicanqui, Silvia Rivera 4

D

Davis, Angela 58
death statistics 170–1
decolonization 3, 5, 23, 33, 45–6, 53, 66,
    101–2, 134, 165, 178, 211, 216
  about asking questions 112
  about Land and healing 103, 114–15
  academic 4
  Blackcentricity and 68
  as *Buen Vivir* 112
  as dynamic process 47
  educational practices 102–3
  Indigenous 105, 109
  link of modernity and 109
  metaphoricity of 103
  as path to recreate/ resurrect past 77
  in reading, re-writing, and re-telling
    stories 112–13
  relationships and 24
  school curriculum 216–17
  settler 103
  social justice as 131
  spaces of privilege 75
  time and space coherence 115
  understanding 7–8
Dei, G. J. S. 38, 56, 68, 209
democratic education 138
denialism 17
deprivation 129
development 15
Diop, Cheikh Anta 38, 67

diversity 209–11
Donaldson, Lester 144
Du Bois, W. E. B. 39, 71

E

economic distributive justice 129
economic marginalization 129
educational inclusion 138
empathy 96
empty signifiers 24
Engels 40
epistemic provincialism 56
epistemic saliency 133–4, 179
epistemology 4, 24–5, 30, 32, 39, 43, 56, 60,
    65, 68, 72, 97, 192–5, 216–17
Equity, Diversity and Inclusion (EDI) 211
equity and social justice education 25
ethnicity/ethnicities 36
Eurocentric conception of African
    traditionalism 40
Euro-modernity 24, 54–5
exonmination 34
exploitation 129

F

Fanon, Franz 38
Fanonian philosophy 38
Farrell, Lennox 15
far-right extremism 1
Floyd, George 1, 19, 82, 88–90
forgiveness 45
Foucault, M. 130
Foucault, Michael 192
freedom 25
Freedom convoy 1

G

Garba and Sorentino 103

Garner, Eric 88
Garvey, Marcus 38–9, 71
  ideas of "Africa for the Africans" 39
  Pan Africanism 39–40
Garza, Alicia 87
Generation Z 6, 48
genetic fallacy 43
geography of Land 66–7
Ghana 11, 13, 16
Ghana Empire 158
Global South 55
Gordon, L. 38
Gray, Freddie 88

H

Harney, S. 216
hate crime 1
Hegel, Georg Wilhelm Friedrich 39
Hume, David 39

I

identity politics 29, 34–5, 39, 210
  Euro-Canadian/American national imaginings and constructions 124
  identity of Muslims 169–70
implicit bias 124–5, 174
Indigeneity 103, 123, 151, 154, 214
  African Indigenous context of community 188
  cartographies of 104–5
  collective awareness and consciousness 117–18
  cultural identities and sense of self 104
  definition 104–6
  distinction between Indigenous and Western societies 104
  Indigenous cosmologies 105
  Indigenous knowledges 56, 106–9, 125–6
  Indigenous modernity 110
  Indigenous resistance 107, 113, 117–18

Indigenous sovereignty 21, 88, 114–15
Indigenous spirituality 135
Indigenous women 105
Land dispossession 47, 56, 60–2, 115–16
links between Blackness and 115
multiple expressions of 106
politics, identity and knowledge 106, 116
queering 105
resistance of 106
solidarity 110, 117
institutional hypocrisy 17
integrative anti-racism 172
intersectionality 169
Intersectionality Theory 38
Islamophobia 23, 37

J

Jackson, Andrew 152
James, C. L. R. 38, 71
  dialectics of freedom 40–1
Jarvis, William 152
Jews 59
Jim Crow 54
Jones, Claudia 71

K

Kaepernick, Colin 90
Kant, Immanuel 39
Karenga, Maulana 67
Karumanchery, L. 209
Karumanchery-Luik, Nisha 209
Kelley, Robin 39, 42, 97
Kemetic (Egyptian) Civilization of 1550–590 BCE 157
Khan-Cullors, Patrisse 87
King Jr., Martin Luther 90
kobene 12
Korchinski-Paquet, Regis 19, 88
Ku Klux Klan (KKK) 29, 54
Kunjufu, Jawanza 67

Kuntunkuni 12

L

Land-based education 47–8
Land occupation and settlerhood 53, 55
   Anti-Colonial Theory (ACT) 66–7
   Colonial exploitation 56, 60–2
   decolonization 103, 114–15
   Indigenous Land dispossession 47, 56, 60–2, 115–16
Larbalestier, Jan 126
LatinX identities 169
Law and Order 90
Lawrence, Sonia 137–8
Laws, Dudley 14
Lenin, Vladimir 40–1
Lenskyj, Helen 16
liberal democracies 25
Locke, John 39
Loku, Andrew 88

M

MAAT principle 48
Mali Empire 158
Marable, Manning 37–9
Martin, Trayvon 87–8
Marx, Engels 40
Marx, Karl 40–1
Mazama, Ama 67
Mbembe, Achille 75
McClain, Elijah 82
McDonald, Laquan 88
McKenzie, M. 61
McKittrick, K. 60
Mensah-Kane, Mr 11
mentorship *see* academic mentorship
millennials 6
Mills, Charles 15
modernity 24, 55–6
Moitt, Bernard 15

Moten, F. 216
multicentricity 132
multicentric knowledge 132
multiculturalism 22
Musa, King Mansa 158–9

N

nation-building and/or national development 129
Negritude Philosophy 38
Negro Citizenship Association 160
neo-liberalism 22, 55
Nkrumah, Kwame 38–40, 71
   Pan Africanism 39–40
North American history 154
North American schooling 157
Nubian Civilization of 3,100–1,000 BCE 158

O

Obama, Barack 28
Odozor, E. 68
Ontario-based of Parents of Black Children (OPBC) 15
Ontario Institute for Studies in Education (OISE) 16
Organization of Black Parents of Black Children (OPBC) 16
Other/Otherness 33, 48, 84, 169
   colonial practices of 58–9
   racialize Others 34

P

Pan Africanism 38–40
Patterson, Orlando 84
positionality 24
postcolonial African schooling and education 16

post-colonial scholarship 32
power and resistance 34
proletariat 40–1
publishing/publication 197–204
   book 202–3
   collaborative work 199–200
   features to enhance 204
   joint 200–1
   Journal 201–2
   sustaining 204

R

racism 1–2, 4–5, 9, 14–16, 28, 32, 90, 172
Radical Black and Indigenous Pedagogy (RBIP) 215
radical inclusion 134
redressing 4
reflexivity 24
relationality 103
Rice, Tamir 88
Roach, Charles 14
Robinson, Cedric 38, 41, 71
Rolfe, Garrett 89
Russell, Peter 152
Ryerson, Egerton 153
Ryland (2013) 84

S

sacred learning landscape 30–1
safe learning spaces 31
Sakuru, King Mansa 158
saliency of race 179
schooling as community 188, 217
self concept 35
Senghor, Leopold 38
senior citizen 13
sense-making 92–5
Skene-Peters, Kwasi 88
skin colour 92
slavery 9, 53–4, 60, 115, 150

Smith, Andrea 54
Smith, Linda 102
social activism 5
social death 84
social justice 126, 129–32, 212
   accountability 130
   for anti-Colonial education 132–5
   in context of occupying Indigenous Lands 131
   as decolonization 131
   effects of globalization 131
   individual and collective responsibilities 130
   power and power relations 130
   promotion of radical education 131
social justice education 121–2, 135–44
social justice warrior 124–5
Songhai Empire 158
Soyinka, Wole 157
spiritual ontologies and epistemologies 134–5
Sterling, Alton 88
structural racism 21
Suahunu 30–1
subjectivity 35
Sunak, Rishi 210–11
Sundiata, King 158

T

Taylor, Breonna 19, 88, 90
theorizing the experiential 18
Thiong'o, Ngugi wa 103
Tometi, Opal 87
transnational corporations 132
trauma free Blackness 215
Troyna, Lee, Dei 38
Trump, Donald 28, 82
Tubman, Harriet 152
Tuck, E. 61
Tulsa race massacre 151
Tumi, Mr 11–12
Tylor, Breonna 82

U

Ubuntu 31
Ultra Conservatives 209
University of Windsor 15

V

Vasquez, A. 68

W

Warner, D. 44
Washington, Booker T 38
Western Sudanese Empires and Kingdoms 158
White nationalism 7, 25, 28
Whiteness/White identity 33–4, 46, 128, 132, 160, 211
as property 128
White privileges 33–4, 82–4, 92, 145
White racism 4, 21
White supremacy 1–2, 7, 21, 23–4, 28–9, 36–7, 54, 72, 83–4, 136, 168, 211, 213
  advantages of 54
  ethnonationalism of 81
  as a protecting army 83
  use of violence 82
  White supremacist violence 82, 88–92
Woodson, Carter G 39

Y

Yancy, George 42

Z

Zimbabwe Civilization of 1100–1,400 CE 158

Studies in Criticality

General Editor
Shirley R. Steinberg

Counterpoints publishes the most compelling and imaginative books being written in education today. Grounded on the theoretical advances in criticalism, feminism, and postmodernism in the last two decades of the twentieth century, Counterpoints engages the meaning of these innovations in various forms of educational expression. Committed to the proposition that theoretical literature should be accessible to a variety of audiences, the series insists that its authors avoid esoteric and jargonistic languages that transform educational scholarship into an elite discourse for the initiated. Scholarly work matters only to the degree it affects consciousness and practice at multiple sites. Counterpoints' editorial policy is based on these principles and the ability of scholars to break new ground, to open new conversations, to go where educators have never gone before.

For additional information about this series or for the submission of manuscripts, please contact:

        Shirley R. Steinberg, General Editor
        msgramsci@gmail.com

To order other books in this series, please contact our Customer Service Department:

        peterlang@presswarehouse.com (within the U.S.)
        orders@peterlang.com (outside the U.S.)

Or browse online by series:

www.peterlang.com

www.ingramcontent.com/pod-product-compliance
Lightning Source LLC
Chambersburg PA
CBHW061711300426
44115CB00014B/2638